HOW TO CARVE WILDFOWL

HOW TO CARVE WILDFOWL

9 North American Masters Reveal the
Carving and Painting Techniques
That Win Them International Blue Ribbons

Roger Schroeder

featuring

Eldridge Arnold, Larry Barth, Lynn Forehand,
Larry Hayden, Ernest Muehlmatt, Anthony Rudisill,
John Scheeler, James Sprankle, and Gary Yoder

STACKPOLE BOOKS

Copyright © 1984 by Stackpole Books

Published by
STACKPOLE BOOKS
5067 Ritter Road
Mechanicsburg PA 17055

First Printing, September 1984
Second Printing, November 1984
Third Printing, January 1985
Fourth Printing, April 1985
Fifth Printing, November 1986
Sixth Printing, January 1988
Seventh Printing, February 1989
First Paperback Printing, August 1997

Jacket photograph of the canvasback hen decorative decoy courtesy of Larry Hayden. Photograph by Les Ward.

Printed in the U.S.A.

Library of Congress Cataloging in Publication Data
Schroeder, Roger, 1945 –
  How to carve wildfowl.

  Bibliography: p.
  1. Wood-carving – United States. 2. Waterfowl in art.
3. Decoys (Hunting) – United States. 4. Wood-carving –
Technique. I. Arnold, Eldridge. II. Title.
III. Title: How to carve wildfowl.
NK9712.S3 1984   731.4'62   84-2598
ISBN 0-8117 2801-3

*to Lynn, Ernie, Eldridge, John,
Tony, Larry B., Gary, Jim, and Larry H.*

Contents

Introduction 9

1 Lynn Forehand – *Shaping With the Foredom Tool* 17

The Artist and His Work . . . Birds and Realism . . . Observation and References . . . The Personality of Wood . . . Power Tools, Hand Tools, and the Art Form . . . Making a Miniature Pheasant

2 Ernest Muehlmatt – *Burning for Color* 40

Birds are Flowers that Fly . . . Arranging Birds Like Flowers . . . Birds of a Shaded Feather . . . Burning for Color . . . Muscles and Bumps . . . Jelutong, Wood from Malaysia . . . Study Skins . . . Colors on a Wheel . . . Washing With Paint . . . Feet, Leaves, and Other Habitat . . . Making Woodcocks and Spruce Grouse

3 Eldridge Arnold – *Putting Wings and Tails on Birds* 67

Designer, Sculptor, Hunter . . . Representational Art . . . An Engineering Feat . . . The Fate of the Art Form . . . Inspirational Materials . . . Telling a Story . . . A Feigning Woodcock . . . Separate Wings . . . Painting – the Less the Better . . . Paper Leaves . . . Courting Doves . . . A Screech Owl

4 John Scheeler – *Feathers As Inserts* 83

The Grand Master . . . Of Clay – and Foam – and Sealing Wax . . . Profiles in Wood . . . Tupelo Gum . . . Inserted Wings . . . Inserted Feathers . . . Making Feathers . . . Making Feet and Support Systems . . . Composition . . . Surf Scoters . . . A Green Heron . . . Louisiana Herons . . . Birds of Prey

5 Anthony Rudisill – *Composition* 104

Professional Painter . . . A Kingfisher Composition . . . Compactness . . . The Base . . . Making a Pattern . . . The Seam . . . Shaping With a Roofing Nail . . . Tupelo Gum Feet . . . Fine Burning and Painted Splits . . . Painting in Reverse . . . A Piece of the Woods . . . Green Heron Pair . . . Black-Crowned Night Heron Pair

6   Larry Barth – *Portraits in Wood*   123

A Degree in Sculpting . . . More Than Decoration . . . Painting With Wood . . .
On The Wing . . . The Essence of a Bird . . . Complex or Complicated? . . . Making
Feet . . . Natural History and Artistic License . . . Fiddleheads, Fluffy Feathers,
and Whirlpools . . . Templates of Clay . . . Roughing Out a Loon . . . Visit to a
Banding Station . . . Anatomy . . . Packing It Up

7   Gary Yoder – *Birds Smaller Than Lifesize*   168

Sketching . . . Implied Motion . . . Shaping and Assembly . . . Flexible
Basswood . . . Texturing and Exaggeration . . . Light Sources and Painting . . .
Vermiculation . . . Swallows, Kestrels, Chickadees, Widgeons, and Mallards

8   James Sprankle – *Waterfowl Alive and in Wood*   195

The Challenge of Waterfowl . . . Aviary Photography . . . Highland Basswood . . .
Separate Heads, Feathers, and Feet . . . Texturing Waterfowl . . . Hollowed
Birds . . . Gunning Decoys . . . Painting on Glass . . . Painting a Shoveler Duck
. . . An Eye for Detail

9   Larry Hayden – *Waterfowl in Living Colors*   232

The Evolution of Realism . . . Painter, Carver, Teacher, Best in Shows Winner . . .
A Study in Subtleties . . . Texturing Without Burning . . . Feather Templates
. . . Crossed Primaries . . . Preparing the Carving for Painting . . . Color Study
Boards . . . Highlights and Shadows . . . Dealing With Colors . . . Jars of Color . . .
Iridescence . . . Bill Subtleties . . . Painting Sequence . . . Brushes . . . Getting
a Handle on the Bird . . . Kiln-Dried Wood . . . Study Bills . . . Aviary Maintenance
. . . Other Bird Resources

Bibliography   251

Sources for Supplies   253

A Sampling of Competitions and Exhibitions   255

Introduction

Sixty years ago in a cave in Nevada archaeologists unearthed a container of handmade ducks fashioned from feathers, bulrushes, and other reeds. Details such as color and shape identified them as canvasback ducks, and dating determined that these decoys were made some 500 years before Columbus first arrived in the Americas.

We owe credit, then, to the American Indian for having originated the crafting of duck decoys to lure wildfowl from the sky. Nearly seven centuries after that container was buried, early settlers became interested in this craft. They quickly discovered that even the crudest decoys could fool the plentiful fowl of the New World.

But as the years went on, when primitive replicas could no longer deceive more cautious wildfowl, hunters started paying closer attention to detail and even studied the habits and habitats of birds. While this was happening, men became market hunters, killing birds en masse for profit.

Though the Migratory Bird Treaty Act of 1918 put an end to this kind of hunting, and the introduction of the factory-produced decoys of the latter part of the 1800s stopped many of these craftsmen-hunters from making their own decoys, the craft still did not perish.

As late as the 1930s, men were turning out these handcrafted birds by the thousands for the sportsman-hunter. Many of these birds were skillfully painted and carved. Some names stand out as early masters of "decorative" bird carving; among them are Elmer Crowell of Massachusetts, Shang Wheeler of Connecticut, and the Ward brothers, Steve and Lem, of Maryland. And the names of two other skilled and talented carvers of birds which were meant to be more than decoys are Wendell Gilley of Maine and Arnold Melbye of Massachusetts.

But it is the name Ward that is particularly significant because, in honor of the brothers, a foundation was established in Salisbury, Maryland to save and perpetuate the recreation of birds. Each spring the Ward Foundation holds the World Championship Wildfowl Carving Competition with its World Championship classes and Best in World ribbons.

It is this prestigious and demandingly rigorous competition, attracting thousands of people and offering more prize money than any other, that provides a standard for excellence in determining who are the best bird artists. And though it is not the only competition in North America, it is extremely important, and its blue ribbons are sought after, more so than even the prize money offered.

Owing, then, to the publicity and awards generated

Lynn Forehand is a keen observer of the natural world, the source for his compositions. He says, "My ideas are a composite of many things observed during the day . . . colors, forms, motions."

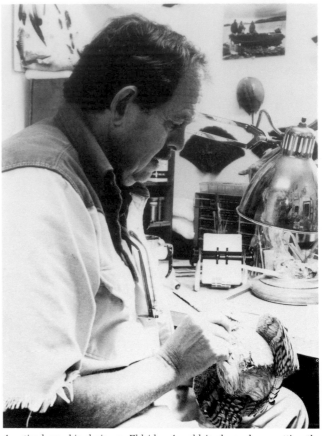

A retired graphic designer, Eldridge Arnold is shown here putting the finishing touches on a screech owl, one project featured in this book.

Ernest Muehlmatt shares his expertise at making birds like woodcocks and grouse, achieving their colors by the way he burns details into the wood.

by this wildfowl carving competition, an idea arose for yet another book devoted to carvers of decorative birds and decoys. But this book would be different from the others. It would be devoted to a select number of wildfowl artists and specifically to the techniques that set them apart from so many thousands of carvers who participate in this craft today.

I have chosen nine men to be represented in *How to Carve Wildfowl*. Their blue ribbons were an important criterion for their selection. The total number they have been awarded is staggering. I believe three for each page of this book would be a close estimate, and that means the number is well over 700. A further distinction, among them, they have won 80 or so Best in Show ribbons, the most coveted of all. But other criteria besides ribbon-winning emerged. While doing the research to determine who would be included in this book, I looked for creativity, ingenuity, technique. I quote one of the nine who later echoed what I suspected before I began writing:

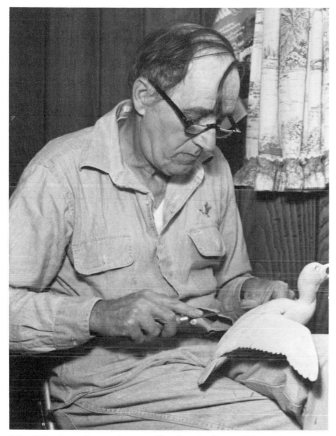

John Scheeler, winner of twenty-five Best in Show ribbons, is a master of decorative birds. Here he works on a shore bird called a willet.

telephone calls. So, because of this fraternity of connections, my original list of six grew to nine when I asked their advice on who should be included in this book. At the end of the selection process, not one of the nine objected to any other he shared the book with, nor could any offer a single addition beyond those I had asked. The book would seem to be complete.

I have been asked if there are some specific characteristics or traits which these men have in common. (Apart from the obvious, their gender, they all wear glasses.) Age is no common link. The oldest is in his early sixties, the youngest in his early twenties. Nor do credentials and education offer any common ground. Art training, sometimes intensive, is common to some, but not to others.

Perhaps geography offers some help. Though there are many bird carvers throughout the United States and Canada, these nine live in a triangular-shaped area, the points of which are Virginia, Connecticut, and Michigan. Nearly all live near water or territory rich in wildfowl, especially ducks. Some of these men have been hunters, others are watchers of birds. None of them lives in a metropolis, and all of them have expressed a deep, personal interest in wildfowl. They are, then, naturalists, even those who hunt, and they share a strong commitment to understanding the wildfowl they observe, both outside and inside with study skins and reference materials always close at hand.

These nine are talented in the many aspects of bird sculpting, each claiming a decade or more of experience in the art. For no one can sit down and produce

In order for a carver to be successful, he's got to have the technical aspects; because if you fail in any aspect of a piece, the whole carving will suffer. And even that may not be enough. You need some spark, some life in the carving that goes beyond just having made it the right colors and the right shape.

This advice was given to me by Larry Barth of Stahlstown, Pennsylvania. The other men I have interviewed for the book are: Lynn Forehand of Chesapeake, Virginia; Ernest Muehlmatt of Springfield, Pennsylvania; Eldridge Arnold of Greenwich, Connecticut; John Scheeler of Mays Landing, New Jersey; Anthony Rudisill of West Atlantic City, New Jersey; Gary Yoder of Grantsville, Maryland; James Sprankle of Annapolis, Maryland; and Larry Hayden of Farmington Hills, Michigan.

What also helped with the selection, incidentally, was what I discovered to be a kind of fraternal order among these men, that they exchanged ideas, visits,

Anthony Rudisill discusses in his chapter his strategies for developing compositions. Shown here he is at work on a kingfisher.

A trained illustrator, Larry Barth strives to create new art forms with his sculptures. The piece he is carving is the loon featured in his chapter.

James Sprankle is one of two carvers in HOW TO CARVE WILDFOWL who maintain an aviary, an enclosure that houses live waterfowl, for reference.

Gary Yoder, a master of miniature birds, shares his knowledge of texturing, painting, and putting birds into flight.

a bird, textured and poised, without a great deal of preparation. The road to success in bird sculpting, I discovered, is posted with signs for a number of skills. As Ernest Muehlmatt revealed, "To be a bird sculptor, you have to be a carpenter, an ornithologist, a painter, a cabinetmaker, a metalsmith, a chemist."

This book examines these skills. For sculpting a bird today is no longer a simple process of applying a knife to a piece of wood. It is a process comprising Muehlmatt's suggested professions and some more.

There is something else in this process of developing skills, a thing that may lack definition. I refer to an excerpt from a letter sent to me by Gary Yoder. He writes:

> My only regret is that I couldn't find the words to tell you about the reasons for carving birds in the first place. Sometimes I really wonder how much of this "art form" is for the people who aren't interested in birds to begin with. Can they understand it if they haven't been out on a green May morning and listened to the redstarts migrating through? Or heard the notes of a woodthrush back in the thicket on an absolutely breathless dusk in June? To me, bird carving goes beyond the cold techniques of carving, texturing, and painting. It must be the final culmination of everything you see, hear, smell and feel if you want it truly to be

Larry Hayden, trained as a commercial artist, is shown here with an early piece, a pintail duck he made that took three Best in Show awards.

The burning tool with its metal tip is used by most carvers to texture their wildfowl carvings for feather details.

This Best in Show blue ribbon is one of over seven hundred ribbons won by the nine carvers featured in HOW TO CARVE WILDFOWL.

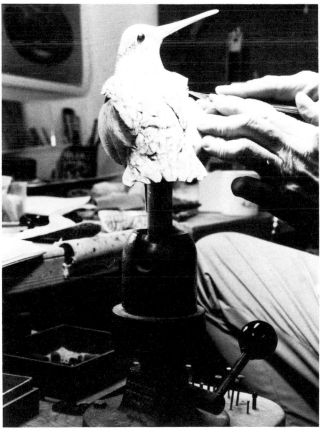

The woodcock shown here without its wings is featured as a project of Eldridge Arnold.

This woodcock, still to be painted, is typical of what Ernest Muehlmatt can do with his burning techniques.

successful. For I get the impression that a lot of people think that learning technique alone will make them good bird carvers. It seems they almost forget the bird itself.

I have chosen to speak to the reader of *How to Carve Wildfowl* in the words of the men themselves, retaining as much of the language generated by the interviews as I could. But besides offering quotations, however eloquent, this book has another, and perhaps more important, strength. I believe hands-on, men-at-work photographs tell the best possible story for a book like this. So many of the 800 photos show the projects in progress.

I refer to the nine men featured in this book as artists. There has been a debate for some time as to whether the carving of wildfowl can be called art and the men who do it artists. As Anthony Rudisill explains it so well:

> This art is still considered by many to be what it started out to be when nobody thought of it as an art — a craft performed by backbay men for the sole purpose of hunting ducks with handmade decoys. The only competition then was 'my decoys are better than your decoys.'
> Then along came two fellows by the name of Ward who started to get a little fancy with their decoys. From there people started to buy them for mantelpieces instead of [for] hunting, and slowly decoy carving started becoming an art. But the average person still thinks we're decoy craftsmen.

I tend to think the material, wood, has something to do with the debate of art versus craft. Perhaps it was

easier to make a choice when baronic families dictated what art is, using for criteria their imported marbles and paintings.

I refer to Larry Barth on this issue. He points out that all the principles of fine art — painting, posing, sculpting, attention to anatomy, working with proportions — go into bird sculpture. "So there's nothing," he says, "to keep this from being fine art except perhaps the subject matter." And birds carved in wood, he says, are not particularly popular with the art critics.

Perhaps the ultimate decision as to whether this is an art form or a craft lies with you. You will discover, from the very first pages of this book, that we are not dealing with those whittlers who invoke an image of bearded men in overalls, sitting on rural porches chipping away at tree limbs. We are sitting down with the masters. The excellence of their work, their perceptions of birds and how to recreate them, their meticulous attention to detail have earned them recognition as the best in the field. Without hesitation, they are called artists in this book.

I caution the reader against thinking that the order of the artists in this book indicates a ranking of talents. If anything, it indicates the order of visitation. Each chapter is devoted to one artist and to his special techniques while at the same time each chapter builds a composite picture of all the techniques and approaches that go into carving birds. Lynn Forehand, the first I visited, suggested that his chapter be devoted to the use of a grinding and wood-removing tool called the Foredom tool, even though nearly all the others use the same machine. John Scheeler, as another example,

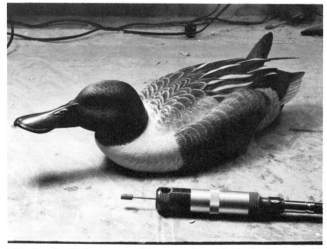

This shoveler duck was carved by James Sprankle. In the foreground is a handpiece, made by Pfingst & Co., for a grinding tool called the Foredom, which Sprankle used to shape the duck.

is especially talented in making individual feathers for his birds (hence, the chapter titled "Feathers as Inserts"), though similar techniques are used by others. I hope you will find that the chapters overlap slightly, and that each one offers new insights to creating birds out of wood.

I also see these chapters as glimpses into the private worlds of nine artists, how they work, what they work with, what they create. When I could, I shared the camera's eyepiece with each of them, so they could see how I viewed their projects. In nearly all cases, they agreed with my "views."

There was something else I shared with them – my love of wood. As a cabinetmaker for nearly fifteen years, I have made sculptured desks, corner cabinets with massive cockleshell carvings, and many other items from toys to tables. This common background helped create a relationship that added character to the book.

I love tools, so I paid close attention to those the nine were using. I found some of the same tools in every studio I visited. The bandsaw used for cutting wood away quickly was one of them. A grinding tool was another. A third was the burning tool with its heated tip that gives definition to feathers. Still, I found, it is not the tool but how it is used that accounts for such exceptional work. I think these examinations will fascinate the reader.

I strongly believe that one does not have to sculpt birds to find useful information in this book. The techniques on painting alone make it a valuable resource for any artist concerned with color. And I have learned things about wood that someday I will apply to my own cabinetmaking.

I would like to point out, because it has bearing on the material presented in the text, that some important precedents helped Stackpole choose me to write this book. In 1980, I met and interviewed a most remarkable South Carolina bird sculptor named Grainger McKoy. The project he was working on at that time was a covey of quail, composed of no less than fifteen carved birds breaking out into space from a field. He and his mentor, Gilbert Maggione, have had an immeasurable effect on the art of bird carving, and they have affected my thinking as well. Yet, both refrain from competitions; neither covets blue ribbons; and they take no birds to Ward Foundation-type exhibits. As a result, they are not featured in this book.

The oriole was created by Larry Barth. Through the window is the view he sees daily as he sculpts his birds. Barth believes in observing wildfowl in their natural habitats.

If there is any bird sculptor who feels he deserved a chapter, I offer apologies. There were, in fact, two noted ribbon takers, fine artists of waterfowl and other birds, I wanted to include, but they had decided on doing their own texts. To them I wish only the best and hope this book offers some help in their ventures. Also, there was an exceptional artist named William Schultz of Wisconsin who, with his consent, would have had a chapter. Regrettably, he died in 1983, shortly before the book was started. He is greatly respected in the field.

My final comments, before you enter the world of these talented men, are in the way of acknowledgments. Such credits seem to me to get out of hand, like cluttered directories of not-so-important people. But a few names need to be noted here. Of course I'm thankful to the nine who offered so much hospitality, both Northern and Southern. A special thank you must go to Stackpole editor Judith Schnell. For if an author is married to his book, Judith is its bridesmaid. It was she who approached me to write and photograph it, and the encouragement was always there when I wondered if I would ever get enough "polished" photos. Cindy Doerzbach of the Ward Foundation is to be thanked for help with the project, as is photographer Paul Olivelli for his invaluable advice. And finally, there are a couple of friends out there named John Kelsey and Jim Beatty who played early roles in making this book possible.

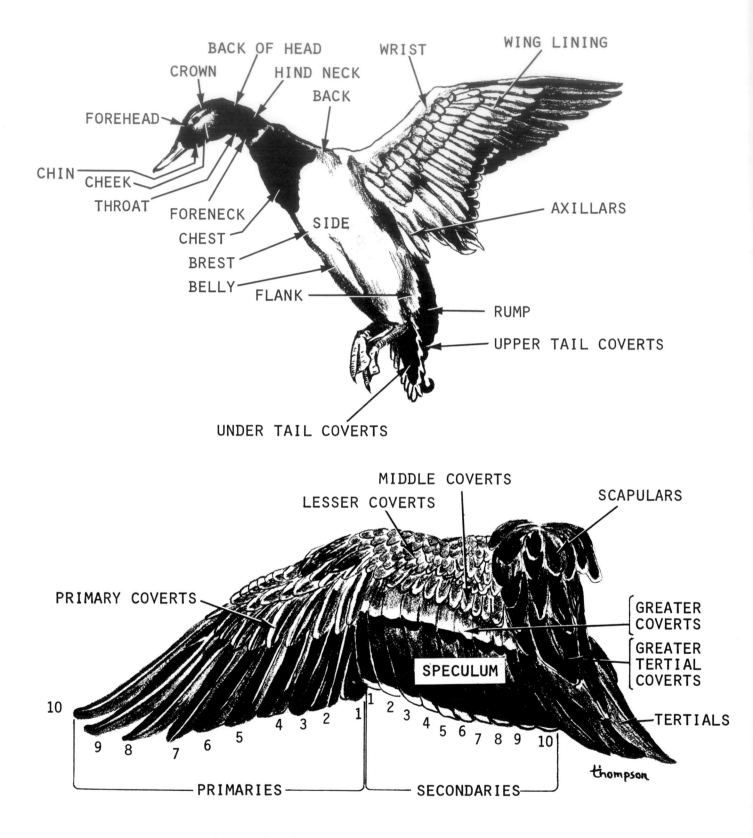

Duck topography and typical wing. Courtesy of Wildlife Management Institute.

1

Lynn Forehand

Shaping With the Foredom Tool

The Artist and His Work

"Anyone sculpting birds for a living probably uses a Foredom tool," says Lynn Forehand. "I can shape a small bird a day with it, then spend a day to texture it, and a day to paint it."

This artist's day, then, is a productive one, for he claims to average twelve hours each day in composing, shaping, and detailing birds, sometimes working seven days a week to keep up with production and make a living.

This man, whose background is rooted in architecture, which, he says, has helped his sense of perspective and his ability to put carved birds in the air, is no newcomer to this field. He began carving decoys when he was about ten years old, though he started as a whittler of pine bark at age six or even earlier. He is typical of many of these artists who have found carving a time for being by oneself. At those times, he says, "you can learn to do a lot with your work."

Over the years his projects have changed considerably from the decoys and freeform sculptures in bark he started with. But there is still a suggestion of youthfulness and individuality when he says of his work today, "Every morning is like Christmas morning. You get up and you know your day is going to end up with something you did yourself with your hands, with no boss to direct you." He's quick to add, "But the mistakes are yours, no one else's."

Lynn Forehand, an accomplished carver of large and small pieces, uses power tools to give shape to birds. Here he roughs out a miniature pheasant with the Foredom tool.

Not all his efforts are done in isolation. He does teach his techniques to others, but, he admits, not everyone can do blue ribbon carving. Succinctly put, he says, "You can give a person direction but you can't give him talent."

He was fortunate to receive good direction from some of the pioneers in the field of making birds out of wood. The biggest advances in carving, he recalls, came early in the decade of the 1970s. During those years, men like Gilbert Maggione and Grainger McKoy brought to shows birds with not only feather inserts, unlike their decoy predecessors, but also birds in flight. As Forehand puts it, "It was getting the bird off its belly and onto its feet, and off its feet into the air, that changed the course of bird carving."

Forehand feels bird sculpture should be considered art, regardless of its handcrafted antecedents. He believes we should look to ourselves and our heritage for art rather than borrowing most of our cultural background from Europe. "We should not have to look there for standards that ultimately must come from within." And how does he define art? "Anything's an art that's done well enough," he says.

Why is there reluctance to accept bird sculpting as an art form? For a long time, Forehand feels, he and others were put into the same category as laborers, though he readily admits they may do fine work. He theorizes that carvers, because of the social climate and work ethic they were brought up in, were at one time considered lazy and unproductive. Consequently, they were forced to work privately, "at night, when the world was dark."

What has also contributed to the art-or-craft controversy are the shows themselves. "Because our work is displayed on a table and not on a painter's A frame," he says, "it is considered a craft." Yet, he points out, the shows have exposed his medium to collectors with money who, with their purchases, have helped dispel some of the prejudices against wood sculpture.

Forehand has seen a benefit in the competitive shows, in that they have helped improve the quality of sculpted birds. He says of his friend, John Scheeler, "The man encourages competitions. That's what makes him such a great guy." This same man, with over two dozen Best in Show awards to his credit, has encouraged Forehand to keep at a piece for competition when frustration was getting the better of him.

Competitions have their drawbacks, however. Forehand, who has been a judge at many, often hears complaints. "Many carvers will complain, after not even placing, that the show was rigged. I've judged shows from Maryland to New Orleans to California, and I've never heard the slightest suggestion among the judges that anything like that was going on. You simply can't do it." And if there were collusion? "It would ruin you," he states emphatically.

What about the individual who says, 'I worked so hard and I didn't win?' That person should realize that there are more brown or consolation ribbons out there than blue ones. And you'd better get used to them." Perhaps this is why Forehand says, "When I'm working on a piece, it's the final product that counts—so be your own judge."

He says, when he is at a show he judges the piece of work, not the carver. And, he feels, the good carvers accept the judge's assessment, though they may not always agree with it.

Is there a supreme carver in this field? Forehand does not believe so, basing his answer on what kind of work collectors buy. "I don't think there is a best artist. If there were, then no one would buy anything but that particular person's work. When you're buying these birds, you're buying an individual's style." This is why Forehand and the others featured in this book strongly urge a carver not to copy a winning piece. "It's a sure way to stagnation." In fact, he adds, "People won't buy your work because it looks like another's. They'll buy it because it's a piece of you."

Birds and Realism

Forehand says that birds have been historically and prehistorically popular, having appeared not only on the walls of pyramids, but also on the walls of cave-dwellers. But there is more to birds than just pictorial or sculpted representations, he suggests. "Birds give more than they take, being part of a healthy ecology. They are not out to change or destroy it." There are even anatomical aspects we should be able to relate to, he adds. "The bird's anatomy is not too dissimilar to our own. It has, by comparison, a forearm, an arm, and a hand."

Recognizing such similarities and developing an understanding of the bird's anatomy have resulted in the biggest changes in Forehand's work. He says, "You must realize that a bird is made of muscle and bone, but at the same time covered with feathers." (Further discussion of anatomy is given in chapter 6 by Larry Barth.) Yet there are differences, for birds themselves differ from one another, a fact the carver must be

Typical of what can be done with the Foredom is this miniature turkey.

In another sculpture, three grebes fight over tadpoles. Still another depicts Ross' gulls fighting over tadpoles. And a fourth piece is titled "Battling Coots." Forehand defends what he sculpts, saying, "This is what birds do. Usually it is to eat. A bluejay, for example, steals eggs, a crow steals young from a nest. This is not violence but acts of natural order. Neither is it cruel. The word 'conflict' is not really accurate, then." Is there an underlying reason for doing such compositions? "These sculptures explain ecology in a way you just can't do with words," he explains.

It should be pointed out that pieces like the jungle fowl and Ross' gulls are large, life-size sculptures. The latter, in fact, measures some thirty inches from the base to the top bird. Forehand says, "I'm prone to a large, complicated piece, but you can't just do one unless you have someone to commission you." His largest commissioned piece to date features two great blue herons in flight, measuring nine feet in height.

Forehand points out that agreeing on a concept for a commissioned piece is often difficult if it's based on the buyer's description of what he wants. Making miniatures, however, takes on, literally, a different dimension. He explains, "There are not many people who have the space to collect life-size birds. With miniatures, you can make a good living, and a buyer is likely to purchase another." For this reason, he adds, decoys are also popular.

Observation and References

Outside Forehand's studio is a crabapple tree. Hanging on it is a feeder to attract birds. Of a small nuthatch he observes while working, he says, "You see him crawling up and down trees, frontways, sideways, upside down. He's a real active little guy. Not a very noisy bird. Very quiet."

Forehand is a careful observer of birds, as are most of the other artists featured in this book. He feels, as do the others, that this is not the only way to develop references for carving or sculpture. Going to a park pond or to the woods, with sketchbook in hand, are other ways to study birds. (Compare James Sprankle and Larry Hayden, chapters 8 and 9, who maintain their own aviaries.) But if you really want to know a bird, Forehand says, "you must have a study skin."

Collecting birds in this country has been limited by laws enacted to protect many species of birds from just that. Yet, Forehand says, there are museums that will loan study skins to a serious artist. The skin for the

aware of. For example, tertials, which comprise a set of flight feathers, may be dissimilar. "And there is even a difference between a beak and a bill," he adds.

Aware now of bird anatomy and its peculiarities, he strives for as much realism in a piece as he can. There are limits, Forehand admits. For example, "There's no way you can duplicate a feather. Maybe someday somebody will, but at present no one's capable of doing that. What's being done today is something that suggests realism." He refers to Ernest Muehlmatt (chapter 3) who burns "hot and cold" to achieve shades of dark and light in a feather. "This is an example of a superb technique," Forehand points out, "but it will likely be surpassed by Muehlmatt himself and others who strive for improvement of today's methods. Such is the inquisitive and exploratory nature of the creative mind," he says.

In Forehand's efforts to achieve realism, there is a conflict that seems, at times, violent. A composition that won the Best in World ribbon at the World Championship Wildfowl Carving Competition in 1979 is entitled "Red Jungle Fowl." In this piece, two birds appear to do battle among a miniexplosion of dandelion fluff.

On the tracing paper overlay, Forehand starts to define the anatomy of the pheasant. He can build up lines or eliminate them on successive sketches. Here he gives some definition to the neck and breast areas.

Shown here is a styrofoam model of a song bird. The material is good for modelmaking, says Forehand, but should be used with caution. Fumes or dust from the styrofoam can be harmful.

By adding feathers, legs, and eye, Forehand begins to get a picture of what he wants as he transfers details he has gathered from specimens and photographs. The sketching is done, he says, "with pencil and imagination."

When making a pattern, Forehand starts with an egg-shaped oval for the body. Then he draws the tail and neck lines and another oval for the head and designates the beak and wing. Making no erasures, he says these are "a few quick lines I can draw on top of."

The final overlay or drawing should be only the outline to be bandsawed. He omits legs and any other cross-grained areas that will break while carving.

Preliminary sketches, a series of overlays, of a miniature pheasant.

jungle fowl, in fact, originally came from Mindinao in the Philippines nearly one hundred years ago. Forehand borrowed it from The Denver Museum of Natural History. Another composition, a black swan study, was done using a specimen loaned by The American Museum of Natural History in New York City.

For other sources of study skins you might consider trying game wardens who often keep evidence lockers of dead birds. Still other specimens are available from the days when dead birds were collectible. The science department of a local school or university may have kept mounted birds or study skins. And some states may have specimen libraries.

What can you do if you can not locate specimens? Forehand suggests that photographs are the next best source. He recommends *Prairie Wings: Pen and Camera Flight Studies* by Edgar M. Queeny. (This book and others used by the artists for reference are listed in the bibliography.)

Valuable too are other books which feature meticulous paintings of birds grouped by regions. One such set is the Lansdowne series. Although many carvers refer to these books, Forehand cautions against following the details in the pictures too closely. Painters often beautify birds to the point where they may not be anatomically correct. "A painter may change the bird somewhat, say, drop the side feathers way down on a waterfowl to exaggerate the wing feathers. In such instances, accuracy succumbs to artistic license. That's why a carver should always work from a specimen."

There is still another reference a carver can work from, and that is a model. Many varieties and materials can be used, from clay to styrofoam to foam rubber, with wings made of sheet metal, cardboard, clay and combinations of the three. Forehand prefers a model made solely of styrofoam.

The advantage in working with a model rather than a mounted bird or study skin is that a model shows exactly how a bird looks in a certain position. Forehand advises, when making a styrofoam model, that you take care not to breathe in the dust. This precludes using a Foredom tool for the shaping. "I just use a knife and slice it," Forehand says. To smooth the styrofoam down, he takes another piece of the same material and rubs it against the carved work. He warns against trying to burn through the styrofoam with a hot wire or blade, because the fumes are extremely toxic. He concludes, "Styrofoam is useful if you handle it correctly, dangerous if you don't."

Some of the other carvers, Gary Yoder (chapter 7)

for example, do sketches of their birds that are anatomically meticulous, sometimes stripping away, like an anatomy text, the feathers and skin to see where the bones are positioned. Forehand's sketches are less elaborate. He will start with a few quick lines, something he can build on. The first sketch may be an egg shape to represent the body. By overlaying sheets of tracing paper, he can build on top of that basic sketch. The next sheet may bring out nothing more than the tail feathers of a bird. He won't make erasures because, he says, "Drawing one line may be better than drawing two that will only confuse me." Instead of erasing, then, he continues sketching and overlaying until he gets a final sketch he can be satisfied with. On that last sketch he overlays one final sheet of paper and traces a pattern or profile for the block of wood to be shaped. Of the whole process, he says, "I'm really making sketches of ideas going through my head."

The Personality of Wood

For his carving Forehand has sampled different woods, not all to his liking. He has used magnolia and

Hard, grainless, and capable of holding fine detail, this piece of tupelo gum comes from Louisiana and is a favorite of many Cajun carvers.

Bandsawed from basswood, this piece will become a miniature pheasant, the result of Forehand's overlay sketching.

cypress (the latter tends to crack), woods more available in his area of the South. He has also worked with white cedar, which was often used to make wood decoys. At one time this was the only wood he worked with until he turned to basswood.

A popular wood with carvers for some time, basswood has replaced even pine as a favorite wood. Somewhat cream colored, it is relatively grainless and sapless. Consequently, it holds detail well, especially the kind put in with hand-held carving tools. Basswood offers a clear and clean surface for paint, one that will not bleed through as a pine surface will, owing to the resins in that wood.

Lately he has experimented with a wood called tupelo gum, the only wood used by Scheeler, and jelutong, used by Muehlmatt. Forehand finds the jelutong too expensive, but the tupelo gum, he says, can be textured for fine detail. The only problem with it may be that it varies, sometimes considerably, in degrees of hardness.

Tupelo gum was introduced by Louisiana carvers known as Cajuns, he explains, probably because it is plentiful in their area. Only the first several feet of the tree are used. Some Cajuns, he says, work the wood wet, although Forehand prefers working it dry. "It can be cut so thin and sanded so finely, it can be read through and can even be cut with scissors," he notes. And though it has all these attributes, Forehand admits it may not be as easy to work with for some as for others.

Regardless of the type of wood used, he believes that each piece of wood has a personality of its own. A piece of wood cut only a foot away from another piece may have all the differences in the world, he claims.

His advice, then, is to find woods that suit the carver, yet ones that are close-grained. Basswood and tupelo gum have that characteristic and are the most suitable for Forehand.

Power Tools, Hand Tools, and the Art Form

The Foredom tool, though not developed for the carving industry, is used by nearly all the carvers in this book. Those who do not use the Foredom use its smaller counterpart, the Dremel Moto-Tool. Along with a variety of bits, both of these power tools are used to remove wood because they can shape quickly and coarsely. They can also remove minute amounts of wood to achieve fine detail.

The Foredom, in particular, with its flexible shaft and cannister motor, is definitely the tool Forehand prefers. He states, "You can visualize something in wood and the Foredom allows it to happen." As a sculpting tool, "it allows you latitude when dealing with a block of wood with its different grain and firmness. I don't know any carver who could survive without the Foredom tool. You've got to use it. It's faster." Yet, he argues, speed does not take away from his art or ultimate product. He says, emphatically, "The use of power tools today is not a deterrent to the art form."

As you study the photographs in this book, you will see a variety of bits and attachments of many sizes used with the Foredom, from coarse, conical-shaped rasps, to ruby-impregnated cutters called ruby carvers, to dental burrs, to sanding drums. (See appendix for a list of suppliers.) The ball-shaped rotary rasp will, for example, permit Forehand to work in concave areas. A conical-shaped rasp does the rough work on convex surfaces. And an elongated, pencil-shaped bit will remove the roughness from the coarse grinding stages. Using a finer rasp with finer teeth, Forehand says, "allows you to get anatomy closer to what you think it is, the area most people have trouble with." And the ruby cutters and dental bits can make the most intricate detailing possible.

Forehand does not believe in using the Foredom for all aspects of shaping and detailing. It is the knife that gives Forehand's birds their anatomical correctness. And it removes the fuzziness from the basswood that is brought out by rasps, burrs, and bits. He advises, when using the Foredom, to "leave enough wood that

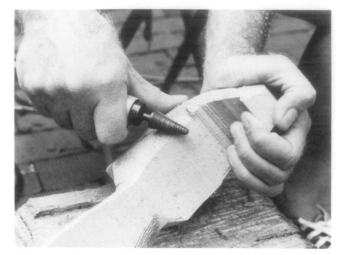

This coarse, heavy-toothed rasp and Foredom handpiece will take the corners off a bandsawed-to-shape piece of wood.

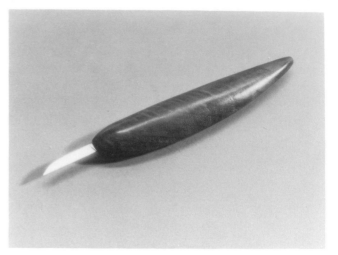

After Forehand is finished with the grinding tool, he uses a Knotts-made knife with a polished walnut handle to put in detail.

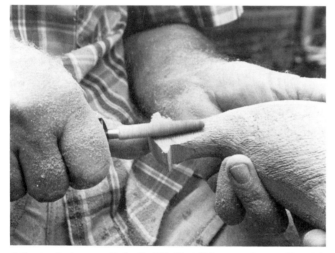

A fine-toothed rasp, called a Karbide Kutzall, has very fine needles sticking out from the shaft. It cuts effortlessly, removing the coarse marks left by the heavy-toothed rasp. Suppliers of the bit are listed in the appendix.

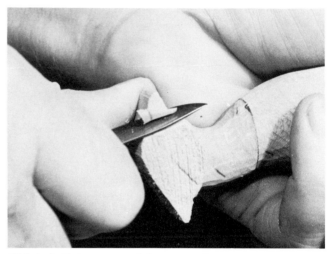

With the knife, he can control the amount of wood he removes. Here he gives shape to the beak of the miniature pheasant.

This is an assortment of carbide cutters, with a few steel cutters in the front, all adaptable to the Foredom tool.

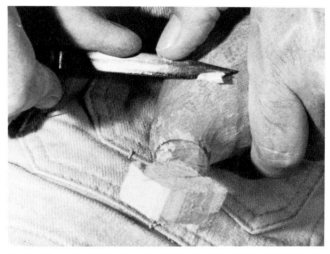

Forehand says that when he pushes the back of the blade with his thumb, he has total control of the knife.

when you cut away the fuzzy stuff, you still have a bird left." He puts it another way, "I use the knife at this point to skin off the rough stuff while at the same time to get a feel of the bird that is in the wood."

Forehand believes the basic technique in using a knife is learning how to make the knife go through the wood. "Don't try to take off too much wood at one time. And remember which way the grain is running. You must go with the grain, never against it. If you do you can chip out something. And once the wood is removed, it's just too difficult to put it back." He adds, "I've seen people liking so much what they're cutting away, they made their birds lopsided."

The knives Forehand has been most pleased with are made by Cheston Knotts of Wilmington, Delaware. (See appendix for full address.) Believing that Knotts supplies ninety percent of the professional carvers who use knives, he says, "He's the only person making a knife worthy of consideration." In fact, Forehand still has his first Knotts knife. The pocket knives he started carving with got dull quickly, and when he switched to Knotts's knives, he never went back to using pocket knives.

Forehand has found that Knotts's steel blades do not "roll up on you," a characteristic of poor steel and stainless steel. Nor do they need a great deal of regrinding. "I can go forever with just touching up," he says. For this he uses nothing more than a piece of hard white buffing compound. As for making knives himself, he says, "It's just not worth buying steel, grinding it down, then making a handle for it." Forehand cautions against using X-acto knives because their points can break off in the wood, causing problems if they are not found and extracted immediately.

For basic tools Forehand does not stop with the Foredom and the knives. Another tool so basic and necessary it is used by all nine artists is the burning tool. (See appendix for manufacturers.) Unlike the old heavy, brass-tipped wood burners, the burners used today have thin wire tips that will add the finest detail to feathers. With one of these burners, John Scheeler can burn in no less than eighty barbs, those hairlike lines of a feather, to an inch.

One such burning tool, developed solely for carvers of birds, is The Detailer, manufactured by Colwood Electronics of New Jersey. Offering a number of interchangeable tips for different, specialized uses, Colwood Electronics has made a burner with a boxed-in rheostat control for altering the heat supplied to the tip. The handle itself is lightweight, made to be used like a

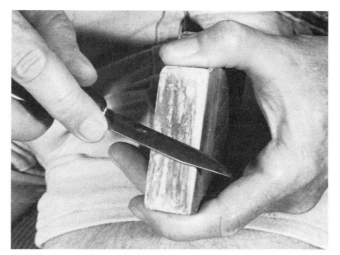
A knife edge can be touched up by stroking it on a cake of hard white buffing compound.

The Detailer is a typical burning tool with a penlike handpiece and a tip for adding detail to birds.

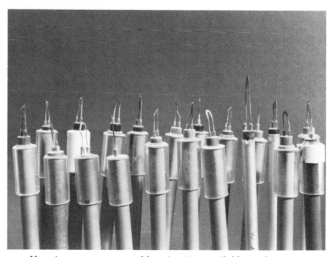
Here is an assortment of burning tips available to the carver.

During the initial development of a piece, Forehand works outdoors with the Foredom to avoid getting the fine dust and chips all over his house. Note the intravenous stand which holds the Foredom motor.

The coarse rasp can help with a great deal of the shaping. Note the amount of shavings thrown off by the bit.

writing instrument, and is usually referred to as a burning pen.

With one of these burners, Forehand can burn in details like the barbs of feathers and their shaft lines. But Forehand has run into problems using the burner on basswood. Although the wood details well with the burning pen, sap builds up on the tip and it must be cleaned frequently. If that's not done, the burning line will widen as the tip grows thick with wood residue.

Forehand shares the last word on tools when he says, "Whether you use a Foredom tool or a knife, tupelo gum or basswood, it still comes down to one thing — the artist who created the piece."

Making a Miniature Pheasant

Forehand's pheasant, only ten inches in length, begins like many of his birds, on the drawing board as a series of overlays. Simple ovals lend shape to the bird as details are added with each new sheet of tracing paper. Finally, after the posture and form of the bird are determined, a pattern can be made.

After the pattern is made, it is transferred to a solid block of basswood, then the wood is cut to shape on a bandsaw. The block, now in cubist shape, can then be rounded and concaved under the tail feathers with the Foredom and its many burrs and cutters.

The solid block might not remain a solid piece. Like other carvers, Forehand may find it advantageous to sever the head, or even the torso, and rotate that part

Forehand advises caution when working near edges. Because of the clockwise rotation of the Foredom, the teeth of the rasp can run around and catch your other hand. Forehand oftens wears a heavy leather glove for this work.

As work on the piece progresses, he checks the thickness of the body with calipers. But he never cuts the wood down to a final size, preferring, instead to reduce the wood in stages. This avoids taking away too much wood in any one area.

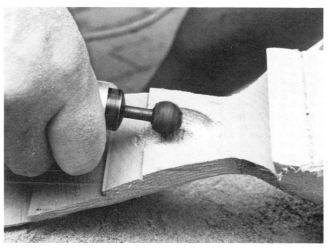

Work begins on the underside of the tail with a heavy-toothed, ball-shaped rasp. This bit allows Forehand to work in concave areas, though they must be bigger than the ball itself.

Continuing to hollow out the underside of the tail, Forehand leaves enough thickness to prevent breaking the feather edges.

At this stage the work of roughing of the body with the heavy rasp is complete.

The roughing has been completed.

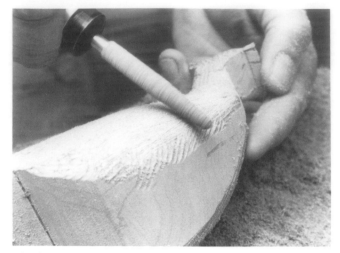

The fine-toothed Karbide Kutzall rasp is used to remove the coarse marks left by the roughing-out work.

Used to make the cut is a fine-toothed X-acto saw, one which removes as little wood as possible. No smoothing of the faces of the joint will be necessary when this saw is used.

Note that with the fine rasp, Forehand works from the head back to the tail.

The head is turned to determine the desired pose. Care should be taken that the head is not cocked to one side.

Now he draws a line on each side of the pheasant's neck. This will be a reference when the head is cut from the body and turned to give the bird a more animated look.

Forehand uses a coffee stirrer to apply a five-minute, two-part epoxy to each face of the joint.

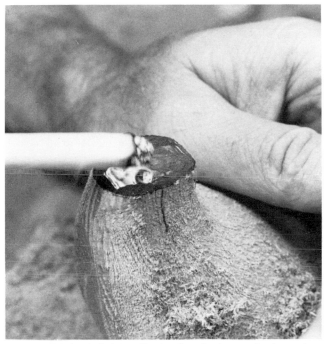

For a very brief period of time, Forehand applies heat to the glue surface. This further liquifies the glue, allowing it to be drawn deeper into the wood. He believes this also makes for a stronger bond.

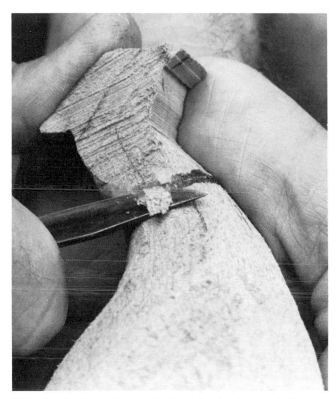

When the glue has set but not hardened, Forehand uses a knife to cut away any excess. A rasp should not be used at this point, because the glue might clog the teeth.

The head is glued in position and is ready for trimming. Note, by the pencil lines, how much it was turned.

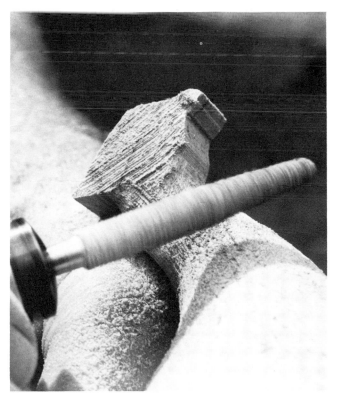

Once the excess glue has been cut away, a fine rasp is used to create a smooth, even flow from the breast, up through the neck area, to under the head.

Note how the head is turned and a smooth flow from the body up through the head has been achieved.

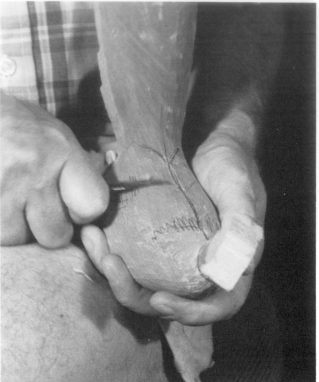

The straight pencil lines are areas to be raised as feather groups. The scribbled lines are areas from which more wood must be removed.

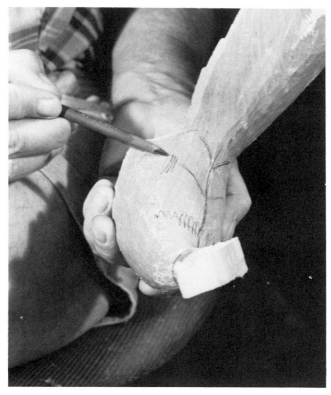

Now all coarse rasp marks have been removed with the knife, leaving a smooth surface to draw on. At no time, says Forehand, should sandpaper be used until the carving is completed. Sanding grit lodged in the wood will dull the knife.

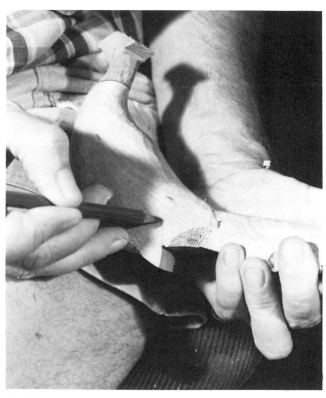

At this point, Forehand refers to his drawing and locates the wings on the carving.

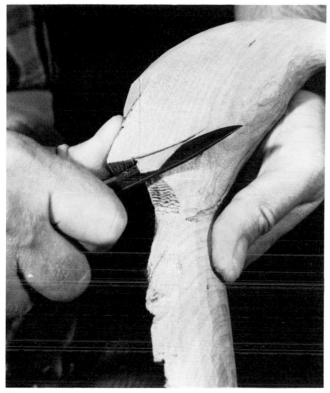

The wing area is raised by removing wood behind it. Wood is also re-moved from the tail area so the tail can be contoured.

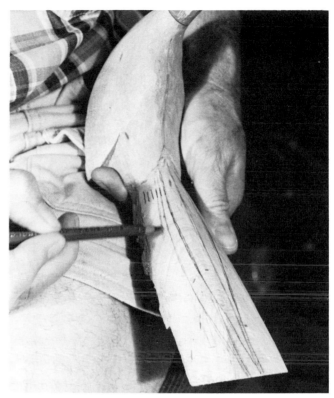

Forehand continues to sketch in the feathers. Note that there are six on either side of the central feather.

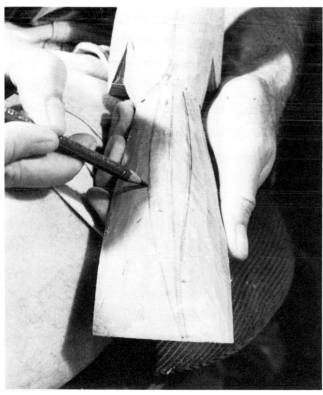

The next step is to draw in the tail feathers, beginning with the central one. Forehand uses a soft pencil, so the lines can easily be erased and will not make an impression in the wood. If changes have to be made, it is difficult to draw over lines made with a heavy hand.

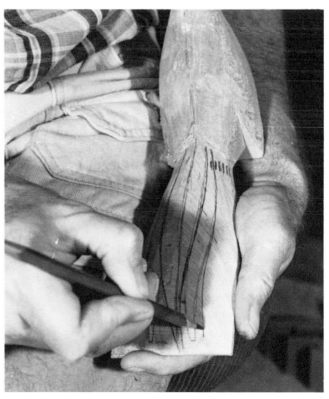

He takes care to divide the area so the feathers will have enough space to run into the body. He also draws them to one side to give the bird a sense of motion.

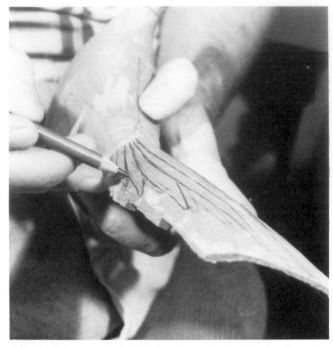

Here the feathers on the left side have been sketched. Forehand consults reference material for the correct number of feathers, their lengths, and widths.

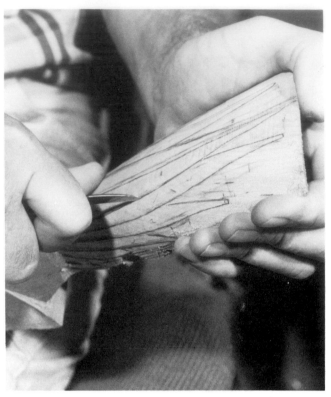

Now that all the tail feathers are drawn, Forehand makes 90-degree stop cuts along the lines. These lines will safeguard against any chipping that may occur as he saws between the feathers.

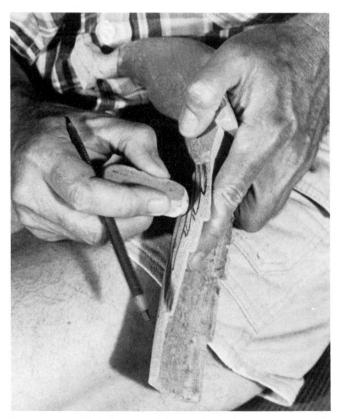

You can expect that changes will have to be made to create graceful, flowing lines. Use a soft vinyltype eraser to clean away the graphite and prevent smudging.

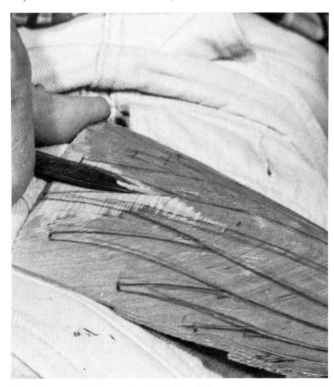

Wood is removed between the tail feathers before sawing. Forehand calls this "shading in."

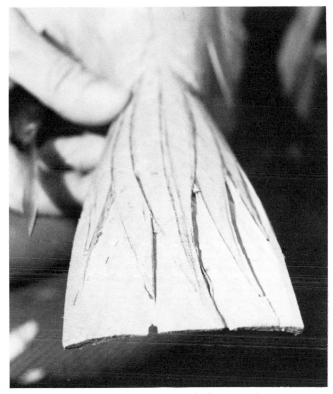

The tail feathers are now ready for separation.

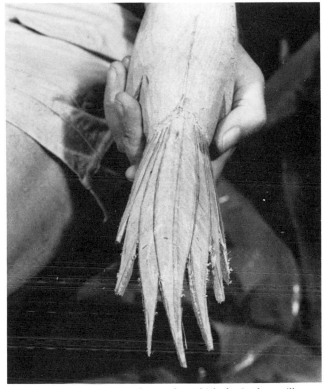

The wood has been removed. Note how thick the feathers still are.

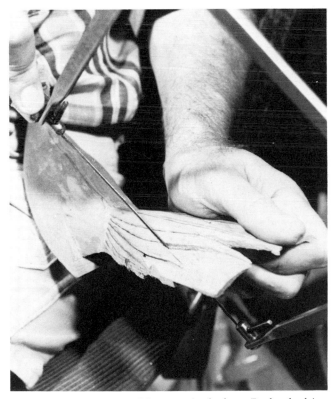

A coping saw removes wood between the feathers. Forehand advises using a fine-toothed blade and working with pull strokes. Those stop cuts made in a previous step will prevent sawing into the feathers.

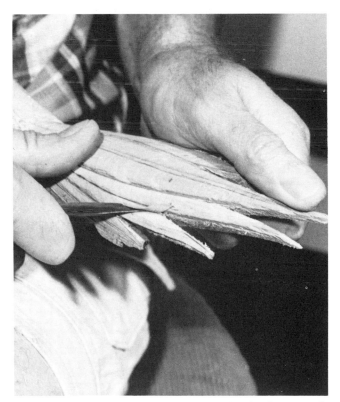

A convex surface is carved on top of each feather, but less so on the smaller ones. Forehand may increase the depth of the stop cuts, but he will only make them deep enough to carve the surface. Too deep a cut may result in so much wood being carved away that the edge of a feather will be lost when it is finally separated from the rest.

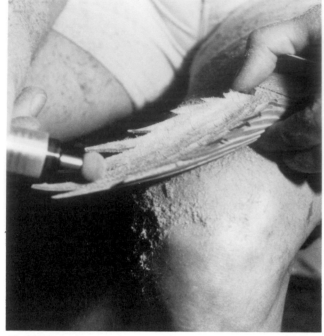

The ball-shaped rasp removes the remaining thickness and forms a concave surface corresponding to the top.

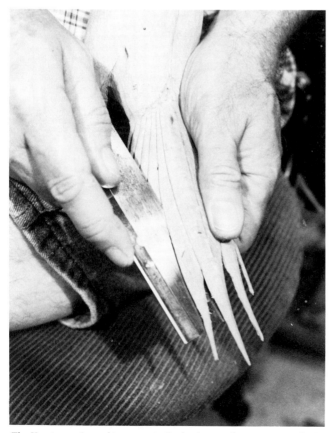

The X-acto saw is used to separate the feathers and create an overlaying effect. Forehand works with a pull stroke.

With the feather separating done, Forehand takes a razor-sharp knife and removes some of the top surface of an underlying feather.

Further separation can be achieved by sanding between feathers. This step also cleans up all saw and knife marks. With a garnet paper, he uses a pull stroke.

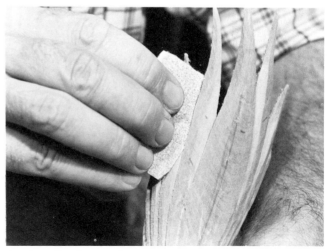

Finish-sanding between feathers is done with fine grit paper. Here he goes in both directions with the paper.

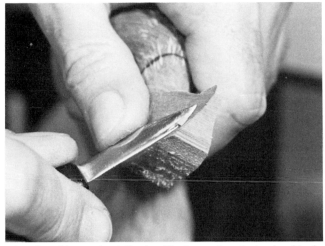

When the tail is completed, Forehand begins work on the head and beak.

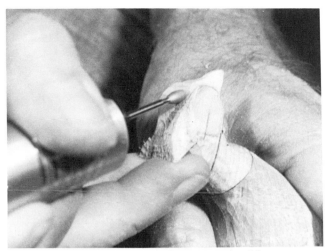

Using another small Karbide Kutzall cutter, Forehand leaves an area above the side of the head to resemble a heavy brow.

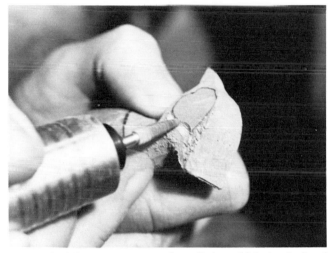

After the beak has been carved, a side profile is established and relieved with a small Karbide Kutzall cutter.

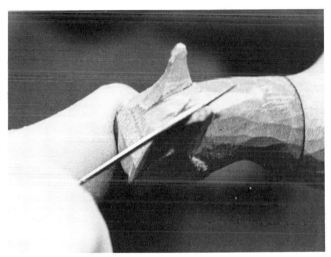

Wood is carved out between the tufts, thereby forming the back of the head.

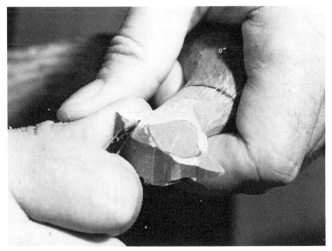

Next, Forehand forms the tufts, sometimes called ears, which stick out behind the pheasant's head.

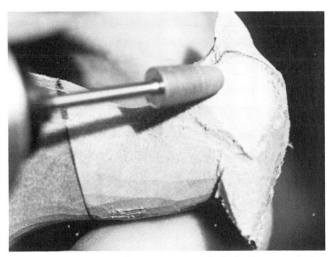

Forehand switches to a ruby carver to smooth the knife cuts and other marks. He can use this tool to form the concave area on either side of the head, sinking it in to bring out more detail. Suppliers of ruby carvers are listed in the appendix.

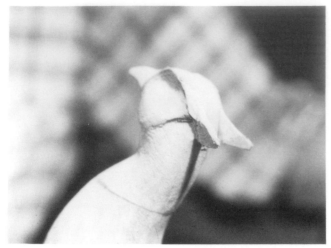

The head, beak, side and ear tufts are completed.

Rendering of these feathers is done in a fashion similar to the tail feathers.

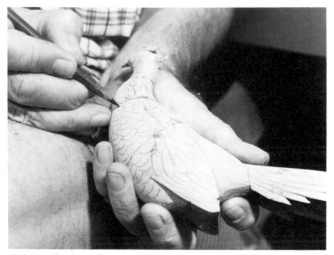

Referring back to drawings, Forehand begins the feather layout. He notes that what appears on a flat photo or drawing will not come out the same way on a rounded surface.

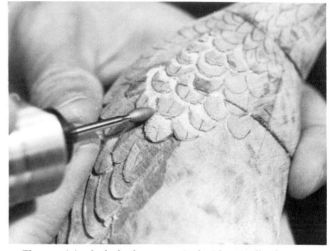

The remaining body feathers are raised with a small ruby carver.

Once the feathers are laid out, stop cuts are made around all the flight feathers, tertials, secondaries, and primaries.

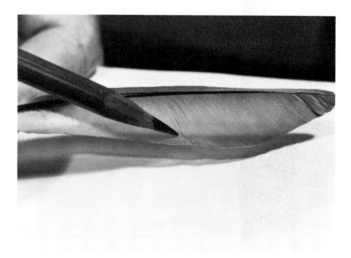

A real feather is shown here to point out the splits and breaks that occur in most feathers. A few like this are done on the body, but this technique is used most often for the tail feathers.

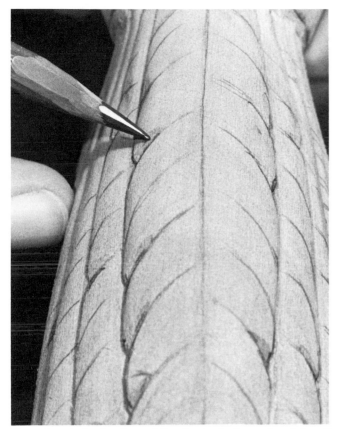

Shown here is the direction to follow for the final texturing of the tail feathers. Occasional stop cuts are made.

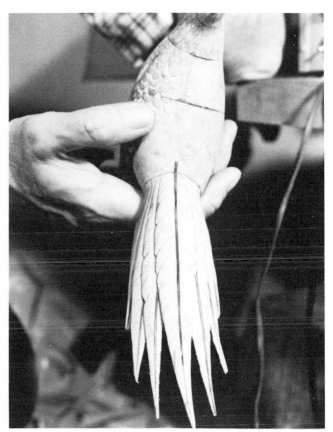

The pheasant is shown here ready for final texturing with a small grinding stone and burning tool.

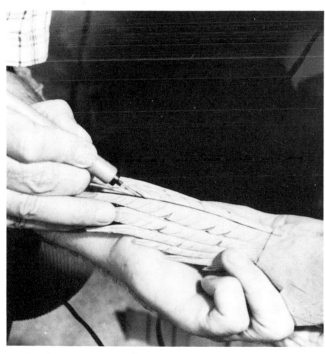

Forehand burns in the shaft lines. These will act as guides for final texturing.

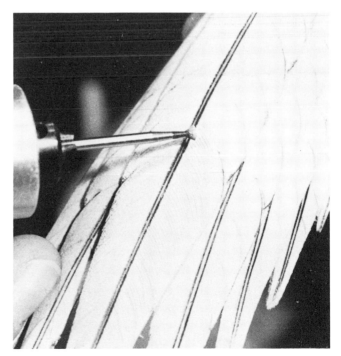

Forehand uses this small, conical-shaped abrasive stone to put in the barb lines that make up a feather.

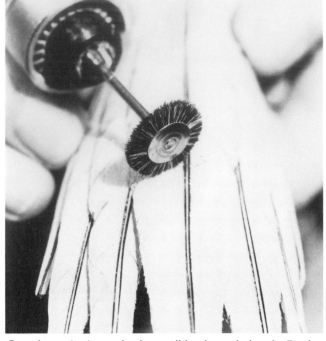

Once the stoning is completed, a small brush attached to the Foredom is used to clean up as much "fuzz" or raised grain as possible. The next step is to touch up the stoning with the burner. The final step before painting is applying lacquer and then "burnishing" the wood with the rotary brush.

of the anatomy. Using a two-part epoxy, that part can be glued in a slightly different position and flared into the body again with knife and Foredom tool.

Once the pheasant has been more finely shaped with a long burr, lines can be penciled on those body areas that need to be removed with the knife.

Asked why he does not make the tail feathers as separate pieces and insert them, as some others do, Forehand admits that it would be easier to do the feathers separately. But he feels the value of his bird lies partly in its being carved totally from a solid block of wood.

Once the feathers are penciled on top of the tail section, with some trial-and-error drawing, they are then separated and given definition with knife, coping saw, and sandpaper. Then the underneath is gone over with a ball rasp to reduce the thickness of the feathers.

Using ruby carvers and knife, Forehand works next on the head. Establishing the eyes and the beak must be done with knife and ruby cutters. Forehand points

Note the layered but relatively smooth look of the turkey's breast.

A close look at the turkey's side will show the effects of stoning for texture.

out that the pheasant is a seedeater. A specialist like the cardinal in that it can crush seeds, it has a beak that is both short and stubby.

The next step is to lay out the feathers with a pencil and detail them with a ruby carver. By outlining them, the effect of feathers laying over and under is achieved.

Not all barbs line up perfectly on a bird. Consequently, there are splits, sometimes resulting in an over-and-under effect. These Forehand emphasizes on the tail feathers, using the point of his knife, while the burning pen can lay in shaft lines in the centers of the tail feathers.

After slightly singeing the bird with a propane torch and lacquering it, Forehand can go over the bird with a small rotary brush adaptable to the Foredom. The friction of the brush against the lacquer irons out the remaining traces of fuzz. The bird is then ready to be painted.

2

Ernest Muehlmatt

Burning for Color

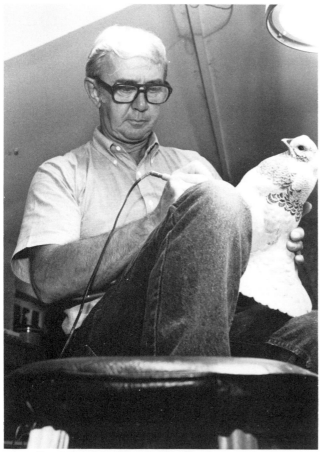

Ernest Muehlmatt burns in the colors on a spruce grouse.

Ernest Muehlmatt burns his colors into wood. Granted, he is limited to shades ranging from brown to a scorched wood black, but the basic tones of his birds are done with a burning tool, similar or identical to the one used by Lynn Forehand.

Before his scorching-for-color techniques are discussed, let's learn something about his background.

Birds Are Flowers That Fly

Though Muehlmatt attended both an art and an advertising school where he learned illustration, layout, and design, much of his adult life was spent in the family greenhouse business, "hating every minute of it," he says, and wanting to do something with his education.

It was not until 1967 when he went to an exhibition of carved birds that he had the opportunity. Impressed with what he saw on display, he felt this was something he would like to do. The following year he returned to the same show as an exhibitor.

Lynn Forehand's theory that carving was not up to acceptable work ethic standards seems not to have been shared by Muehlmatt, although he started, he says, "making birds in the greenhouse boiler room early in the morning before anyone got to work." He carved part-time for five years, doing as many as ten birds a

Muehlmatt describes this baby chickadee as "a little flower arrangement," an obvious reference to his background. The base is walnut and the bird stands on a manzanita root.

day and selling them for six or seven dollars apiece. He says that "now it's doing something I love and making a living at it."

When he finished school, he went into the flower business, doing mostly floral arrangements. Of this experience he says, "I liked the Japanese influence in arranging flowers with S-lines and their portrayal of heaven, earth, and man, with the heaviest colors and the heaviest masses down low, while the lighter colors are up top in reeds and grasses." He feels he was good at this type of arranging. "After twenty years you had to be." The experience left an impact on what he does today. He admits that the influence of flower designs affects the way his birds are arranged in their habitats, recalling someone having said that "birds are flowers that fly."

Arranging Birds Like Flowers

In good flower arrangements, a focal point must be created to attract the eye of the observer. The focal point is the heaviest mass, the darkest color, Muehl-

An arrangement may begin with a base and a piece of wood. This wood was chosen because its straight grain will coincide with a woodcock's beak.

Here the bird is positioned so the beak follows the grain of the wood.

The leaves are added to form a "design line" that will lead the eye to the rear of the bird.

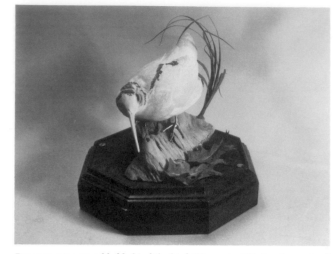

Paper grasses are added behind the bird. The curl will bring the eye back to the woodcock's head.

matt explains. But there must be a line to it, one that allows the eye to move out, yet return to that focal point. This way, he says, "your eye doesn't get annoyed." If there are too many heavy colors, too many focal points, the eye won't know where to go. "Your eye will jump around, the arrangement will annoy and bother you, and you may not even know why." He notes that this was also true of what he studied in advertising school. "I learned how to lay out a page with a focal point."

And the same, he says, is true of his bird arrangements. For even if the bird is accurate and has attractive feathers, he explains, it cannot overpower the arrangement with its color or position. This axiom

Sometimes Muehlmatt will put more than one bird in an arrangement. Here are three woodcocks sunning themselves in a woodland setting.

This painting, which Muehlmatt did from a carving, shows the Japanese influence on his arrangement.

This is the carved head of a bald eagle. The feathers are carved in a circular direction at the bottom, unlike the real eagle's, so the eye will come around and back to the beak. Muehlmatt says he sculpted this piece in the shape of an oval.

offers the crucial reason for choosing the birds he does — woodcocks, grouse, and quail.

Asked what mental processes lead to the actual arrangement of a bird and its habitat, Muehlmatt says he starts out with a mental picture of what he wants, with the major rule being, "I don't want something antagonistic to the eye." He may even make some sketches, though that will depend on how familiar he is with a bird he may have done before. Invariably he finds his piece comes close to the original sketch. "As in the flower business, I make a design and fit my birds to that."

Specifically referring to the Japanese influence, he relates the making of a sculpture he did of two least bitterns. When first viewed, the birds seem to be alike. But actually they are not, for their attitudes are reversed, he explains, which demonstrates the Japanese S-curves. This piece won Best in World in miniatures at the World Championship Wildfowl Carving Competition in 1981.

More typical of his sculptures is a woodcock (the focal point and heaviest mass) standing on a piece of wood (a neutral color of gray). The woodcock's long beak seems to point down to its feet at leaves of a color similar to, but not as strong as, the woodcock's. The eye, instead of returning to the bill, will continue on to a branch or grasses behind the bird. Only then will the eye return to the woodcock. "I keep you entertained this way," Muehlmatt explains. The circularity of the arrangement is complete.

He has done sculptures which have not included habitat, but he still follows the rules of arrangement. Two eagle heads, because of the combination of form, beak and feathering, move the eye along the piece without moving off it. He says, "I didn't want anything that would shoot your eye out and away from the head."

Birds of a Shaded Feather

Woodcocks are birds of earth tones, with shades of brown, black, autumn gold, gray, and white. Muehlmatt, like Eldridge Arnold (chapter 3), finds a fascination for the bird that goes beyond its coloring. Noting that they "have big beautiful eyes," he says their eyes are high up on the head, making it impossible to sneak up on a woodcock.

Living in moist woodland, swamps, and thickets, the woodcock eats nothing but earthworms. Its bill, which can be used as a probe, has adapted to its habitat in such a way that when it digs for food, only the very

There is a compactness to this carving of a golden eagle's head. Used for a bronze casting, it was left unpainted.

tip need be opened. Muehlmatt says, also, that if an area looks dry of worms, the woodcock will spread out its wings and flutter them. This movement, which sounds like raindrops falling on top of the earth and leaves, brings the worms to surface, since they do not want to be in the ground when it is raining. The woodcock's habitat, then, is made up of leaves and low branches, both of which are integral parts of Muehlmatt's sculptures.

The spruce grouse, with colors similar to the woodcock's, is also an appropriate subject for Muehlmatt's arrangements and burning techniques. Muehlmatt says they are beautiful birds that live in the northern parts of the United States and Canada. Found in a habitat

Here is the same golden eagle's head painted. Muehlmatt set it on a piece of marble not only to give contrast to the golden brown bird, but also to represent the eagle's mountain habitat.

One feature of the woodcock that appeals to Muehlmatt is its eyes.

Quail are also birds he burns for color. This print was done from an actual carving.

Because of its coloring, Muehlmatt will do birds like the spruce grouse. The mount on the left stands in contrast to the carved bird yet to be finished.

Muehlmatt has a fondness for doing baby chickadees. He has, in fact, carved over 2,500 of them.

of coniferous forest, the spruce grouse eats only spruce needles ("They have a terrible taste," he comments.) and berries. These grouse are fairly tame. When flushed they may fly to the lower limbs of trees and remain there. "You can hit one with a stick," he says.

Muehlmatt has also done quail, and among them he finds many variations of color from pure white to a burnt sienna color to black. Probably one of the most popular game birds in the United States, the bobwhite quail, Muehlmatt says, "is an ideal subject for coloring with a burning pen."

And though he has done songbirds such as chickadees and shorebirds, usually he chooses game birds like woodcocks and quail because of their shades of brown and black.

This pair of semipalmated plovers carved by Muehlmatt are sleeping with their heads into the wind.

Burning for Color

Credit goes to a Louisiana Cajun carver named Tan Brunet for giving Muehlmatt the idea of using burning lines as a basis for a bird's coloration. Noting that Brunet burns very neatly and precisely, Muehlmatt had seen a pintail duck Brunet brought to a show. He had burned in barbs and shaft lines, but he had left the bird unpainted. Muehlmatt recalled how soft the duck looked without paint on it.

Most important to Muehlmatt's technique is the burning pen and its tip. He does most of his feather detailing with a tight round point, one that he invented and is now supplied by Colwood Electronics. "It's a very fast point," he says, "because you can backstroke with it." He points out that many other carvers, like Forehand for instance, use a skew-type point, but "you can't back up with it. You have to drag it toward you and hold it at a forty-five-degree angle." With the tight round, he can work almost perpendicularly. He adds that he can burn a bird twice as fast with the tight round than with another point.

Muehlmatt will start burning very lightly, barely scorching the wood. At this stage he sets the burner's rheostat at a number two on a one-to-ten scale. For a slightly darker shade, he will set the burner at three and go over the same burn grooves, either partially or totally, depending on the feather color. This technique works well for woodcock feathers, for example, because they are not one solid color but have patches of color bordered by light tones. For later detailing, he may change the tip to what he calls a fat tight round, "good for getting different tones." On some areas of the bird, he will burn in tiny, black dots with a writing

To save time, Muehlmatt will use three burning tools, each with a different tip. One will give a light burn, another a medium, the third a dark burn.

This tight round point was invented and named by Muehlmatt. He uses it for nearly all his burning except the very black tones.

A 600-grit sandpaper, backed up with a block of wood, is used to remove the haze that builds up on the burning tool. He has found that the point burns cleaner lines when it is shiny.

Here Muehlmatt uses a 3 mm drafting pencil to pencil in a woodcock's feathers. He prefers a mechanical pencil, the kind in which the lead is inserted, so that he does not have to bother with sharpening. He tries to vary the feather sizes as well as stagger them.

The first step in burning is using the tight round point for the bird's quills and barbs.

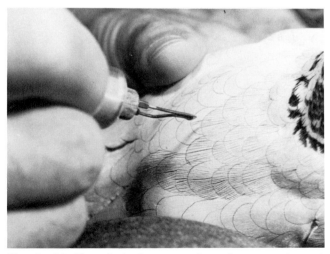

Burning tool tips have other uses besides burning for color. On the golden eagle's head, much of the texturing was done with a burning pen tip called a writing point. These are effects, he notes, that cannot be made with a paint brush.

Note that Muehlmatt limits the amount of area done at one time with the light burn. Each of these areas is completely burned before he goes on to another.

point, noting that "the less metal in the tip, the hotter that tip gets."

Regardless of the point used, it will need cleaning to remove what Muehlmatt describes as a haze. To clean the point, he runs it across a piece of fine sandpaper backed by a block of wood.

Is there a special burning tool he uses? Muehlmatt recommends The Detailer, the same tool used by Fore-hand, but says "all the burning tools are good."

What procedure does Muehlmatt follow for detailing the entire bird? When burning, he starts with the head first, then goes on to the rump, the back and chest, every place except the area he is holding. "I don't like to touch any of the burned areas because the more you touch them, the smudgier they get," he says. "You want to leave them nice and crisp, which you'd lose if you kept touching them." The last areas, then, to be burned are the primaries and wing areas.

On the body, he will burn four or five square inches at a time, which for him is about a day's work. "I'll burn the area completely, the first, the second burn, the shading, the dark stuff, and tune it up with little dots if I have to." Then he will go on to another area. He would rather do this than go over an entire bird with a light burn as the first step. It takes him from six to seven days to completely detail a bird like a woodcock.

Muscles and Bumps

Muehlmatt says he does as much for the bird as he can with the burning and does little to hide it if he gets the shades he wants from the burning instrument. There are preliminary steps he takes that, in fact, emphasize the burned-in tones.

"Muscles and bumps," he says, "give the bird a fluid look." He notes that wherever there is a change in feather patterns, he makes a distinct bump. He may exaggerate, he admits. "A feather pattern may not have a rise, but I do it anyway. It produces a distinct change. I may even exaggerate a little grouping of feathers." He may create a bump even if there is a change in color. "For some reason it looks good," he says.

What does he use to make these bumps and muscles? The Foredom and ruby carvers are the mainstays for shaping these anatomical features. Of the cutters, he says, "They cut real well, they don't load up or clog up with wood, they never get dull, and they're fairly inexpensive." Muehlmatt agrees with Forehand when he speaks of the grinding tool. He says, "You can do so very much with the Foredom tool."

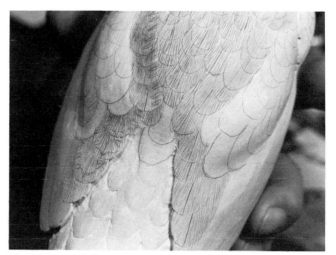

The lightly penciled-in marks on the burned feathers indicate where the dark burns will be.

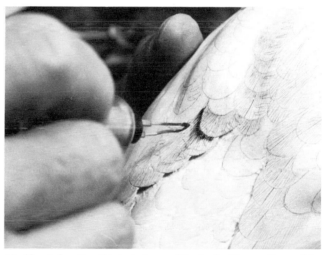

Muehlmatt describes this technique as "shading" with a small round tip. This tip is used for dark brown and black burns.

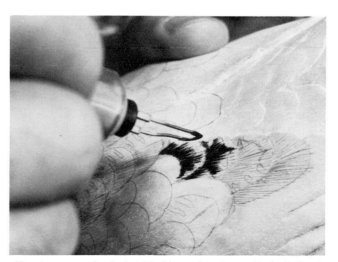

Here is an example of what Muehlmatt describes as "dark shading."

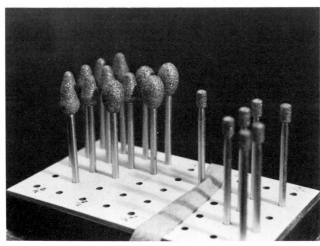

On this unfinished woodcock you can see the muscles and bumps Muehl-matt puts on a bird. Note that a woodcock, because of its eyes and anatomy, can see as well behind as in front. It has, in fact, 360-degree vision.

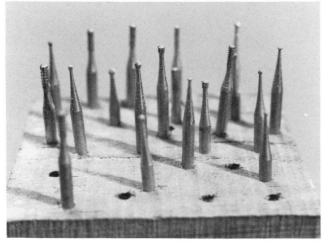

These are the ruby carvers which Muehlmatt uses for much of his detailing.

Dental bits are used for confined areas such as those around the beak, for shaping the eyelids, or for doing minute detail.

When asked if he makes separate pieces such as wings and feathers to emphasize anatomy, Muehlmatt answers that he never made a practice of doing inserts, claiming that he enjoys doing a solid bird instead. "To me a solid, one-piece bird can be just as intricate and just as interesting as a feather-inserted bird," he says. "Also, I find a great challenge in doing birds with open tails or wings out of a piece of wood." He adds that with precise cutters such as the ruby carvers he can achieve very fine detail.

Jelutong, Wood from Malaysia

Muehlmatt has a favorite wood, but it is not basswood. He uses jelutong exclusively. A Malaysian wood, it does not have the fuzz basswood has. Consequently, it sands a lot smoother. When a Foredom tool is used on jelutong, the wood is pulverized. With a ruby carver, he says, "the wood disappears in front of your eyes."

Jelutong does have limitations. It is not as strong as basswood, and it does have a tendency to crack. Another drawback is that with knifework, jelutong can

The tail feathers of this spruce grouse are not separate pieces but are carved from a solid block of wood to a thickness of one-sixteenth of an inch.

easily be split, especially if the knife goes against the grain. However, Muehlmatt uses no knife, relying instead on the Foredom, which can go with or against the grain. "With the Foredom, I have better control over my birds than with a knife," he says.

Jelutong has little grain and no sap, and, Muehlmatt points out, "whether it's my imagination or not, I'm pretty sure it burns with a browner tone than basswood." He adds that "once you get used to jelutong, I don't think you'd go back to a wood like basswood if that's what you started with."

He says the price of the jelutong is about the same as basswood, and it is available at some lumberyards and carving supply houses in thicknesses up to four inches. Anything over that width can be glued up with good results, he adds, recalling a spruce grouse he made from three separate pieces of jelutong.

Study Skins

Muehlmatt agrees with Forehand that study skins are essential to doing bird carvings. He says, in fact,

Though three pieces of jelutong were glued together for the spruce grouse, no glue lines show because Muehlmatt used a thin, watered-down application of glue.

that he would never work without one. However, while working, he will refer to illustrations or paintings from books like those done by Lansdowne, an artist, Muehlmatt says, "who tells you where he saw the bird he's painted, how it lives, and offers pencil sketches of how he developed his painting."

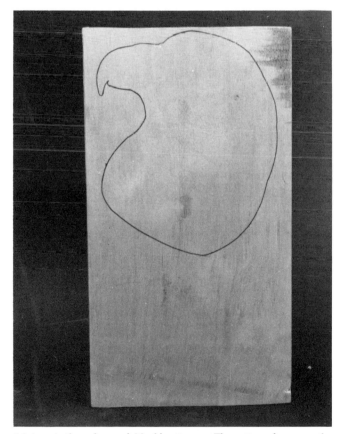

Jelutong is the only wood Muehlmatt uses. The pattern drawn on the wood is for the bald eagle's head.

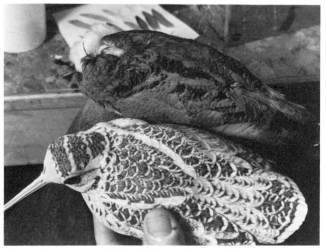

Study skins are essential to Muehlmatt's work. Here he compares a study skin of a woodcock to a carving he is preparing to paint.

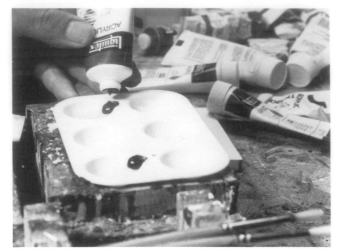

Muehlmatt begins to paint by mixing a pea-sized glob of acrylic paint with a tablespoon of water to make a wash.

A wash has a thin, transparent consistency that will blend with other washes. He compares the application of washes to laying colored sheets of cellophane over the bird, though much of the mixing, he says, is done by the eye.

A constant stream of hot air from a hairdryer will dry the washes. Muehlmatt cautions that when you touch the bird, if it feels cold, the paint is still wet; if warm, the wash is dry.

Although he claims he can do a woodcock carving with his eyes closed, Muehlmatt says that he sees something different every time he picks up a study skin of the bird. He will, in fact, look for a particular feather when burning or painting. "I decide what feather I'm doing on the bird, then pick out approximately the same feather on the study skin," trying to duplicate it. Yet, he notes, every skin has a different design to it. There are different designs he has become aware of on birds. The woodcock, for example, has at least a half-dozen different ones.

Muehlmatt makes an interesting observation about birds. "When a head is turned, the feathers are no longer arranged the same way. They slide around." Knowing this gives him a decided advantage in working from a dead bird. "You can get one and twist its head around," he says. This enables him to burn in the feathers as they are found on the bird.

Colors on a Wheel

Basic to painters and most artists are colors and color harmonies – that is, the combining of colors. Basic pigments which cannot be broken down into other colors are called primary. Secondary colors are a result of mixing two primary colors. Tertiary colors or intermediates lie between the secondaries. When these colors are laid out in a schematic circle, the result is a color wheel. (For more on color, see chapter 9 on Larry Hayden.)

On the color wheel, yellow, red, and blue are the three primary colors. Mixing red and blue produces

Ready to paint, Muehlmatt checks a woodcock wing for reference.

violet; blue and yellow make green; red and yellow create orange.

"I burn my birds basically brown," Muehlmatt explains, "but some areas are gray. Now brown is somewhere in the oranges. And combining opposite colors can produce a neutral color like gray. So if I have a brown bird that should have some gray in it, like the woodcock and spruce grouse, I put a blue wash over my brown burning, and that makes a gray."

Washing With Paint

Muehlmatt uses acrylic paints mixed with water until a thin consistency is achieved. He does not mix colors on a palette or in a paint tray. "I take colors right out of the tubes and mix them on the bird," with, of course, the addition of water.

Painting this way cannot be done with a single application. Muehlmatt explains, "If you lay one wash on top of another, it must be completely dry. If you do it wet, the new wash will lift off the old wash, and you won't get anywhere." The solution? Muehlmatt uses a standard hairdryer to blow a stream of hot air on the bird to dry the wash. "When it's dry, it feels warm; when it's wet, it feels cool." He adds, "You can't tell this by looking at the carving. You have to put your finger on the bird. This is what takes up most of the painting time—you have to wait for things to dry."

Explaining the overlaying of washes, he says, "Put a blue wash on a brown wash; the color is grayed up considerably. With the right amounts, you can get a nice soft gray. If, after drying, you look at it and it's

Painting begins by enhancing areas with "warm" black paints. These warm blacks do not come in tubes but must be created by combining primary colors.

Here a blue wash is applied to "gray up" an area that was too brown.

Colors in the wing are matched with swatches of paint on paper.

A burnt umber is put on the bird to duplicate the color on the original wing.

Two feather stripes are made gray with a mix of burnt umber and ultramarine blue.

Now to blend the areas together the white edges of the primaries are painted with a thinned-down mixture of burnt sienna and ultramarine blue.

Primaries are painted with ultramarine blue and burnt sienna, while the white edges are left unpainted.

These feathers are not carved. Instead, Muehlmatt underlines the lower edge of each feather to create the illusion of overlapping.

Periodic comparisons are made to check the progress of the washes.

The secondary feathers are darkened with burnt umber washes.

still brown, put another blue wash on it. If it's too blue, you go back and put some brown on it."

Successive coats or washes are necessary to see how the bird is coloring. Muehlmatt describes this way of working as a safety measure. "Once you get the area too dark, you can't get it lighter, even if you put a real light coat over it. Anyway, a light mix looks better, more transparent. This is the depth you want by putting on one thin coat after another, which you can't get by doing it all in one shot." He compares it to furniture finishing, for which many successive coats are better than one heavy application of a finish.

Not all his painting consists of graying a bird. Some areas need to be whitened. For this he uses not acrylics but oil paints. When the bird is completely burned, Muehlmatt sprays it with 1301 Krylon acrylic spray. Acting like water, it soaks into the wood and seals it. The light areas (those lighter than the lightest burn) are done with a white oil interior house paint. DuPont Ovalite is a brand he uses. Mixed with an equal part of turpentine, the paint becomes a thin mix that can be brushed on. As with the grays, it takes Muehlmatt three or four successive coats to get the white he wants, "that many to get a pure white, though I may want an off-white or a beigey white."

He does all the white areas in one day, with the following day devoted to acrylic washes. For that he will use brand new Windsor Newton sable brushes, series 233. He says this series points up well, though it is not the ultimate in brushes. A small series 7 brush may cost twenty-five dollars, and a larger one eight times that. After he uses the brushes, he will either throw them out or use them for the oil paint application, "which is the graveyard for them."

Muehlmatt points out a basic inconsistency in using oils and acrylics, when it comes to putting the final washes on the bird. "You're not supposed to be able to put acrylics on top of oils, because oil is supposed to repel watery paints. But they don't the way I do it. The flat white oil undercoat dries very flat, and for some reason, it's a great base for the acrylic washes."

After you've worked with washes, it should become clear to you why Muehlmatt does not do birds like cardinals. "If I did a bird like that, I'd have to white out the burning before I got the real, true red. It just wouldn't work putting the red over the burning. The same would be true with a blue or a yellow bird. You'd lose a lot of the burning detail."

But a bird like a female cardinal, he admits, may be more appropriate for his technique. The barbs of this

Muehlmatt again compares his carving with a study skin to see how the washes are working.

Here the study wing is compared to the finished painting. Note on the bottom how closely the color of the real primaries matches the painted wood.

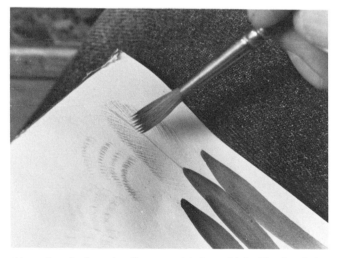

At one time, barbs and quills were painted on a bird with a brush that had flared-out bristles.

This chickadee was not burned. All the details were painted on the wood.

from it overnight and come back, right away you can see if there is something wrong with the piece." Then one or another wash can be added.

It should be pointed out that all the carvers in this book burn in detail and paint over that, but burning has not always been an accepted step. At one time burning was not done at all, and all the detail was painted on the bird. Muehlmatt explains that in the early days of decorative birds, barb and quail lines were painted on. To do that you needed a brush that flared out and was trimmed or "manicured" so that the brush hairs were absolutely even. Water-based paints were used, and using them required a great deal of skill. "There were a few very good painters of feathers," he says. "I was supposed to have been pretty good at it."

bird, he says, are red and green, a natural combination which mutes the red resulting in a "buffy brown."

To paint birds, Muehlmatt says, the only thing you have to know is what color combines with another color to get the effect you want. "If you want a gray, you never use a black and white combination, especially the black." This color, he says, is dead-looking. And one like a Mars black he describes as "icicle cold." To make a black, he suggests using a combination of green and red. Mixing it with a deep brown can produce a charcoal brown for dark washes.

Another tip he offers is to apply washes in an afternoon and let the bird sit until the next morning when you can look at it with a fresh eye. "If you get away

Feet, Leaves, and Other Habitat

Feet can be a difficult aspect of the anatomy to re-create, especially if they are to hold the weight of a carved bird. (Compare Scheeler's and Barth's techniques for making feet.) Different materials can be used, although for major competitions such as the one sponsored by the Ward Foundation, feet must be made by the artist. For commercial purposes, many carvers, including Muehlmatt, purchase feet cast in pewter. (See appendix for supplier.)

For leaves, Muehlmatt uses brown craft paper to make his own. (Arnold's techniques in the following chapter are comparable.) He says he will go out into the woods and get some beech leaves or oak leaves, lay them down on the brown paper, and trace their outlines. With a pair of scissors he can cut out the paper tracings. Then with acrylic paint mixed with water, he can add the colors he sees in the originals, using such paints as burnt sienna or a yellow-brown mix. After the replicas have dried, he can re-wet them, lay them out on a towel or soft surface, and burn in the veins using a blunt-tipped burning pen. He can even put in little marks and holes or distress the leaves with the pen. "Burning the leaf curls up the side you're burning on," he adds. "Then you can turn it over and recurl it if you want."

Other elements of habitat may include a piece of wood and some paper grasses. If he wants to create an earth-effect on a base, however, Muehlmatt may resort to an epoxy. Using Tuf-Carv, a brand he prefers, he

These pewter feet for the spruce grouse were bent to conform to the base. This is possible because pewter is a soft metal. Suppliers of these feet are listed in the appendix.

With the feet permanently attached to the base, the bird rests on the feet and can easily be removed to be worked on.

This oak leaf was made from brown paper. When the paper is wetted down and a burning tip is applied, the edges will curl.

can make earth, pebbles, and even rocks. (For more on this technique, see Scheeler's chapter.) Similar to an autobody putty, the epoxy is mixed with a hardener and can set up in five to thirty minutes. As it solidifies, it can be shaped, carved, and sanded.

The base was filled with Tuf-Carv, a filler that can be textured to simulate earth. Muehlmatt worked the filler by poking at it with a stiff brush before it set. Poured on waxpaper and fitted into the octagon base, the filler could be worked after it was semihard.

Muehlmatt makes his habitat leaves from paper. The leaf on the right is a real one.

Sometimes habitat may consist of nothing more than a piece of wood. This piece became the base for a chickadee.

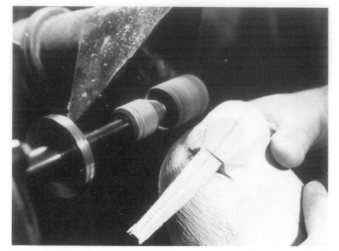

To rough-shape the woodcock Muehlmatt uses a one-and-one-quarter-inch diameter rotary rasp on a stationary bench motor.

Muehlmatt uses this tool to take off 99 percent of the wood. Here the edge of the rasp underlines the bottom edge of a wing.

Because the changing grain patterns may weaken areas, the beak for this woodcock was added as a separate piece.

Making Woodcocks and Spruce Grouse

After Muehlmatt decides on the basic elements for a composition like the woodcock, he begins with a bandsawed block of wood. He might not go immediately to the Foredom, but instead he might use a motor-mounted rasp for much of the rough shaping of the wood.

From there he can go to the ruby carvers and Foredom. He starts with the head and adds details to areas such as the eye sockets and the beak, which he applies as a separate piece of jelutong. Is the jelutong beak brittle? It would be if he did not coat it with a hardener such as Krazy Glue. "It makes the beak like a piece of plastic," he says.

The eyes are a very important part of Muehlmatt's scupltures and an area he works on as soon as he can. He says, "I get the eyes in as soon as I carve. If you can get the expression in the face and eyes as soon as possible, it helps you to visualize what the rest of the bird will look like," even if most of the body is still in a rough block of wood.

As nearly all carvers do, Muehlmatt uses glass taxidermy eyes. (See appendix for suppliers.) With a ruby carver, Muehlmatt can cut a hole on each side of the head for the eyes, making sure one hole is not higher than the other. On eye sizes, he advises, "You can't go wrong with too big of an eye, but you can with too small an eye," giving the bird what he calls a "beady-eyed" effect. "If a woodcock takes a ten- or twelve-millimeter eye and you can't make up your mind, go with the twelve," he says.

After shaping and sanding, and putting in muscles and bumps, Muehlmatt pencils in the feathers, beginning with an area that does not have to be held. After he makes an initial burn on a small portion of the bird, he can go over the lines a second time, depending on the amount of darkness he wants and where he wants it.

What does he do with the areas he wants to be white or beige in color? These, he says, are whitened out with a pastel pencil. "I would forget where I was as I went from a white feather to a black feather, or a black feather with a white edge," he says, if he did not do this. These areas, then, get whitened out, but the pastel can be brushed off before painting.

The washes come next, and the study skins are an aid to getting the right tones and shades of color. Mixing the washes is really done as much by the eye as with the brush. "When you step back six feet, your eye naturally mixes two washes together."

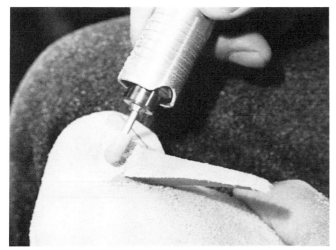

Fine texturing and reducing the width of the head slightly are done with a carbide cutter and Foredom.

A depression is made for the right eye.

Use the same tools to shape the top and side profiles of the beak.

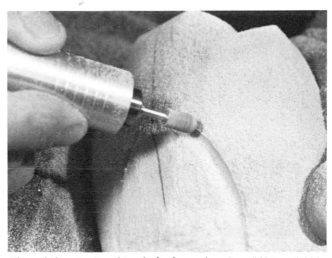

The carbide cutter is making the back muscle or "cape." Using a bit like this, Muehlmatt says, is comparable to outlining with a pencil.

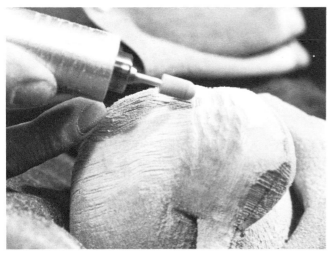

Here Muehlmatt works lengthwise on the side profile of the head.

Even if it is ground away, the centerline should be redrawn to act as a reference, Muehlmatt advises. If the bandsawed profile were exact, carving away the sides should not remove this line.

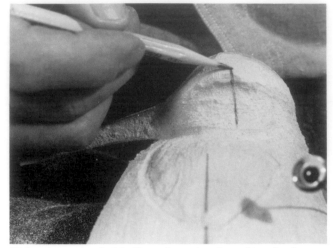

With a glass eye handy, Muehlmatt determines the positions for the eyes.

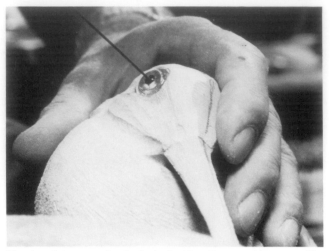

The size of the eye socket is checked with a 12 mm taxidermy eye. The sockets must be not only big enough, but also deep enough to hold the eye.

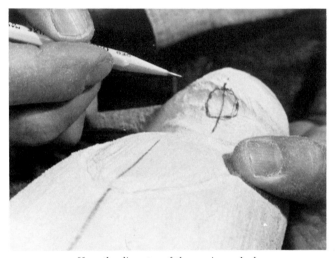

Here the diameter of the eye is marked.

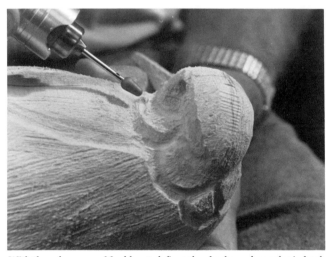

With the ruby carver, Muehlmatt defines the cheeks and muscles in back of the head. He can also make individual feathers by undercutting with it slightly.

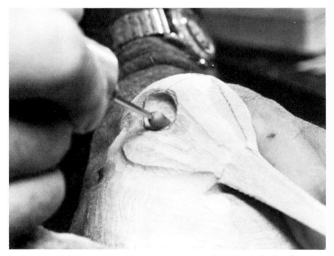

A one-eighth-inch diameter ruby carver makes the hole for the eye.

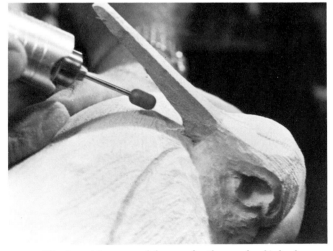

Wood must be removed from under the woodcock's beak.

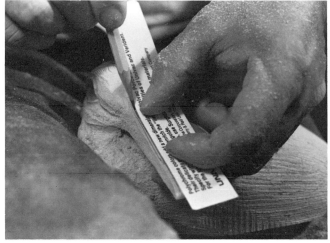

Putting a centerline on the beak helps achieve symmetry when wood is removed on either side.

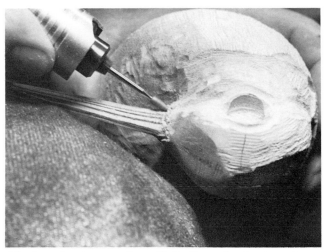

After he makes the separation with the "burner" and a depression on either side of the burn line with the ruby carver, he outlines the transition area, where the beak meets the head.

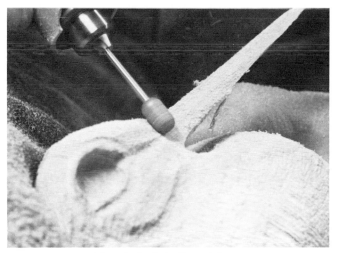

Here the beak is slimmed down.

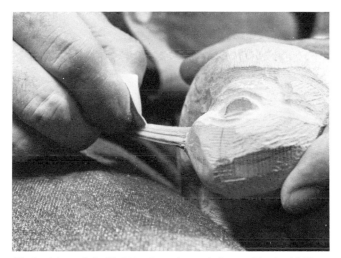

The beak is sanded with 280-grit sandpaper before soaking it with Krazy Glue to harden the wood.

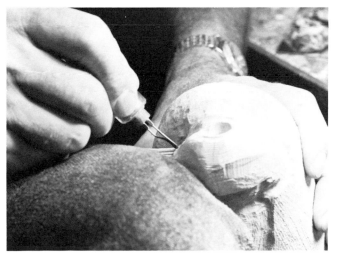

Muehlmatt uses a burning tool to create the bill separation.

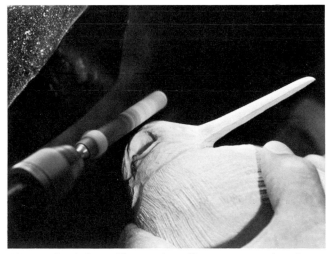

More sanding is done with 280-grit wet/dry paper mounted on the stationary motor.

A slotted brass spindle holds one end of the wet/dry sandpaper. The rubber band keeps the sandpaper from unwrapping. When the end gets worn, it can be snipped off. Muehlmatt says that one-sixth of a sheet of sandpaper is enough for a small bird.

The woodcock is ready to be painted.

These feathers were not carved in. Instead, Muehlmatt burned darker under the leading edge of the previous feather.

Here is a good example of the detail and tone that are achieved by burning. Dots, done with the tip of the burning pen, break up the heavily darkened areas.

The texturing on the woodcock's underside was done with the tight round burning tip.

The spruce grouse, about thirteen inches high, is lifesize. Note that Muehlmatt burned from the head to the rump.

The texturing around the eyes was done with a pointed burning pen tip.

Muehlmatt points out that this bird has tones of gray, burnt sienna and burnt umber. When he burns and paints to get those effects, he will always use a study skin.

Each feather was penciled in after the initial burn to indicate light and dark areas.

Here the rump was burned to represent the grouse's black and gray feathers.

This is the first burn on the grouse's upper tail coverts.

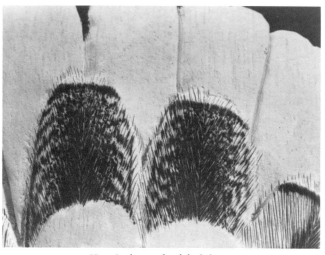

Here is the result of dark burns.

Each feather of the grouse's tail has a slight rise. The separations were done with a small circular saw adaptable to the Foredom.

The underside of the grouse must also be burned. Here the carved and partially burned bird is compared to the mount.

These are the undertail coverts. Note the pencil lines that indicate where Muehlmatt will burn.

There are really only two shades of color for the chickadee, with no dots.

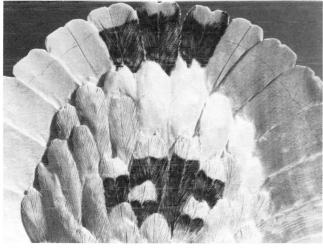

Also burned are the lower portions of the undertail coverts, with the white tips left unburned.

In comparison to the spruce grouse, this chickadee was a simple bird to burn. The head was burned black, with a medium burn on the back and a gray wash put over that.

A slightly more difficult bird to do is this mourning dove. Has it just landed, or is it ready to take off? This is an ambiguity Muehlmatt sometimes tries to create.

Rarely noticed is this bird's iridescence or sheen, which is seen as shiny spots on the feather edges of the dove's neck.

Muehlmatt will also try to create a look that suggests his bird has just confronted a human.

The rump of the dove is composed of subtle tones of purple and pink.

This yellow legs, a shore bird, is posed to have a startled look that would come with confronting a human. Note how the grasses follow the leg lines and flow around the bird.

Here is a good example of feather groupings that are carved in to break up a smooth surface. They also catch light and make shadows on the neck.

Because the pewter legs were bent, they were not strong enough to hold the bird in position. A piece of wood was used as a support under the chest.

The yellow legs is mostly white and black. After the first light burn, the bird was burned dark and white was painted around each black spot.

The Carolina wren poses a challenge for burning with perhaps three shades of color burned in.

The back of the bird has many more dark areas burned into the wood.

These baby chickadees were bandsawed from jelutong and are ready to be carved.

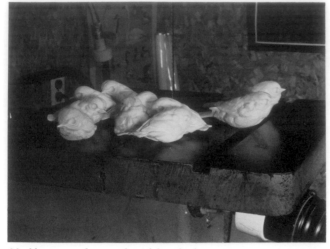

Muehlmatt may do a number of these birds at a time. Note the muscles and bumps carved into the chickadees.

Describing these chickadees as three weeks old, Muehlmatt says that they have just left the nest and are ready to fly. The first night out, they group together for security.

These chickadees have had all their details painted in. No burning has been done on these pieces.

The procedure for doing a larger bird is basically the same. The spruce grouse featured in this book is also made from jelutong, but it was made by laminating three blocks together instead of from one solid piece. Muehlmatt uses Elmer's Glue which has been watered down, even though the three pieces are well clamped together. Why a thin consistency of glue? He explains, "If I hit a glue joint that has too much glue with the burning pen, the glue would bubble up on me." He uses as little glue as possible.

The fanned tail of the grouse, carved from the block, was thinned down in areas to as little as one-sixteenth of an inch. The tail was the last area to be done to avoid for as long as possible any damage to such a fragile piece of the sculpture.

The finished bird was set on pewter feet that were glued to its base. This was done for easy removal when shipping the bird.

Muehlmatt notes that the spruce grouse was carved "in a strutting position, advertising his splendor to a nonchalant female."

3

Eldridge Arnold
Putting Wings and Tails on Birds

Designer, Sculptor, Hunter

Although Eldridge Arnold started sculpting birds
professionally after most of the other artists featured
in this book began doing it, he feels his background
has given him some decided advantages. Arnold began
recreating birds in 1976 when he sold his graphic design business, and he says his experience and training
in color, design, and art gave him a head start. Indeed
it has, for in the span of a relatively few years, he has
taken six Best in Show awards and numerous blue
ribbons.

His interest in carved birds began with decoys, because he was a duck hunter and an avid bird enthusiast.
"But after a while you get to love birds so much you
want to recreate them," he says. "A psychiatrist may
say I have a guilt complex—maybe I do—but I don't
think that's something to let bother you."

Arnold's love of wildfowl is shared by a good many
Americans. He says that "Americans are bird happy
people, and the English and also the Japanese." He
points out that Americans and the British are the only
people who have laws to protect migratory birds to
any great degree. In other countries, he notes, "people
eat anything they shoot, and they will shoot a great
many birds. We passed in this country laws to protect
wildfowl. And many of them wouldn't be around if
this hadn't been the case." He sees, then, a tradition of

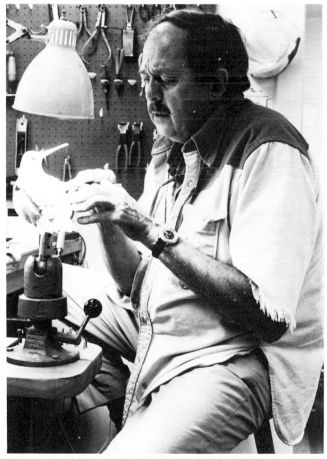

*Eldridge Arnold has combined his love of birds with his background
in graphic design to contribute to the art form. Here he works on a
woodcock.*

preservation that is carried over into the carving and sculpting of birds.

Representational Art

With his professional experience and talents, Arnold is concerned that what he and others in the book are doing be accepted as art instead of craft. "I don't like the term bird carver," he says. "Bird sculptor is a much more current way of describing it, because it's more than a little guy up in Maine whittling on a piece of wood. I see this as representational art in a dimension that a camera and photographer can't see." He adds that just as a portrait painter uses sittings and photographs to capture his subject on canvas, he is representing the bird, through painstaking research, as realistically as he can in wood.

An Engineering Feat

Arnold's commitment to realism is founded in a deep understanding of the birds themselves, a knowledge not unlike Lynn Forehand's. Speaking of feather patterns, for example, Arnold says, "I'm intrigued with the way everything overlaps, how waterproof everything is in the bird." Describing this as an engineering feat, he goes on to say that "the bird is one of the only animals that lives outdoors with almost no shelter at all. Most other animals find it, perhaps only a hole to crawl into. But most birds don't do this. When it rains, it rains right on them. It's the same with snow and wind. They live with the elements and they survive.

Study boards are an invaluable reference. This one of an American woodcock has such information as bill length, notes on pose and habitat, and painting of some of the features which he will refer to later.

They can take a terrific beating because of an intricate feather structure that can expand to create insulation and warmth." The recreation of such attributes and characteristics is not overlooked in the birds Arnold sculpts.

The Fate of the Art Form

What does Arnold foresee for the future of bird sculpting? He answers that if the art form is to improve, overall quality needs to get better. "You go to an exhibition and less than twenty-five percent of the work may be any good." (Compare Larry Barth's criticisms in chapter 6.) He also believes that what he does is an art form, but it is not *fine* art, especially when compared with bronze and marble sculptures.

Inspirational Materials

Arnold is inclined to sculpt birds he hunts or ones he simply is fond of as an avid observer and researcher of birds. His sculptures, then, may include grouse, woodcock, quail, shorebirds, and songbirds. To prepare for a piece, he says that "you have to start with an inspiration even before the block of wood is touched." Inspiration can come from a photograph of a particular pose, one he may have taken when he was on a hunting trip as far away as South America. He is constantly perusing magazines like *Audubon* and *National Geographic* for ideas.

But perhaps more indispensable as a source for ideas is the mounted bird. He, like many other carvers, uses

Study mounts, which he designs on paper before turning them over to a taxidermist, are an invaluable aid. He describes a Wilson snipe he designed as a fast flier.

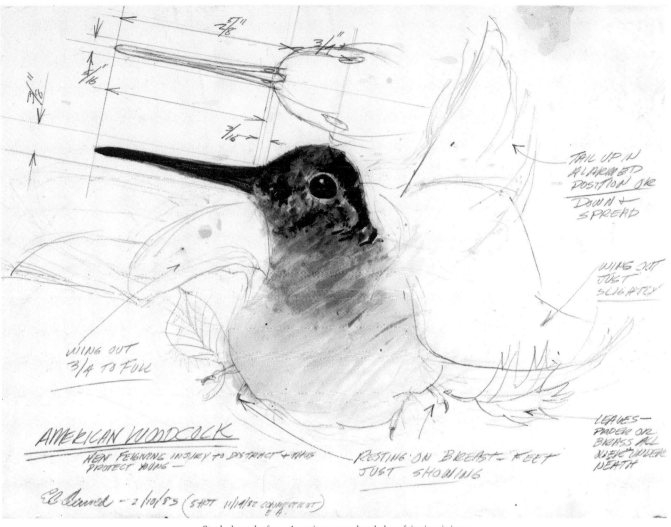

Study board of an American woodcock hen feigning injury.

stuffed birds, but what may be a unique feature of the way he works, he will make sketches of how he wants the mount to be posed. These sketches are followed by a taxidermist when he prepares the bird.

To prepare himself, Arnold will spend a lot of time doing study boards. He may do one, not from a mount, but from a bird that has died very recently, a couple of hours at the most, taking from it important measurements such as beak and eye sizes.

He can start determining painting colors by actually mixing blotches of acrylics on the illustration board.

Telling a Story

Arnold strives to do more than just preserve and represent three-dimensionally the look of a bird. He also wants to tell a story. "Birds do more than just sit on a branch. That's the way you usually see them. I'm interested in putting a bird in a posture most people will never get a chance to see," he says. He may have a bird preening, in flight, confronting another bird, or feigning injury. A cuckoo he made, for example, is ready to take off from a branch with a bit of nesting material in its beak. He describes this as a story of nest building.

Habitat may also tell the story, as it does in a sculpture of three dunlins, members of the sandpiper family. For this composition, he has the birds in a sleeping position in grasses which are bent as if from the effects of a strong wind. This climatic effect is as much a part of the story as the birds, he says. "They decided to doze instead of fly. It was just too windy."

Study board of an old squaw drake.

A pair of Wilson snipes he made are held in the air with the aid of grasses made of metal. "I was trying to show action with the two birds flying and dropping down evasively and very quickly," he says, adding that the speed of these two fast fliers is what his story was about.

What he calls a story of confrontation is a pair of birds that meet in the woods. One is a ruffed grouse, the other a much smaller northern water thrush. "Both of these are forest birds. And who is to say that a grouse walking along isn't going to run into another bird," with neither liking the other's presence.

A Feigning Woodcock

Arnold points out that often the only way to see some birds is through the eyes of a hunter. This, he says, is the case with the woodcock, a bird that lives near the edge of the forest. Like many other birds, the woodcock will leave its nest and feign or fake injury when the nest is threatened by a predator. Arnold explains that the bird fakes injury by extending its wings in

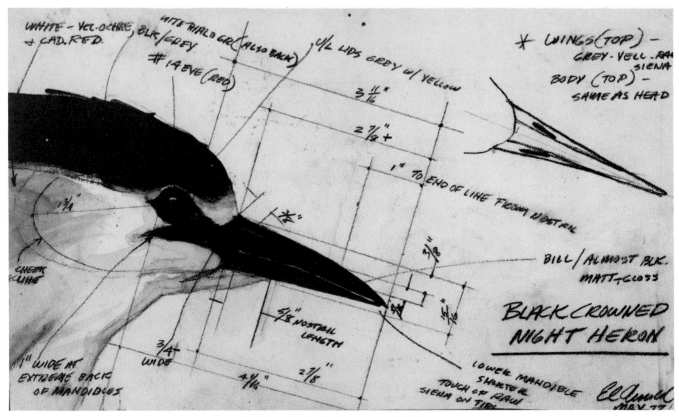

Study board of a black-crowned night heron.

The woodcock, done in 1983, is a bird rarely seen except by a hunter. The sculpture tells a story of how a bird will feign or fake injury to distract a predator threatening the nest.

such a way that it appears unable to fly. But recreating both wings and body from a solid block of wood is difficult. Arnold made the wings as separate pieces.

Separate Wings

For both the wings and the body of the woodcock, Arnold used basswood. Though he has tried tupelo gum (a screech owl he did is partially made from it) and jelutong, he prefers the basswood. He explains that if it is well seasoned, or aged, and dried, the wood carves and burns or textures nicely. To make the wings, Arnold started with a block of basswood a full one-and-one-half inches thick. He bandsawed the block to shape, and then used a rotary rasp and Foredom tool.

He points out that some wood carvers do their roughing with a hatchet and rasplike file, "the old traditional

Though Arnold could have made each feather separately for the wings, he chose to do them together from a solid piece of basswood.

Each wing fits into a slot or cavity on the bird. Note that some of the texturing on the body is not done until the wing is glued in place.

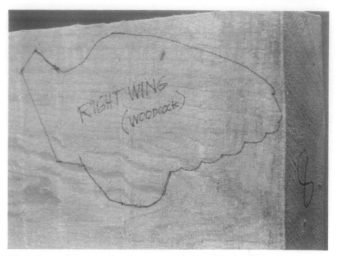

The wings of the woodcock were cut from a block of basswood a full one-and-one-half-inches thick.

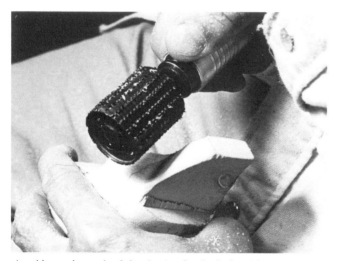

Arnold can do much of the shaping for the body with a rotary rasp. Arnold describes this attachment, along with the Foredom, as replacements for the traditional hatchet once used to shape decoys.

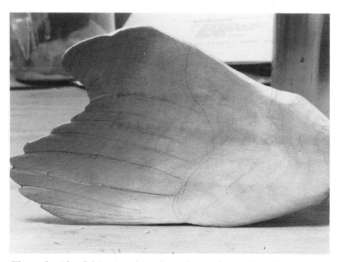

The underside of this wing shows how the wood was shaped. The pencil lines indicate the outlines of the separate feathers. These will be slightly undercut.

An assortment of these rasps is always on hand in Arnold's studio.

The top side of the woodcock's wing shows the amount of texturing Arnold does with a burning tool. Note that the exposed parts of the overlapping feathers are different sizes. This is done to avoid a scaly effect.

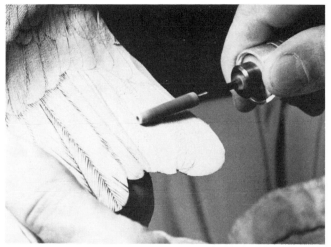

For shaping and defining features, Arnold favors these diminutive sanding drums called cartridge rolls.

This trial-and-error procedure of joining wing to body was done after the wing had been shaped but before it had been textured.

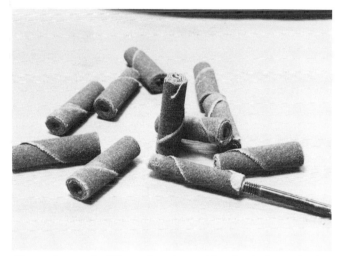

These rolls come in different diameters and lengths. An interesting feature—wearing through one layer of sanding cloth reveals another. They are used with a one-eighth-inch mandril.

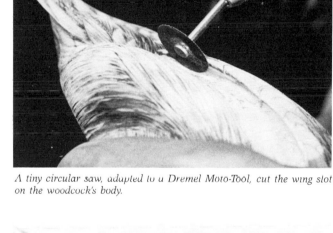

A tiny circular saw, adapted to a Dremel Moto-Tool, cut the wing slot on the woodcock's body.

In order to know where the wings would go, Arnold had to hold each one to the body and then make the cavities.

Though the saw is small, it is extremely sharp and should be used with caution.

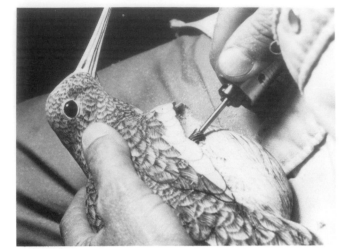

The next step in making the wing slot was using this steel cutter to remove wood.

The work done by the rifflers is shown at the rear of the woodcock.

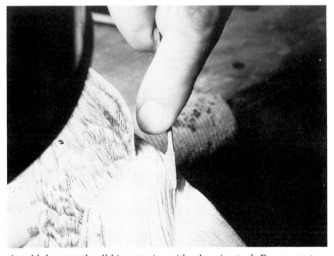

Arnold does not do all his texturing with a burning tool. For coarse textures, he will utilize this riffler, a kind of file. Its biggest advantage is that it can remove wood slowly.

Arnold advocates redoing an area, if necessary, after carving and texturing it. Here he felt an area was too flat, so he went back with a knife and made some changes.

Rifflers come in a variety of sizes and shapes as shown here.

Like many carvers, Arnold will use a Knotts knife like this one. He finds the blade extremely sharp.

Arnold uses the cartridge roll to smooth out the area that was knifed away.

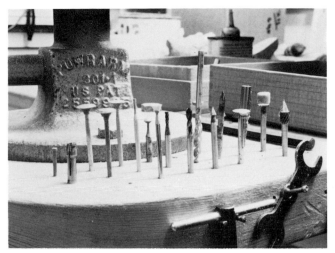

Shown here is an assortment of stones, cutters, and drill attachments.

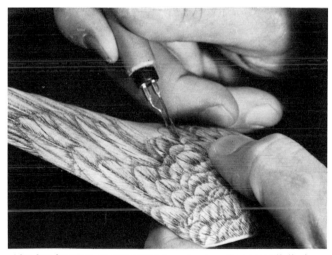

After handsanding, he will retexture and reduce the area with the burning tool.

Stoning areas raises a fuzz on a wood like basswood; to remove it, he first brushes the area with a bristle brush.

If Arnold wants a texturing tool that is faster than the rifflers, he will choose a grinding stone, shown here with a Dremel Moto-Tool.

Shown here is the brass bristle brush he uses. It will remove much of the fuzz.

The next step is to burn off the remaining fuzz with a propane torch. After that, he will apply a flat lacquer to seal the wood before painting.

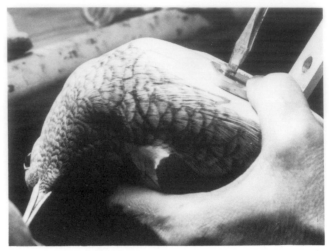

A steel bracket must be screwed to the underside of the bird. This bracket, in turn, can be attached to the vise.

methods of wood removal." He compares the large, rotary rasp to a round hatchet.

In the following two chapters, you will find that Anthony Rudisill and John Scheeler not only make separate wings, but separate feathers as well. Arnold will do this also, but not for his winged woodcock. He explains that "in this case you can get the same idea by just carving the feathers in." After he has sketched in the separate feathers, he uses a knife and small, rotary sanding drums (coarse and fine sandpaper rolled into elongated cylinders) to carve in the feathers. He can also use these tools for shaping and defining the muscles and bumps of a bird. Arnold uses Knotts knives, ones, he says, that "hold a good edge and sharpen nicely."

Another tool which Arnold finds useful is this power vise. Able to lock in different positions, it allows him to work on a bird with both hands free.

When working a piece like the woodcock, Arnold may find it necessary to saw the head off, reposition it, and glue it to the body. Note that no glue line can be seen.

The difficult aspect of this woodcock sculpture came with the joining of the wings to the body of the bird. After each piece had been shaped, but not textured, Arnold held each wing to the body to see where it would be inserted, for he would not glue the surfaces flush or flat together. Instead, he cut a hole or large slot into which the wing would fit. "I moved a wing over to the body and determined how much space it was going to take up," he says. The rest, he admits, took some trial and error, a method, he says, he uses often. This is particularly the case since he does not work with patterns of how parts of anatomy fit together. Cutting the wing slot was done with a small circular saw that adapts to the Foredom. Extremely sharp, it can cut in a straight or curved line. He removed the rest of the wood with a steel cutter and the power grinding tool.

Arnold cut the head off the carving and repositioned it to have the head turned. This was done in much the same manner as Forehand explains it in the first chapter. What is important to Arnold is that the head and body have a flat bonding surface. This, more than anything, will help hide a noticeable glue line.

Arnold feels that there is nothing wrong with going back and redoing an area of the carving. If, after texturing and even painting, he finds an area too high or too flat, he will remove it with the knife and sanding drums and retexture and repaint it. "It's a matter of going back and correcting because you're striving for perfection," he says.

Other tools which he finds useful are rifflers. These are files with different shapes and contours which he

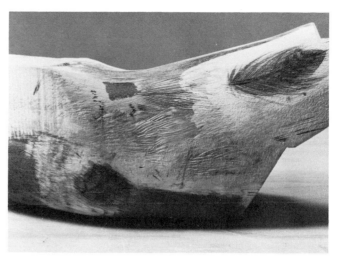

Before going to the bird with grinding tools and paint, Arnold may practice on a roughly shaped block.

can use for the coarse texturing that is invariably part of a bird's makeup. The biggest advantage in using rifflers, he says, is that you can work slowly with them. "You can watch what you're doing so you won't make many mistakes." For faster texturing, Arnold can go to a small grinding stone and Foredom to put in lines on the wood.

As Forehand and others have found, basswood raises a fuzz after being carved. (This is especially true of ground areas.) Arnold's solution is to burn that fuzz off. But before applying the flame of a propane torch, he will scrape the wood with a brass bristle brush. After "flaming" the wood, he will then apply a DuPont flat lacquer to seal the wood before painting in the bird's colors.

Painting—the Less the Better

Arnold compares some of his painting techniques to Muehlmatt's—that is, he uses the burned texture to combine with the paint to produce the effects he wants. And, like Muehlmatt, he uses many thin washes as basic colors. Then he can come in with dark colors over the washes and put in highlights and outlines of feathers. He says, however, that "painting is a very personal thing. I find the less paint you put on a bird, the better it looks." He feels, incidentally, the same is true with the carving. "It's not what you put into it, sometimes it's what you leave out."

He explains that the danger of applying too much paint is that it can give the bird a "porcelain look." He indicates that birds generally are not shiny. Instead,

The alternating shades on these woodcock feathers are made with paint, not lighting. The different shades are created by building up many thin washes of paint.

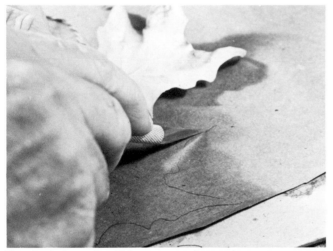

This X-acto knife can be used for some fine texturing. But Arnold prefers to use it when making leaves for some of his birds' habitats.

To make the leaves, he will first trace a real one on lacquer-impregnated brown craft paper. Then he will cut it out with the X-acto knife.

they are rather dull in color. So he strives for what he calls a dull or matte finish. He points out that many carvers will spray their birds with a dull varnish after they have painted them because they find the birds too shiny. Arnold believes he can get the same effect without spraying by applying as many as ten thin washes of paint. He did this on the feigning woodcock, but he also introduced an interesting variation. On alternate sides of the quills, he varied the intensity of the washes, achieving an alternating light and dark effect, yet one without a sheen.

Paper Leaves

Habitat is important in Arnold's work, but he believes it has its limits. "You don't need a lot of stuff on a base," he says. "It's extraneous and it detracts. A bird doesn't have to be in a setting necessarily." Though he used to feel habitat was more important, he believes what he is doing now makes the bird more a piece of sculpture.

For the feigning woodcock, he uses a base composed of only a square stone and a few leaves. The base is a soft material called wonder stone. He places the leaves, maples and others, strategically under the bird, "just to give it a touch of its environment, a little bit of background." He adds, "It's easy to overdo this, it's hard to underdo habitat."

Although at one time he used copper and brass for leaves, he presently uses paper. He feels that the brown craft paper which he coats heavily with lacquer gives him a better painting surface than the metal foils. To make them, Arnold takes a real leaf and draws the out-

Here he removes the maple leaf. It's now ready to be textured.

He puts in the veins of a leaf by scoring the paper with a sharp instrument such as an awl or ice pick.

line of it on the paper. He then cuts out this outline with an X-acto knife. To make veins in the leaf, he scores the paper with an awl or some other sharply pointed instrument. He may even put in worm holes, again using the X-acto knife.

For the painting, Arnold may mix washes of burnt umber, white, and ultramarine blue acrylics to get "the browny look" of a fall leaf. Because of the rejecting effect of the lacquer to watered-down paint, a number of coats are needed. Between coats, he uses a hairdryer. To get the spots often found on fall leaves, Arnold soaks a toothbrush with a paint mix and spatters the paint across the leaf. Once finished, the leaves will be glued to the base.

After he applies a wash of paint, he dries the leaf with a hairdryer before he applies another wash.

Courting Doves

Arnold sees little difference between making the wings and the fan of a bird's tail. "Creating a spread tail is just as complicated as making a wing," he says, because he has to deal with the same problems. Such is the case with a sculpture of mourning doves he is working on. Comprising three birds, this composition will tell the story of courting. He will have two of the doves displaying their tail feathers as they do when they are courting. A third, "the rejected suitor," will not. In the courting posture, the two birds touch each other with their heads and bodies together. "I don't think anyone carving has done two birds quite this way," he says.

Arnold points out that when a dove is on the ground feeding, you never see its tail spread. Only in the few

This basswood mourning dove is one of three birds that will tell a story of courting and rejection. Note the muscles and bumps that Arnold puts in with the cartridge roll.

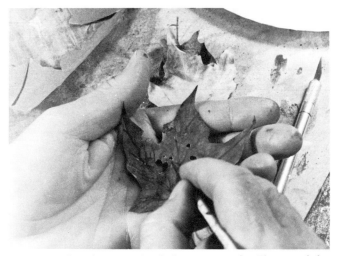

He uses washes of paint to give the leaves some color. The worm holes were made with the X-acto knife.

Shown here is the coarse texturing on the bird's underside that can be done with grinding stones or rifflers.

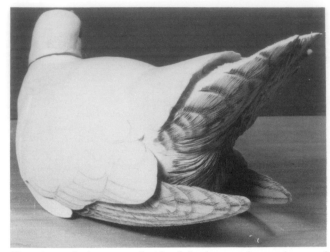

The primary feathers on each side of the dove are done as basswood inserts.

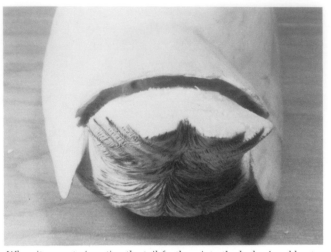

When it came to inserting the tail feathers into the body, Arnold cut a curved slot with the tiny circular saw. The curve was made so the feathers would not lie in a straight line, which would look unnatural.

Here are the two inserts for each side. The one on the left is called the alula or thumb. On the right is the primary insert. All ten of the feathers were detailed on a single, thin piece of wood.

moments of flight can it be seen. The tail he describes as beautiful, and it is the main reason he likes the bird.

Not all the feathers of the courting doves' wings are carved and inserted. He makes only two of the primaries for each side, in addition to pieces for the birds' alulas, or thumbs, which are sometimes called spurious wings. Each tail, however, will be composed of some fourteen separate pieces, including transitional feathers that will get progressively smaller as they fade back into the dove's body.

He makes all the feathers by starting with real ones. After studying these, he works up cardboard templates, which can be transferred to thin pieces of basswood. Once cut to shape, the wood pieces are inserted into a slot. The fit and size of the slot is important. If the slot is not the right size, the observer will notice how

When it came to doing the tail feathers, Arnold made each one separately. He began with real ones, made paper templates, and transferred these to wood (the three steps are shown left to right).

Here can be seen how the tail feathers are temporarily inserted and held together with a piece of tape.

All the feathers are inserted in the tail area. The smaller ones in front are transitional feathers that help break up a sharp division from the body to the longer ones.

The dove's head was made as a separate piece, so the grain of the head would run in the direction of the beak, which is a delicate and fragile area. If the grain of the head ran across the beak instead of with it, the beak might easily break off.

the feathers are inserted. Arnold points out that the tail slot he cuts has a curve to it. "A lot of amateurs make the mistake of cutting the slot almost straight across," he says.

Also made as separate pieces are the doves' heads. He does this to counteract any problems with the grain of the wood. He explains that a small beak is extremely fragile, and if it is made along with the body, it might break off because of a change in grain patterns. So a separate head, with the grain running out along the length of the beak, has to be used.

A Screech Owl

A far more complicated piece done by Arnold is a screech owl. This bird has a total of over seventy sepa-

This screech owl leaves the ambiguous impression of either taking off or landing. The body was made from tupelo gum, while the wings and feather inserts are basswood. The head was cut off and repositioned to get the stiffness out of the pose.

Arnold notes that these feathers must be brought into the body another half inch. He also points out that the spread tail is a display of courtship when the bird is on the ground.

Arnold wanted his owl to have a fierce look.

These tail feathers were inserted on the owl. Note the rough edges of the feathers that allow air to pass through without making a sound.

This is an individual tail feather Arnold made but later rejected. Again, notice the rough leading edges called barbles that allow the owl to come down out of a tree noiselessly.

rate pieces as feathers in the wings and tail. Here too is a story. Perched high up on a branch, the owl has one foot in the air. This, says Arnold, shows a certain tension that asks the question: Is the owl putting its foot down to land or is it picking it up to take off? "A lot of carvers will show the screech owl with the head turned one-hundred-and-eighty degrees, which it can do. But I wanted to make it interesting in a way most people don't see it." And, he adds, "your imagination should be able to run a little bit."

Apart from the fierce look he gave the piece, he points out some of the other features of the bird. He describes the owl as very "hairy" on the underside of the wings. Consequently, it can come down on an animal from a tree and make no sound, because as the air goes over and under its wings, the sound is muffled by the roughness of the feathers. (The leading edges of all the owl's feathers have very pronounced barbles that also help reduce the sound of the wings in the air.) "It is unlike a flying duck which you can hear because that bird has a very stiff and smooth wing."

4

John Scheeler

Feathers as Inserts

The Grand Master

Ernest Muehlmatt was not the only one strongly affected by carved bird exhibitions of the late 1960s. John Scheeler also foresaw a career change for himself after attending one. He explains that at that time he was making a few decoys for pleasure. "I thought I did a pretty nice job on them," he says. "Then I heard about this wildfowl show in Salisbury [Maryland] and went. It blew my mind. I saw the possibility of making a living at it and doing it professionally."

He did get started soon after, and immediately he won his first competition with a Best in Show ribbon. To date, he has won approximately twenty-five of these awards and seven Best in World ribbons at the World Championship Wildfowl Carving Competition. His record has been so outstanding, some call him the grand master of bird carvers.

He makes some revealing comments about being such a consistent winner. "It's nerve-racking because the more you win, the more people expect of you. If you slip a little bit, they wonder what's the matter with you. They think your eyes are going bad or you're sick." Yet, he adds, perhaps with some irony, that he does like the competitiveness. "It keeps you sharp," he confides.

John Scheeler, shown here, uses few patterns to achieve the animated look of his birds.

A model of a pair of least terns is done in Plasticene, a modeling clay.

Typical of his work is this life-size surf scoter.

These models do not have to be very accurate but are useful for getting the design of a piece. Note that a pencil holds the upper bird aloft.

Of Clay—and Foam—and Sealing Wax

Like the other artists in this book, Scheeler uses study skins and he will read up on a bird he is sculpting. Observing a bird, especially one in its natural surroundings, is essential to his work. He tells of wanting to do a roadrunner once. When he told his friend, Gilbert Maggione, of his plans, Maggione asked Scheeler if he had ever seen one. When the answer was no, Maggione told him not to do it. He has followed that advice ever since. "Now," Scheeler says, "if I take a ride, it's going to be some place where I can see some birds. I have binoculars with me all the time."

Patterns are also some help to him when he is working the wood, but sketches he finds of little use, saying that he is limited to only two dimensions by them. As for artists' renderings, he may refer to them, but only for compositional purposes.

The reference Scheeler utilizes most frequently is the model. And, like Forehand, styrofoam is basic to

Pieces of aluminum flashing cut to shape with scissors give body to delicate areas such as wings in these models.

This clay sculptor's tool is all Scheeler needs to give some definition to the modeled birds.

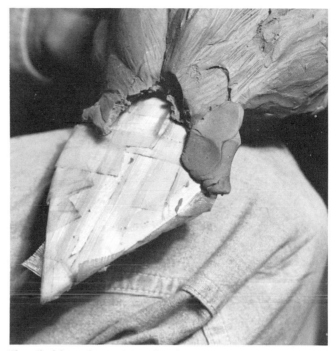

The tail of the surf scoter is taped cardboard. Taping prevents the paper from drawing moisture out of the clay.

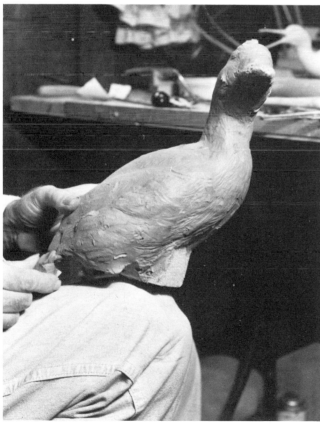

This is a clay model of a surf scoter. Note the styrofoam armature sticking out of its underbelly.

This model of a ptarmigan is made solely of styrofoam and cardboard wings.

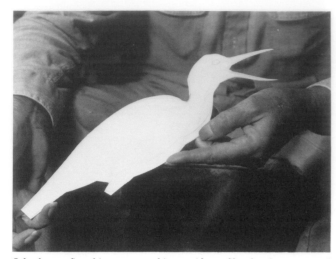

Scheeler confines his pattern-making to side profiles, but he may spend an entire day doing the pattern. Still, he may make changes along the way. This pattern is of a willet.

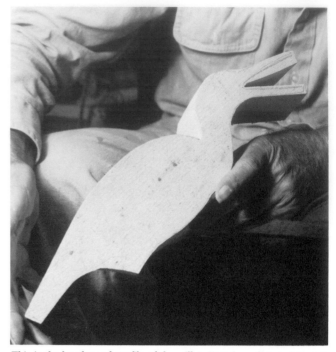

This is the bandsawed profile of the willet. Note how distorted the bill appears before it is carved.

his modelmaking. In addition, he'll use other materials including Plasticene, which is a clay substitute, aluminum flashing, cardboard, and even wax. The clay-like material acts as a workable skin to cover material like the aluminum, which can be shaped into wings. The metal is flexible and can be cut with scissors. For the body and head, the styrofoam acts as an armature or filler. (For comparative information, see the chapter on Larry Barth.) If the head is a separate piece, a toothpick can hold it to the body, enabling Scheeler to turn the head to the position he likes. "You can put a twist in the neck and things like that. It's a big help."

He can use the wax instead of the Plasticene. He tells of once doing the head of a hawk, from memory, shaping the wax on a piece of styrofoam. For another model he did, a surf scoter, he used styrofoam and Plasticene for the body and cardboard for the tail, putting tape over it so the cardboard would not draw moisture out of the Plasticene. Scheeler points out that you do not have to be very accurate with any of these materials, but they are valuable for defining the design of a piece.

Profiles in Wood

It is remarkable that so much of what John Scheeler shapes, sculpts, and composes is determined almost solely by eye. Using only a Foredom tool, he can shape a block of wood into a bird starting with only a band-sawed side profile and a center line. Although many of his birds have turned heads, Scheeler will not saw off the head just to reglue it in a different position. Nor will he make and bandsaw a top profile.

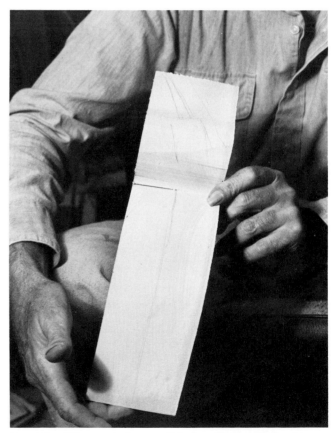

To get the stiffness out of a pose, Scheeler will draw the head to one side, an attitude which is conducive to his technique of grinding in an arc. The hardest part for him is doing the beak.

Here is the willet nearly finished.

He uses this ball-shaped cutter for most of the grinding

Is this difficult? Of working this way, he says, "It looks confusing and terrible with so much wood to remove. You don't think you'll ever be able to work it out, but you can." Beginning from the center line and the high points of the bird's body, Scheeler works to "flow the piece around." He says, "I use my big cutter and always grind the wood on an arc to get the flow into it." Still, he admits, one of the hardest things is keeping the bill straight, especially when the bird's mouth is open.

Scheeler does not do a profile casually. He may, in fact, spend the biggest part of a day trying to get the pattern accurate. "The problem is," he says, "it looks right on paper. Then you bandsaw it out on a piece of wood, and it looks like it grew."

Tupelo Gum

Unlike Muehlmatt, Scheeler does not do the long beaks of his birds as separate pieces. What makes this possible is the type of wood he prefers. Tupelo gum, he says, "is a pretty tough wood. And it doesn't have any grain you have to worry about, which is ideal for a turned beak." He will, however, coat the beak with Krazy Glue (as Muehlmatt does) to harden it. But he will not apply the glue right away, "because I want the beak to be a little limber in case I hit something with it. And once you put that glue on, you can't do much more with it. The beak gets so hard, it gets just like plastic."

Scheeler also likes tupelo gum because of its lack of fuzziness, a problem with basswood. Some carvers, he points out (James Sprankle is one of them), use an

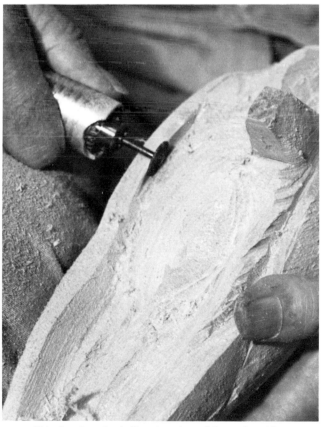

This disc-shaped grinding stone is used for undercutting.

alcohol spray to raise the basswood's fibers for a final sanding. The alcohol is used because it dries so quickly. But, he has observed, a heavy tool will bruise basswood. So when the alcohol is sprayed on it, welts will come up where the wood was disturbed.

Obtaining his tupelo gum from the Louisiana Cajun carvers, who frequently use it for their decorative decoys, Scheeler notes that it is really only the first four feet, the bole of the tree, that is used. This is where the grain is at a minimum. And its characteristics are such that it can be worked either wet or dry. When put into a heated oven to remove some hot melt glue, the wood, Scheeler discovered, did not crack. This would happen to most other woods when brought below a certain moisture content. In the case of the oven-heated tupelo gum, nearly all the moisture was released.

The Cajun carvers in particular use this wood green or unseasoned (meaning the moisture content is high), and they actually keep the wood wet when roughing out the bird. At the end of a day working it, Scheeler says, some of these carvers will put the wood in a re-

Typical of the fine detail tupelo gum can hold is this head of a clapper rail.

frigerator or wrap it in a wet towel. Then, if it is a floating decorative decoy (see James Sprankle's techniques for making one), the Cajuns will hollow the bird out and let it dry.

When asked about carving the wood, Scheeler says it is comparable to cutting a potato when it's green. It can be worked nearly paper thin, a definite advantage in doing feather inserts.

Inserted Wings

Like Arnold, Scheeler does his wings as separate pieces. But he does not make them to be inserted as finished wings. As he explains, "It's hard for me to make a wing and finish it, to make a bird and finish

This block of tupelo gum was sent in the mail to Scheeler by a Louisiana carver. The wood, he says, is smooth, soft, and burns nicely.

One of the reasons Scheeler is reluctant to use jelutong is because there are imperfections in the wood. Here is one in the body of a Hungarian grouse he was carving.

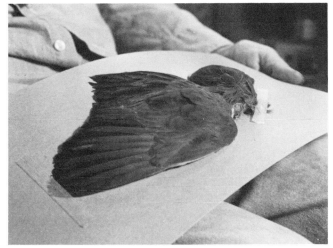

To determine how he wants a wing to look on a bird, he will take a study wing and tape it to a piece of cardboard.

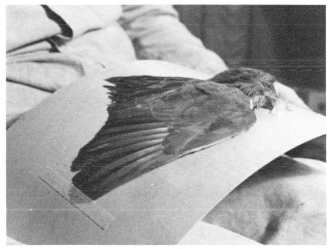

By bending the cardboard, he gets an idea of how he wants to curve the wing so that it will follow the curve.

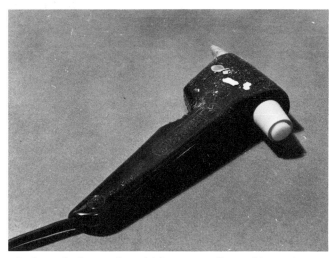

This hot melt glue gun is useful for temporarily attaching a wing to a body.

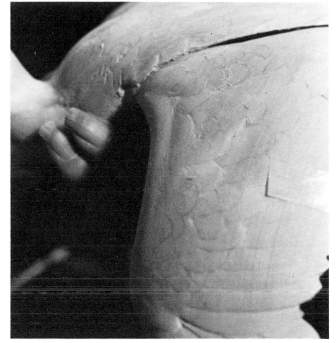

Here the wing and body are attached. Only a small gap remains.

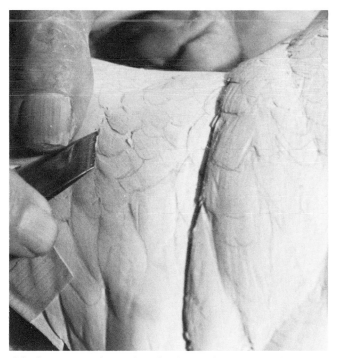

Scheeler can proceed to work on details with the wing and body attached or separate.

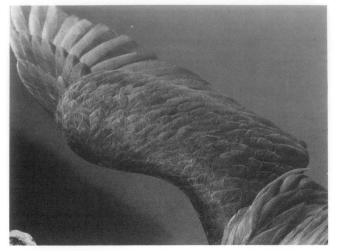

The top of this green heron wing shows the detail he puts into the bird while doing no undercutting of feathers.

A favorite tool of Scheeler's is this offset skew chisel made by Chester Knotts. Comfortably held in one hand, this knife enables him to cut in and around a feather to give it definition.

it, and put the two together perfectly." What he does, then, is rough-carve the body and fit the somewhat roughly carved bird wing into it, securing the two together with hot melt glue. "It's real strong with the glue," he says. Then he can finish separately both wing and body after getting the proper fit. "By temporarily gluing them together, I can look at the bird from different angles and see what I have to do," he says.

How does he get them apart to allow for further detailing? By putting the winged bird in the oven at a moderate temperature, the wings will fall off. And, if he has used tupelo gum, there will be no cracks in the wood.

Wings, like birds, are not static; they have motion. Scheeler has a special technique for getting the contoured look he desires. Using the study wing of a bird, he will tape it to a piece of cardboard. Since a wing is flexible, he can bend the cardboard convexly upward, thus having a model to carve from.

Inserted Feathers

Feathers, too, are inserted as separate pieces, and Scheeler is a master at this technique. Knowing the number and sizes of primaries and secondaries and their locations, Scheeler will draw their arrangements on a piece of cardboard and cut out the profile achieved by the feathers' outlines. He checks this for size against a slot and shelf cut into the wing itself, where the finished feathers will be glued. (For more, see Rudisill's techniques in the following chapter.)

Scheeler can use the cardboard template to check

Here is a fine example of feather inserts, ten primaries and ten secondaries, on the wing of a green heron.

Even with a large skew chisel, he can work fine detail into this willet.

the size and shape of each feather as he makes it. Then he can tack-glue them to the cardboard until all are shaped and detailed.

Making Feathers

Scheeler makes all his feathers the same thickness — about one-sixteenth of an inch. Instead of cutting out their profiles with a knife or scissors, he burns the feathers out of the wood, using a burning pen with a fine point. Scissors "tend to mash the wood and put tiny splits in it that you may not even see," he says.

The feather detailing and contouring come next. He first burns the shaft lines in. Then he sands the edges of the feathers down to get them as thin as possible. He will not, however, sand the middle, which he wants to remain thick for strength.

Working on a curved piece of wood, Scheeler explains that the bend in the wood combined with the heat from the burning pen can give a curve to the feathers, which will match the curve in the wings. It helps, he says, to do the top first, burning in the barbs off the shaft at the angle he wants. Then he can turn the feathers over and burn the undersides. That will help create the proper bend in the feathers.

Sometimes Scheeler will want to put a twist in the feathers. Putting a thin piece of cardboard over the feathers to avoid scorching or damaging the burn lines, he can use the burning pen as a burning iron, heating and twisting the feathers at the same time. The only difficulty, he says, is that if you do this, you will want to determine a common bend so that when the feathers

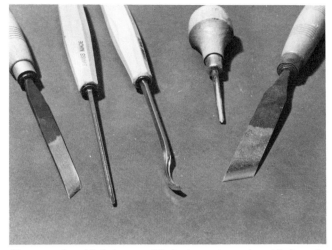

Here are other chisels he uses. His basic carving tools, aside from the Foredom, are few.

Another example of inserted feathers is the wing of this clapper rail.

Before Scheeler begins to make his feather insertions, he will study the real feathers. These are from a Virginia rail.

Shown here is the wing of a willet.

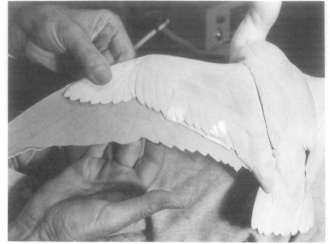

Here is an example of a cardboard pattern for a willet's primary and secondary feathers. Note that each one is penciled in.

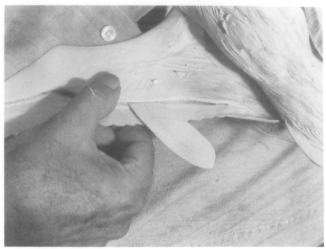

Here an untextured feather has been inserted into the slot on the underside of the wing where it will eventually be glued in place.

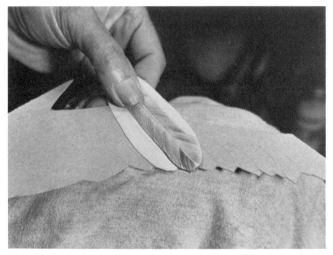

Using this pattern Scheeler can determine the size and location of feathers to be inserted in the wing.

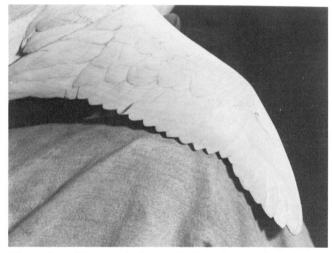

These edges of the carved wing are fragile and can easily be broken.

The pattern, underside shown, is taped to the wood and rests on a shelf carved into the wing.

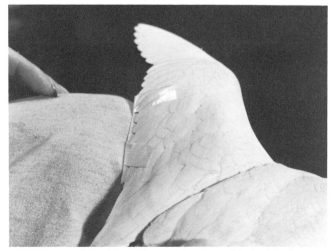

To protect the edges while working on the wing and body, Scheeler tapes a protective piece of cardboard to the underside.

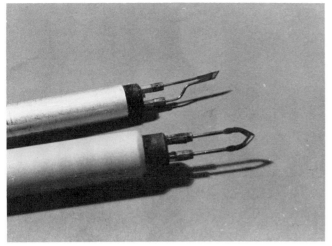

Here are two types of burning tips which Scheeler uses. The top one is for burning in the barbs of a feather; the bottom he can use for bending and shaping a feather.

By applying heat to one side of the feather, he can lift it to change its shape. He notes that the wood will always bend toward the heat.

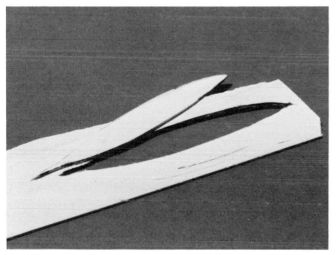

From a thin, flat piece of tupelo gum, Scheeler burns out the feather by running a hot burning tip around its outline. Burning, rather than cutting with a knife or scissors, keeps the edges from fraying.

Using the same method of applying heat, he can also put a twist in the feather.

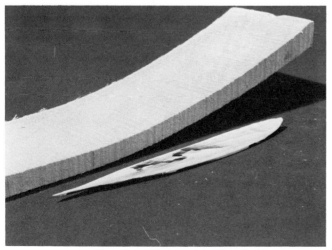

This concave piece of wood acts like an ironing board when it comes to changing a feather's shape. Using the same board for all the feathers, Scheeler will have each feather sharing a common curve.

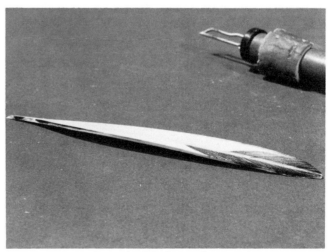

Here is the result of the heat-and-twist technique.

Scheeler can burn in from 50 to 80 barb lines per inch of feather.

These delicate legs of this clapper rail are made of tupelo gum. The bird is depicted as a noisy one.

are put together, they will align properly. He adds that some carvers will use hot water or steam and then bend the feathers with their fingers. He advises, however, that a hairdryer should be used to dry the wood.

How detailed does Scheeler get with his feathers? Using the same fine point he uses for cutting out the feathers, he can burn in as many as eighty barb lines to an inch. But he feels that fifty lines per inch are just as effective in achieving the look of a feather.

Making Feet and Support Systems

It is remarkable, considering their size and delicacy, that Scheeler does not resort to using pewter or cast feet. Instead, he carves them in wood, and tupelo gum lends itself to that. On some birds, he uses added support for strength. What he will do is cut a groove up along the back of the leg and run a heavy-gauge piece of wire along it to extend out into the bird's underbody. The leg wire can then be covered with an epoxy putty.

One bird Scheeler carved, a clapper rail, stands on only one foot. Into the base he set a length of square tubing, the kind that can be purchased at a hobby store. (This tubing was put into a hole filled with a five-minute epoxy.) From the body of the bird he extended the leg wire one-half-inch under the foot. With the foot already attached to the bird, he slipped the extended bit of wire into the tubing. Since it had not yet hardened into place, he was able to turn the assembly until he got the stance he wanted. After holding the clapper rail for five minutes, he was able to remove the bird and wire insert assembly, leaving the square

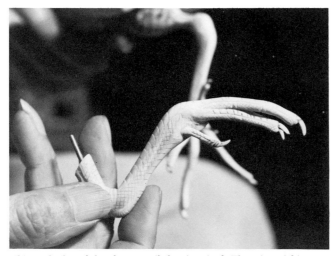

This is the leg of the clapper rail that is raised. The wire sticking out allows it to be inserted into the body of the bird.

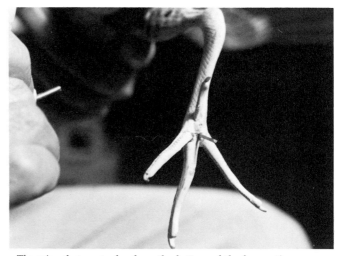

The wire that protrudes from the bottom of the leg continues on up through the back of the leg. This end will be inserted into the base of the bird.

tubing permanently in place. He did, however, add some grease to the joint in the event that glue got into the tubing.

Composition

Scheeler believes there is more to a good sculpture than separate wings, detailed feathers, and carved legs. Many things, he says, are involved in doing a good piece. And one of them, composition, which involves textures, colors, and arrangements, is his specialty.

On textures, Scheeler says, "For every smooth part of a carving, I feel you should have a heavily textured area somewhere else to balance it. You just wouldn't want to make the whole thing smooth."

In designing the composition, Scheeler advises that you should make sure everything complements the main subject, the bird. This is especially true of colors. "I see it happen a lot of times where a fella may make a bluebird and then make a blue flower for it. I'd pick some flower that's orange because orange is a comple mentary color."

Colors, then, should be balanced and complementary. He goes on to say that if there is a color in the beak or the legs, the same color should be found in the base composition. "I did a couple of ruddy turnstones once. They're reddish. On the base I used things you find along the beaches – shells, some seagrass. But I also used a pincer from a rock crab that had turned red from the sun. It just tied the whole composition together." He did the same with a green heron, using in the base plants with the same colors as on the bird.

Here the legs are secured on a mossy composition base, though the clapper rail can be removed so it can be transported safely.

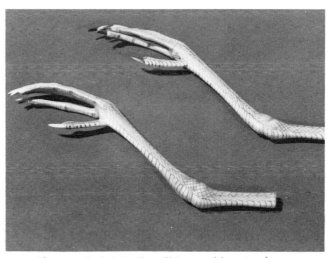

These are the feet for the willet, carved from tupelo gum.

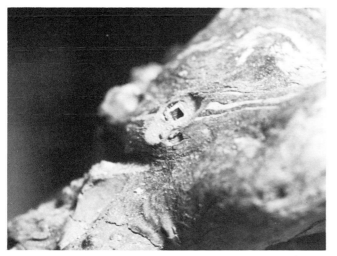

The leg wire is inserted into this square piece of tubing that can be purchased in a hobby store. The tubing is set into a five-minute epoxy so it can be turned as the bird is positioned.

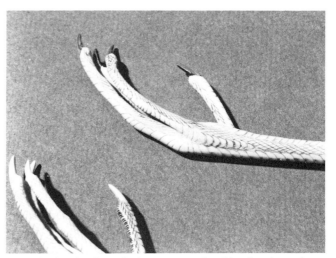

The fine details on the legs were put in with a burning tool.

A typical arrangement of two birds for Scheeler is this pair of Louisiana herons. He prefers to do large birds like these over smaller song birds.

In composing a piece, eye placement is an important feature of the bird. Scheeler may put in the eyes and take them out perhaps a half dozen times. This is the head of the green heron.

Scheeler feels he has had a great deal of success with his arrangements, saying it is a way of keeping his compositions interesting. One of his best may well be his pair of Louisiana herons. Here, two birds stand on a piece of wood, one higher than the other, in a preening attitude.

"It's really hard to get much going for you when you're using a single bird," he says. With two birds you can make an arrangement. And the more birds, the better the arrangement. It's like a bouquet of flowers," Scheeler says in words not unlike Muehlmatt's.

Arrangement also applies to putting a bird in the air. "You have to give the bird direction, a sense of flight by twisting or extending its neck and pointing it in the direction it's going."

It should not be surprising that eyes play a vital role in arranging a sculpture. "I work on the eyes a lot. Sometimes I'll have them in and out of the head a half-dozen different times to get them to where they look right."

Scheeler says of arrangement and composition that many of the new carvers he has met are great on technique and even on painting. "But they can't seem to

arrange their birds or make a bird look convincing at what it's doing. Eventually you've got to make the bird interesting to look at because there's so much of that static stuff around, or copies of what other people have made." It comes as no surprise that Scheeler avoids the kinds of carvings others are doing.

Surf Scoters

A sculpture which typifies the elements of good composition is a pair of surf scoters, ducks found along the northern shores of the United States. Scheeler says there are three kinds of scoters along the coast, and all of them are black. But a surf scoter has more white on it than the other two (the common and white-winged

Here is a pair of surf scoters. Native to New England, they are America's only true black duck.

The tail feathers of the birds were inserted. To achieve the color, he used a Rustoleum black spray.

In composing, Scheeler strives for both smooth and textured areas, as well as light and dark ones.

The pads of the webbed feet were done with an epoxy putty.

For the heads of the surf scoters, Scheeler wanted an alert look.

Typical of the birds' habitat are the oyster shells and rocks. The dark spots on the tupelo gum shells complement the color of the birds.

scoters). "It's the only really true black duck we have, and it's a bird few people see up close," he says. It was that color that Scheeler was able to utilize so well.

He likes scoters, he adds, because he finds they have interesting heads, yet somewhat simple faces. Combining this with his interest in their basic black color, he wanted to see what he could compose. He picked, then, two drakes or males because they have a stronger black color than the females.

With these elements in mind, Scheeler put his two surf scoters on basically white stones. "They are rocks with a lot of texture and variety, in almost stark contrast to the birds." Yet the color of the stones complements the white on the birds' heads and bills. Also, there is a white in the oyster shells in the base, while the heart of the oysters is dark like the birds' feathers. "The black mark on the inside of the oyster shells matches the color of the birds. And I also picked up the color of the birds' bills in the shells." There is even an old feather, white in color, on the base. Of the base he says, "I wanted it to look like a piece of driftwood, so I scratched it up and tried to give it a weathered look."

Basically, Scheeler sees the piece as a contrast between the rocks and the birds. Yet, both belong to the same habitat. "You see stones like that up in Maine," Scheeler says. "That's the habitat of scoters." And they are birds found often around oyster beds—hence, the presence of oyster shells.

Though the scoters are carved, as are the shells, from tupelo gum, the rocks are made of basswood. And how did he get their textured look? After rough-

The distressed base was made to look like driftwood.

Scheeler added an old feather, carved and painted white, as a contrast to the black on the birds.

shaping the stones, Scheeler began with a heavy outdoor latex paint used on houses. Leaving the can open for a few days to thicken the paint, he brushed on a heavy coat and stippled it. This is done with the end of a brush to raise up different areas. The next step was to sand the rocks down, which meant sanding off the points left by the stippled paint. Then he mixed up thin coats of acrylic stains and washed them over the rocks to make them gray. To get back some white on the high spots, he again sanded the high places, leaving gray in the remaining areas. Then he dulled the white with raw sienna and burnt umber acrylics.

Muehlmatt points out that a black acrylic taken directly from a tube should never be used. What Scheeler utilized to give his birds their natural color came from a can of Rustoleum spray paint. "I didn't use an undercoat because my burn marks are deep brown. Some of that comes through the paint. But then I had to spray a gloss coat of clear lacquer over everything to bring the color of the birds back to life."

The basswood rocks for the composition have both a rough and smooth texture. This was done by stipple-painting them — that is, raising up some areas with heavy paint, then sanding them smooth.

This green heron piece is set among pitcher plants and moss, the latter made from wood shavings. Scheeler did the base first, then decided on the bird.

A Green Heron

Although this may contradict his thoughts on composition, Scheeler carved the pitcher plants of this piece a year before he made the bird. "They were so interesting looking," he says of the pitcher plants. "I arranged their stems in a piece of soft wax until I got the design I wanted." But at that time he did not know what to make with them. Finally, it occurred to him to use a green heron because it picked up the same color in the plants. And there may have been another reason. At the time he was picking the pitcher plants, he saw a green heron in the area.

On the base of the piece are stones and moss. The stones are made of Durham's Wood Dough, a putty. "It's a powder you mix with water," he explains. "But because it's so awfully heavy, I used styrofoam pellets as a base and put the putty over them. If I want a granular look, I can make small pellets out of it and fuse them together with water from an atomizer." The moss, he says, is nothing more than shavings produced by running a very coarse cutter on the Foredom over wood that has been wetted down. A green stain gives the wood its color.

Underneath the wing of the green heron, Scheeler inserted feathers to break up the transition from the body to the inserted wing.

Louisiana Herons

Scheeler feels this pair of birds exemplifies a vital element in his compositions — there is nothing distracting in the sculpture.

Made of tupelo gum, the herons were chosen for their lines. Scheeler describes their look as almost

Note the relatively smooth texturing in contrast to the underside of the wing. This technique plays a strong role in most of Scheeler's compositions.

These tail feathers on the green heron are inserts.

The pitcher plants are also made of tupelo gum.

Here is the underside of the green heron's tail feathers. Note how finely done the barbs are.

oriental and notes the Japanese use of herons in print. The necks in particular lend themselves to twisting curves that have a flow that goes up and returns. "It's continuous," he says. What aided in carving the piece was making the heads and necks as separate pieces.

Scheeler points out how the leg of the top bird follows the plane of its wing, while the heads and necks curve around in their preening positions, keeping the eye from drifting off the sculpture. He also says his original idea was to have a longer base with the two birds, but he compressed them instead.

Scheeler says that the body of a bird, heron or otherwise, is a rigid frame, that there is no way the body can bend, unlike humans who have flexible backbones. "So the only things you can change on the bird are the wings, the tail, the legs, and neck." He decided, then,

Typical of what he can do with wood, these feet are made of tupelo gum and detailed with a burning tool.

The stones for the green heron composition are made of Durham Wood Dough. Sometimes Scheeler will use styrofoam pellets as armatures to reduce the weight of stones or rocks.

This is another base for which Scheeler has not decided on a bird. What appears as the end of the driftwood is actually part of the base that has been carved.

This area on the back of one bird shows the heavy texture Scheeler puts into a piece.

to tip the herons' bodies to get the effect he wanted, in conjunction with getting the legs and necks away from a stiff pose.

Interestingly, he simplified the birds' underbellies, doing the feathers more as groups of burn lines, pointing out the need for contrast with the heavily textured wings. He justifies this simplification, saying: "Sometimes it's a mistake to put down on a carving even what you know is there."

Birds of Prey

Though it would seem that Scheeler favors shore birds, he is really partial to birds of prey: hawks and

This pair of Louisiana herons is preening. Note how the wings, beaks, and legs follow the same plane.

In contrast to heavy texture on the wings is a relatively smooth breast on this heron.

The heads and necks of the birds were done as separate pieces.

He says the hawk is keeping its eyes open for any movement below.

Note how one of the tupelo gum feet is tucked under the bird's feathers.

One of Scheeler's birds of prey is this sparrow hawk.

Unlike the other birds featured, this sparrow hawk has no inserts.

falcons. He says: "I like the expression you get in the faces of these birds. There's a fierce and wild look." And the goshawk, he adds, "is about the fiercest of them all." It was a sculpture of such a bird and its prey, a crow, that won him the Best in World ribbon at the 1982 World Championship Wildfowl Carving Competition.

It is the "ruined" crow, though, that is particularly interesting. Actually, Scheeler carved a featherless crow, a technique he had used before. Only after carving a "skinned" crow did he add the wooden feathers. But he carved the head separately. He made it funnel-shaped and squeezed it over the feathers on the neck.

Why did he choose a crow, one that he painted using the same technique as he had with the scoters? "Its color didn't take anything away from the main subject. In other words, I didn't want it competing with the goshawk."

5

Anthony Rudisill
Composition

Professional Painter

Although he is not the oldest of the nine artists in this book, Anthony Rudisill has been interested in birds for more years than any of the others. He can trace his interest back to preteen years when, as a boy scout, he was encouraged to look for birds. Later, he started painting them, copying Audubon paintings to learn about birds and their colorings. With the exception of a few years in high school, Rudisill has been involved with birds and art for over forty years with many awards and gallery exhibits to his credit.

Still, with all this background, the sculpting of birds out of wood is a fairly recent achievement for him. It was John Scheeler who took an interest ten years ago in Rudisill's paintings. Soon, Scheeler was loaning Rudisill tools and wood, and in 1976 he began carving birds. In such a short time, his accomplishments with wood have been remarkable. His first piece won a blue ribbon and his third carving, a pair of bobwhite quail, won Third Best in World at the World Championship Wildfowl Carving Competition. In 1978 he took the grand prize, Best in World in the Decorative Lifesize Pair, with two clapper rails. He repeated that achievement in 1983 with a pair of black-crowned night herons.

"I enjoy both painting and carving," he says, "but carving is a lot more rewarding in the end because you have a lot more involved, such as composition. With a painting, the composition comprises only one

At home on the bay, his source for inspirational material, Anthony Rudisill is an artist on canvas and in wood.

104

view, whereas in a carving, you want it to look good from all sides."

A Kingfisher Composition

Rudisill is in the process of developing a composition of a kingfisher and habitat typical for the species. (Compare Larry Barth's interpretation of kingfisher and environment in the following chapter.) Kingfishers, Rudisill says, sit on pilings or anything high. In the case of a freshwater stream or pond, it will be a tree limb. Unlike some birds that look for fish while flying, the kingfisher looks from its perch. The pose for his bird is a typical kingfisher attitude, he explains. "I watch them all the time outside my home. That's the way they sit, not necessarily looking down."

Why did Rudisill choose to do a kingfisher? Apart from the fact that he is familiar with the bird, Rudisill says, simply, that he had a specimen to work from. "This bird is a challenge because for years I've been

Rudisill also did these red-bellied woodpeckers. Note the meticulous attention to habitat which is also reflected in his carving compositions.

Typical of his wildlife paintings are these bluejays done in a medium gouache.

Painting birds is something he has done for most of his life. Here is a yellow-billed cuckoo.

Standing on a piece of wood piling is this kingfisher. On its base are oyster shells and blades of grass and sand, all carved or duplicated by the artist.

Calipers are a standard tool he uses to check proportions and dimensions when he is working with a mounted bird.

Also helpful are dividers, used here to compare bill sizes, although Rudisill knows that a bird's beak will shrink after it is dead and mounted.

Rudisill compares his partially finished kingfisher to the study mount. Using a mounted specimen eliminates a great deal of guess work and Rudisill feels it's important to use one, even if it is incorrectly mounted, like this one, with shoulders the bird does not have in real life.

Again using calipers, he checks the distance between the wings on the mount.

trying to get a kingfisher specimen. You can't go near one with a camera. It's the most timid bird I've found." He adds, "It seems all the time you're controlled by what specimens are available. But that's what dictates the beginning of a piece." He also adds that though this is one of the smallest birds he has done, preferring to work with larger ones, "for many buyers it's an ideal size and more affordable."

But as other carvers in this book warn, mounts can be deceiving. He says the kingfisher mount he worked from was not a good one, having, for example, shoulders where they did not belong. Plus, as James Sprankle and Larry Hayden point out in their chapters, parts of the anatomy such as bills and feet shrink and change color after the bird has died. So a novice might look at a bad mount and say it has to be right because it is the real bird. Despite these drawbacks, the specimen remains an important reference for Rudisill. As he says, "There's not a lot of guessing if you have the bird. I think the guys who come in last all the time in the competitions do some guessing. And if they do have the specimen, they either don't look at it or don't have the ability to copy."

Compactness

Rudisill notes that when some carvers are planning compositions, they have a tendency to "let things fall apart." He explains that when pairs of birds are too far apart, or when a bird is too high off its base, the composition lacks compactness—it falls apart. "Birds may

When composing a piece like the kingfisher and its habitat, Rudisill is very conscious of what he calls compactness. Holding the bird on top of a piling, he points out that it is too far from the base.

Placed lower, the bird gives the overall composition more shape and tightens the sculpture.

The same measurement can be taken on the carving.

This wood was once a piling, but rot has reduced its once large size. Running through the piling at one time were two bolts, as indicated on the center left of the wood. The projection to the right is the remains of a knot.

Rudisill's original idea was to have water, made artificially from resin, in the base. On the bottom is a coarse sand held with glue. It was painted a dark color to give the water depth.

be like that in real life, but for art's sake, they have to be compacted."

He says this could have been the case with the kingfisher composition. The piling the bird sits on was originally higher. To reduce it, he cut it down a full one-and-one-half inches. "By lowering it," he says, "I feel the piece has more shape to it, instead of leaving a skinny piling with a bird on top."

Compactness is also a factor with what Rudisill describes as overworking a composition. At first he had thought of having two kingfishers, one perched lower than the other on a bolt that had originally run through the piling. This would have overdone it, he says. "Overdoing something is not knowing where to stop, adding extraneous things like an insect, for example. It's redundant. Even adding an extra leaf can be too much. Knowing when to stop probably comes from my years of drawing and painting."

The Base

The wood the kingfisher sits on was originally a pine piling reduced in size by rot from a considerably larger piece, leaving only the core and a knot.

But a good composition for Rudisill does not stop with finding a base. He points out that many carvers, being preoccupied with the bird, neglect the base. "We're creating a piece of art, not just a bird," he says. "So we should consider every square inch of it as art. That's what separates it from just a decoy." He adds, "I

The reeds, which appear in the final composition, are also part of the kingfisher's typical habitat.

These reeds are made from brass shim stock, only .005 of an inch thick. The material can be purchased from an auto supply store.

Rudisill will collect materials from the shore or forest that he will later duplicate in wood.

think the fellows who are successful feel that way. For when you see their work, there's nothing left undone."

Rudisill explains his reasoning in the development of the kingfisher base. At first he was going to have water with reeds in it. He had even sprinkled coarse sand on Elmer's glue on the inside of the base. This he painted a dark green to make the resin he would add later look more like deep water than if he had left white sand in the base. But his thinking changed. For though he stayed with the reeds he had planned on originally, he added a sandy composition and oyster

Here he has placed some shells he collected in the water and sand base. This gives him a feeling for overall composition.

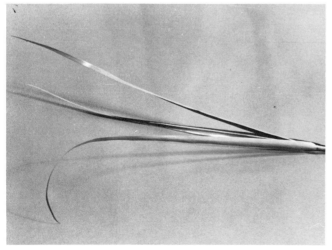

When heated, the brass can be made pliable. If bent, a blade can easily be reshaped.

When it came to the final composition, all these shells were carved and painted.

The shells were textured with paint splattered on with a toothbrush, and the holes were put in with a sharply pointed instrument.

Sketches of various shapes for a base.

An artistic challenge, these white shells with their black spotted interiors complement the colors of the kingfisher above them.

shells. "I thought the oyster shells would add a lot more atmosphere and give me a chance to do more artwork."

It is not unusual, then, for Rudisill to collect shells, acorns, or whatever he might need as models in a composition, but he has a predisposition to and love of the bay. He says, "Most everything I've done has something involved with that habitat such as reeds, mussels, oysters."

Like the other artists in the book, Rudisill is an ingenious manipulator of materials to achieve habitat. To create reeds in the kingfisher piece, he used brass shim stock, .005 of an inch thick that can be purchased from an automotive supply store. To make the metal pliable, he took the temper or strength out of it by heating it with a propane torch until it was red hot. After being bent, the brass will stiffen up again. He notes that taking the temper out of the brass is not critical because the reeds are not supporting anything, and if one gets bent, it can easily be reshaped.

The base for this composition is teakwood. Rudisill finds the grain of the wood attractive, with every piece having something different to offer in terms of grain. Yet his underlying motive for using it is its availability.

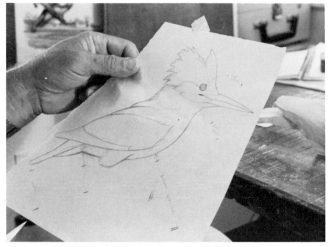

To make the pattern for the kingfisher, Rudisill starts with a piece of tracing paper, on which he plots out some basic dimensions such as bill and tail size.

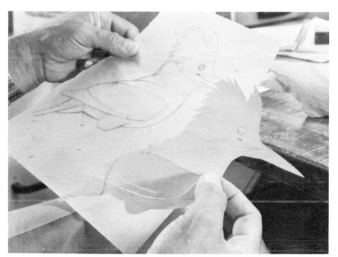

From the tracing paper he makes a working pattern, something more rigid to work with.

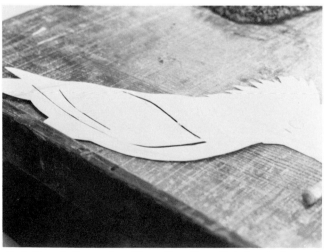

Rudisill works from only a side-profile pattern. Note how he has made a thin cutout to indicate where the wing on the wooden bird will go.

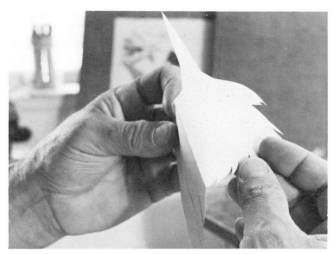

Here the head, shown as a separate piece, is taped to the rest of the bird. This was done so he could make a separate head with grain running differently from the body. With the grain running along the beak, the wood will not be so likely to break.

He obtains teakwood scraps at no cost from local boat-yards and turns the teak himself on a lathe. This, he says, is cheaper than having someone else do it, and he can get the precise shape he wants.

Making a Pattern

Like Scheeler, Rudisill disdains the use of detailed illustrations in preparing for a piece like the kingfisher. Beginning on a piece of tracing paper, he draws out his pattern, conscious of how important the head is. He says, "I'll get the head drawn just super, but I may not get the rest of the body right, especially if it's a bird in flight. So I'll keep the first paper with the head that's been measured accurately." Then he can do a new pattern.

This method has a decided advantage for grain patterns. For though Rudisill draws the entire bird in his preliminary work, he may want to make the head separately, especially if there is to be a change of grain. The pattern, then, can be cut at that place where he wants the head to be separated from the body.

The Seam

Rudisill says he would have preferred the kingfisher to have been made from one piece of wood, but the long bill of the bird would have been subject to changes in grain, which would have weakened it. So the head was made separately. But a problem may still arise.

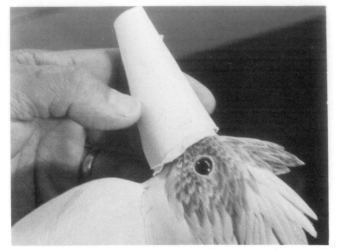

Still, he feels it necessary to protect the beak. Consequently, he has made a cardboard cone to fit over the beak when he works on it.

Shown here is the seam, the result of the head being joined to the body. Note, in spite of this, how relatively grainless the two pieces of basswood are.

For "everytime you add a piece," he points out, "you get involved with a seam."

It should be noted that even with the grain running along the length of the bill, it can still be potentially fragile. To protect it, Rudisill fashioned a piece of cardboard, a cone really, to fit over it. This, he feels, will protect it from being dented if bumped.

Rudisill tries to put the seam to use by taking into consideration its position on the bird. The strategy for the kingfisher is laying neck feathers over the seam. "I selected a place to put the seam where these feathers will be. I'll try to have enough of them to stop at the seam to break it up, get rid of it if I can." He does admit, though, the seam may still come through after painting because of the way paint will be absorbed differently by different grains.

Rudisill works, then, from basically one pattern. Top profiles, he feels, are unnecessary; he uses only a side pattern. But this includes such detail as the positioning of the tail on the body, shoulder width, and head measurements. And he may even have a pencil-point-wide cutout of where the wing will be. He says, however: "It's not really final, but at least I know where I'm going with it."

Shaping with a Roofing Nail

The crest with its tossled head feathers "depicts what a kingfisher is all about," Rudisill believes. To help achieve that effect, he has devised his own tool—a steel roofing nail. Nicked with a grinding stone in a Foredom tool, the nail will fit into the Foredom and cut the notches of the crest. It can also be used to

A good way to disguise the seam is with neck feathers, which help Rudisill determine where the seam would go in the first place.

The crest, he feels, is an important characteristic of the kingfisher, one that distinguishes it from other birds.

define the individual feathers on a carved wing. The rest of the crest shaping can be done with a knife.

Tupelo Gum Feet

Though the kingfisher body is carved from basswood, the feet are tupelo gum. He finds it pliable, especially when working on features like the toes. It will bend to a certain degree, he says, before it breaks. And it can be finished smoothly.

Why didn't he use wire to make the feet, as others such as Larry Barth and Gary Yoder do? He answers that as long as the legs and feet can be made out of wood, they should be. "When they can't, you go to something else." He adds, "I get a lot of pride out of saying I made these feet out of wood. And a lot of people are amazed. But that's not to say the other guy didn't work as hard making them out of epoxy. Still, for small birds like song birds, you may have no choice."

Rudisill's support system is the same as Scheeler's — wire running along the back of the legs, emerging at the bottoms of the feet. The wire is then inserted into a piece of square brass tubing, which will keep the bird's round wire from turning. A small amount of Vaseline makes removal easy.

Fine Burning and Painted Splits

"A bird's not the perfect thing you think he is," says Rudisill. "He has feathers out of place, for example. So the more of this you can incorporate into a piece, the more natural the bird's going to look."

When laying out the feathers, Rudisill will do his

And here is the head of the finished bird.

To achieve these separations on the head feathers, Rudisill uses a steel roofing nail. By nicking its edges, he has made it into a tiny circular saw.

Here he draws in the head feathers with the wood to be removed between them.

The same nail can also be used to make feather separations on wings.

Rudisill will spend a great deal of time doing feather layout. By varying the sizes and shapes of the breast feathers, he tries to avoid a fish-scale effect.

This wing belongs to a baby bluejay.

When it comes to texturing, he burns his lines as closely together as possible. This will create a soft look when painting.

Rather than use artificially-made feet, Rudisill chose to make his from tupelo gum. The kingfisher's feet, then, were carved and detailed by him, though a wire runs along their backsides for support.

Though the primaries of the kingfisher were inserted, the rest of the feathers, including the tail, were carved and textured on the solid block.

Shown here is the block before the tail feathers were given definition.

He might paint in feather splits on the breast of a bird.

Relying on his painting skills, Rudisill will occasionally paint in feather splits rather than carve them. Here he illustrates how a darkly painted line can imitate a split.

Using a dark color and a fine brush, he can create a shadowy effect. Large splits are carved.

On the back of the kingfisher, some splits are painted in, while others are carved.

best to avoid what he calls a fish-scale effect. He will spend a great deal of time drawing and erasing feather patterns on the body until they look right. And he will insert feathers where he feels he wants special emphasis. "I think putting in all the feathers is a waste of time unless you want that special effect. In most cases, it's a lot of unappreciated work." For the kingfisher, he inserted only the primaries.

Perhaps most crucial to the look of the bird is the burning or texturing. He tries to get his burn lines as close together as possible. "The finer or tighter you burn, getting all those little barbs almost on top of each other, the better your piece is going to look when painted." He says the wood will maintain a soft rather than a hard look. "Birds have a sheen owing to the light reflecting on the barb lines, and burning them in gives the carving the same feeling."

Occasionally, he will revert to his illustration skills by painting, not burning or carving in, feather splits, using a dark color that will create a shadowy effect. These are not big splits, however, and a very small brush is used. He confines the painting to areas such as breast feathers and the upper coverts. "It's like painting on canvas," he says. "For that you have to create your own shadows. You can do the same on wood." (For more on similar techniques, read about Larry Hayden's approach in chapter 9.)

Painting in Reverse

Though he will carve the head of a bird first, Rudisill paints from the tail and works toward the head. The reason, he explains, is that all the feathers overlay toward the rear, so he is working over what he has painted just as the feathers overlap. Consequently, he paints the tail first, then the rump, the wings, on up the back and breast, and the head last.

A number of carvers use gesso, a white primer, as a preparation for painting their birds. Rudisill prefers an undercoating called Lok Tite. It has a lacquer base that both seals the wood and gives a white undercoat. "I like the white underneath because it's like working on illustration board," he says, adding that "it gives light under the colors." Why doesn't he use gesso? He points out that it is waterbased like acrylics and will raise the grain of the wood, a defect of many carvings.

For a game bird such as a grouse, though, he will put a coating of gray over the white Lok Tite and work over that. "It makes the browns nice and warm," he says.

Rudisill does not use gesso as an undercoat; instead he prefers a primer called Lok Tite. He applies his paints to this base, working from the tail toward the head so that his strokes overlap as the feathers do. This way, the edge of the feather he's painting finishes off the previous one.

He admits that at one time he used watercolor washes and sprayed them with a matte fixative. "But I didn't know how permanent those colors would be or what the fixative would do over a long period of time, so I started working with acrylics." These, he says, are as permanent as you can get. Also, with acrylics he can work over them, though the watercolors tend to stay soft in tone and the different colors can be "pulled together" with a little water. But, he points out, he was constantly worried about pulling up the last layer with watercolors.

When working with acrylics on an area such as the breast, he will work the paint as thick as he can when he begins. This slows down the drying time, he says, and he can "push and pull the colors together." He will use thin washes, however, if he wants to change the tint or hue.

A Piece of the Woods

A composition Rudisill is in the process of working on demonstrates again his close attention to the base. On turned teakwood he has created an earthy composition of stones, a log, and two low-growing swamp oaks. Rudisill says, "It is the most natural-looking base composition I've ever done. It looks like I walked into the woods and dug it up." He spent, in fact, an entire day in a forest looking for what he wanted.

The bird for this composition will be a ruffed grouse in flight. It will have a steel or heavy aluminum feather inserted into the tail which will be touching the log.

Before starting the bird, which will be hollow to reduce its weight, Rudisill made a styrofoam and cardboard mockup, the first time he had done one. "You have to make a model for something like this, so you know where you're going with the bird. For more static poses, I think it's a waste of time."

At the time of our visit, the body was roughly shaped; it was carved from two thick pieces of basswood hollowed and joined. The head was nearly finished. As Rudisill says, "If the head is right, the rest of the bird will be right." And like the kingfisher, the ruffed grouse's crest feathers were defined with his roofing nail. Why was the head made separately? This was done, so it would not have to be bandsawed in half, as it would if it were still part of the body.

For this composition Rudisill worked from a single, side-profile pattern. Here again he was able to decide how big the head would be and give attention to changes in grain between that part of the anatomy and the rest of the body. Using the pattern he was also

Typical of the grouse's woodland habitat are acorns and brown leaves, suggesting a fall setting. Both were made by Rudisill.

Low-growing swamp oaks are also part of the habitat.

This base, which might be called "a piece of the woods," is ready for an as-yet-to-be-finished ruffed grouse.

These oak leaves were made from a metal foil and textured.

What gives the leaves support are slivers of bamboo.

The same putty can also be used to make small stones.

Also part of the habitat is an earthlike composition.

The base, which Rudisill turned himself, is made from one of his favorite woods—teak, a grainy, brown wood.

Durham Wood Dough was used to make the pebbles and sand.

The habitat is not put directly on or into the teak base. Instead, it was built up on a piece of plywood which in turn was set into the base.

Here is the styrofoam model of the ruffed grouse, held where it will be attached to the log by one tail feather made of steel.

The roughly defined body of the grouse was hollowed to reduce its weight.

Here the head of the ruffed grouse is shown as a separate piece, with much of the detailing already done. It was made independently of the body so it would not be sawn in half when the bird was hollowed.

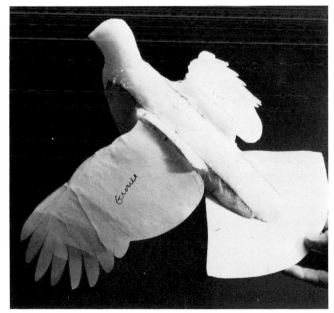

This is the first styrofoam and cardboard mockup Rudisill had ever done. But it was necessary to determine the pose of the flying bird, something that is difficult to do on paper.

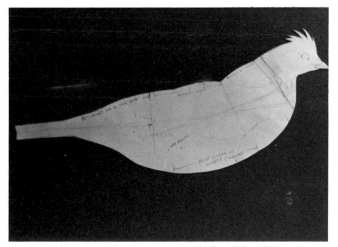

This is the pattern for the grouse, marked with key dimensions.

Shown here is where Rudisill determined the head would be attached to the body.

This is the right wing stub positioned on a paper underlay. The paper will determine the placements of the primary and secondary feathers of the grouse.

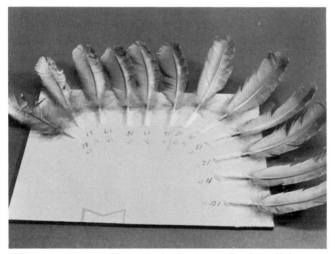

When it comes to making wing feather inserts for the ruffed grouse, Rudisill uses the real feathers from the bird for later tracing on the wood. Here he has removed the primaries and secondaries.

The underside of the same stub shows the slot for feather insertion.

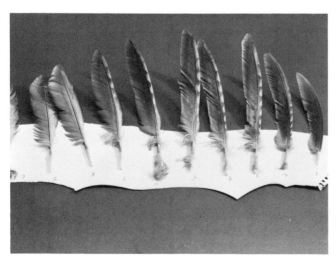

The feathers are ready to be traced.

These are the left and right wing stubs, with only one textured.

This pair of green herons is a composition of display and balance. Compact, with the birds confined to the area of the base, the piece can be rotated while at least one bird will be visible from any angle.

able to decide on the overall dimensions of the bird, the placement of the tail, and the width of the shoulder.

The grouse, unlike the kingfisher, will have both primaries and secondaries inserted into separately made wings. Using real feathers from a ruffed grouse, Rudisill will number and trace them on thin pieces of basswood. What Rudisill uses is a special technique limiting his burning of the barb lines on the feathers. To do this, he inserts the feather into the wing to see how much is hidden in the slot. This portion he will not burn, because he feels that it is a waste of time to texture what is not seen.

The habitat, Rudisill says, is a fall one. "It's hunting season for this kind of bird, and the colors in the base complement the bird's." He also points out that he kept his oaks at just the right height to blend with the overall composition."

It should be noted that Rudisill did not build his

habitat directly into the twelve-inch diameter base. Instead, he stepped down the inside of the base a half inch and fitted into it a round piece of plywood. On the plywood he affixed his oaks, log, and Durham putty stones and pebbles and sand. (He made them as Scheeler described in chapter 4.)

Green Heron Pair

Rudisill made these birds for the 1979 World Championship Wildfowl Carving Competition and they won Third Best in World. For this piece, he created a habitat of a saltwater marsh mudflat with mussel shells and the herons are fighting over a fiddler crab. This confrontation, he says, "makes good use of the herons' long necks."

Perched on a teakwood base, the birds have their wings spread, "for display and balance," he says. "But the main reason was to show off the wings. They impress people." And, not surprisingly, he says the crab was as much of a challenge as the birds.

This pair of black-crowned night herons features an adult and immature bird. Note the use of mussel shells and reeds in the base. This won Best in World as a decorative lifesize piece at the 1983 World Championship Wildfowl Carving Competition.

Rudisill sees this piece as having pleasing symmetry. Explaining the use of the term, he says that the composition can be viewed from any angle and look good. And, in fact, at least one bird can be seen no matter how the base is rotated. "With a good carving, you can position it anywhere and it should look good."

He also points out that the piece is compact, indicating that the birds are confined within the area of the base. The composition, then, "does not fall apart."

In designing a piece like the green herons, Rudisill may do what he calls thumbnail sketches. He'll take this approach most often with two birds, he says. "With a single bird, you could finish him and then decide what you want to do with him. With two birds they have to work together." So simple sketches can help him see how the birds stand in relationship to one another and how they will appear from different angles.

Working sketches of the green heron pair that won Third Best in World in 1979.

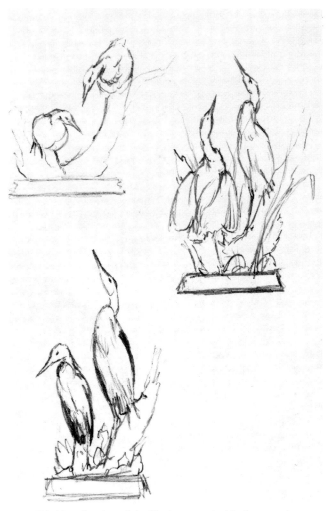

Working sketches of the black-crowned night heron pair.

Black-Crowned Night Heron Pair

These two birds represent an immature and an adult heron. "My thought," Rudisill says, "was to show the immature and adult because both sexes are alike. Doing this lent an educational value." But there was another aspect to his choice. "I chose to have the adult bird above the immature one to show a protective attitude. The feeling's there of having a parent-child relation." He also thought of having the birds facing in opposite directions, but he felt this would not work compositionally.

The base, like that of the green heron pair, also has mussel shells, adding, he says, "realism and artistry." And like the kingfisher piece, he included reeds made of brass shim stock. This part of the habitat was especially important to Rudisill. He says that when he finished the birds and base, he had not as yet put the grasses into the piece. When he did finally add them, "everything just came together. It was as if the grasses gave everything else a reason for being there. I've never experienced anything so definite. They had to be there to finish the composition."

6

Larry Barth
Portraits in Wood

A Degree in Sculpting Birds

Larry Barth's background is unique among the nine artists. His formal training has given him what could be called a college degree in bird sculpture.

His direction developed early. "I've always been interested in birds as a result of my mother's influence," he states, while his father, being a woodcarver, contributed to his sculpting talents.

During his first years in high school, he began to carve birds in a smooth, stylized fashion. In 1975, he enrolled at Carnegie-Mellon University's College of Fine Arts to pursue a career in illustration because, at that point, his carving did not seem to offer a feasible career.

The factor that would sway him toward sculpting birds professionally came during his freshman year of college while he was on a trip with his family that took him through Salisbury, Maryland, where the Ward Foundation's Wildfowl Carving Exhibition was being held. There he saw an entire convention hall of bird carvings, some similar to his own style, others highly detailed.

He says of this experience, "I had been carving in isolation. It just hadn't occurred to me to take what I was doing that far. But once I saw what could be done with birds, my skills developed quickly, and I began to see this as a potential career." As a result of this revelation, he redirected his curriculum at Carnegie-

Larry Barth has made significant contributions to the art of bird sculpting. Here he puts the final touches on an oriole.

Barth sees the making of a piece like the oriole more than decorative art. Rather, he sees the sculpture as capturing the essence of what a bird is all about.

Mellon to enable him to take courses that would help him carve birds professionally.

"There were no courses at school on how to carve birds, but there were courses that would make me a better artist," he explains. "I took courses dealing with design principles, composition, color, and anatomy, and applied all these to my carving." The result, in part, was not a written thesis in his senior year, but instead a sculpture of great horned owls, an adult and two young, and slides of the project in progress. That same year Barth entered the piece at the World Championship Competition where it took second place in World Class Decorative Lifesize. A week after the show he graduated and has been carving fulltime ever since.

Barth says, "I think my background has given me an advantage for my future. Most of the carvers I've met are people who pick this up in their spare time. My advantage, apart from working full time, is having known so young that this is what I wanted to do." And he admits that he has never been too far from this field. "I started with drawing and painting birds," he says, "now I'm carving them, which is satisfying because I've moved from two to three dimensions; I'm creating the whole bird."

More Than Decoration

Nearly all of this book is devoted to decorative works, but Barth objects to the term decorative. He says it suggests that a piece is pretty to look at but nonfunctional, the decoration being put on as a secondary step. He believes there is more to the work than that. He even suggests that the term decorative may have been meant as an insult, "originated by people who did working decoys and applied it to others who got fancy with their carvings."

Barth goes on to explain that when he is making a bird, he is trying to capture the essence of something he's seen, something he considers both naturally striking and naturally beautiful. "So I don't see putting wings and feathers and other details on a bird as decoration. To me it's a marriage of form and function. That's why I dislike the term decorative. It sounds artificial."

He also feels that the term may be making it difficult for the critics to accept bird sculpture as an art instead of a craft. He also thinks that many of the com-

Here the singing oriole pauses momentarily on the delicate and high-up branches of a cherry tree.

What Barth describes as a three-dimensional portrait or full painting in wood is this kingfisher composition. This, he says, is an entire scene of a kingfisher's world.

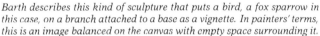

Barth describes this kind of sculpture that puts a bird, a fox sparrow in this case, on a branch attached to a base as a vignette. In painters' terms, this is an image balanced on the canvas with empty space surrounding it.

The kingfisher, miniature in size and not highly detailed, gazes down into the center of an eddy.

petitions are holding back the artistic growth of the field by imposing too many restrictive rules and guidelines. As an example, for the World Class Decorative Lifesize category, only pairs of birds can be entered, and the kinds of birds that can be submitted change each year.

It's interesting that he claims that the novice table is where fresh ideas are to be found. "Here people may not have gotten their skills together, but there are good ideas to be found, innovative ones that don't get credit because the bird may be bad." He adds that "it's the idea, the composition, the piece working as a whole that should determine its worth, not just the hand skills."

Painting With Wood

When discussing bird sculpture as an art form, Barth speaks of the painter's canvas and uses the terms vignette and full painting. In a vignette, he says, the image is balanced on the canvas, but there is empty space surrounding the image that is not used. (Compare

Another piece he describes as a portrait is this pair of loons. He likens this to a full painting of two birds in their natural setting.

Strong lighting on the piece can create some dramatic effects, a decided advantage to this portrait in wood.

Muehlmatt's paintings of a quail and a woodcock.) In a full painting, the image "spills off the edges."

Most of the carvings done today, he says, fall into the vignette category, including ones he has done, his oriole, for instance. He sees the vignette approach contributing to the craft image and calls it "the bird on a stick on a base" stereotype. While there is room for innovation and excellence in this format, it is often just a bird on a stick on a base.

There are pieces Barth has done that he considers three-dimensional, full paintings. One of them is his kingfisher composition. The bird, miniature in size and not highly detailed, is perched on a wood snag in a stream. This is a full painting, says Barth, because it's "an entire scene. It's the habitat, the atmosphere, the mood. The bird is an inextricable part of its environ-

ment. It more completely represents, then, the kingfisher in his world." He adds that it is as different from just a kingfisher on a stick as a full painting is from a vignette.

As a composition, Barth feels the piece works. Instead of using synthetics such as resin for the water, he carved it out of wood. A branch he has corkscrewing down into the water forms an eddy, which is the center of piece, he notes, and the kingfisher's gaze goes directly down into the center of that eddy.

Barth has also carved a pair of loons in their natural setting. In this piece the surface of the water is rippled by the passing loons, an element which likens the sculpture to a full painting.

These pieces are examples of Barth's efforts to bring fresh ideas into the field of bird sculpture and get away from the bird-on-a-stick-on-a-base formula. He goes so far as to say that "the loons and kingfisher are my strongest arguments for this being art instead of craft." And he will do more of these kinds of pieces. He anticipates doing a carving in which the water spills over the edge of the base rather than being confined in a manmade pool. He envisions another sculpture hav-

Here Barth points out that the shape and form of the piece become more important than the color of the loons.

Barth describes this ruffed grouse composition as "a running take off." He feels it is important that there are no conspicuous or distracting signs of what suspends the bird in flight.

ing no formal base at all, just rocks and flowing water composed to create graceful lines, something he sees as artistic.

On the Wing

What does Barth have to say about carvers who put birds into the air? Putting a bird in flight differs from anchoring it onto a stick, but most bird sculptors use the same technique: wingtips touch other wingtips or they touch a branch, a blade of grass, or some other part of the habitat. (For a comparison, read chapter 7 on Gary Yoder who puts miniatures in flight.) Barth says that with a flying bird, the first question asked consciously or subconsciously is how is the bird held up. "I think that can be a problem if the method of support draws attention to itself and away from the bird and the composition, which are, after all, what's really important. I don't think the viewer's eye should catch on conspicuous signs of technique. The finished piece should appear to be effortless. It should be enjoyed without questions having to be asked."

Barth has done a composition of a ruffed grouse in which he feels the method of support is neither conspicuous nor distracting. To anchor the flying bird as inconspicuously as possible, he placed one of its legs against a log. "The leg touches the log, but the toes still hang free, so visually it still reads as airborne." This way, he feels, it is anchored but not conspicuously or distractingly so. And he says that even though the contact can be seen, "you don't worry about it. You don't get hung up on how the bird is suspended."

The Essence of a Bird

Barth says the legs of the ruffed grouse are crossed like a skater's, a gesture that tells the viewer where the bird is going. Feet, he says, can tell a great deal about what birds are doing. This is an important aspect to making a grouse or an oriole, pieces he describes as three-dimensional vignettes.

He goes on to say that the parts that are not feathers, the feet plus the eyes and bill, "have a whole lot more to do with birds looking real than do the feathers." Feathers he describes as being variable. "You have a lot of liberty with them; they can do almost anything." And though a carver has to get them correct anatomically, "it's the eyes, the bill, and the feet that you've really got to get right."

Barth pays close attention to such details as eyes and beak. On the kingfisher he points out that these are areas that must be anatomically correct.

The way Barth shapes a bird is not unlike what has been described in previous chapters. Even the wood Barth uses, basswood, has been discussed before, though the very first wood he used was sugar pine. It was around the house, he says. He soon discovered basswood, finding that other people were using it. "It's a well-behaved wood, no knots, no pitch, no hard and soft rings." Pine, he points out, does not burn evenly. Because of that characteristic, the grain can be seen after burning. And pine does not have as much strength. Basswood, then, "has the strength to hold all the detail I've ever wanted to put into a bird. Until it's unable to hold the detail I want to put into it, I won't look for another wood."

The feather texturing technique which Barth uses on birds is a mixture of burning and grinding. Strong,

Barth notes that details like this eye and beak on the fox sparrow can only occur when the artist knows his subject thoroughly.

Barth both stones and burns the textures on his birds. For softer feathers like those on the breast of the oriole, he will use a small stone.

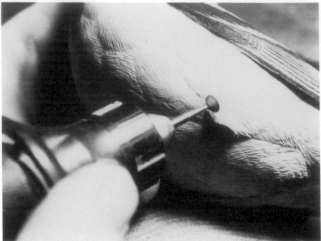

Here he demonstrates how the stoned texture is achieved.

distinct feathers such as those on the wings and tail are burned, while the softer, looser body feathers tend to be ground with a small stone. For the grinding, Barth uses a tool that is not always found in the other artists' workshops or studios. The Dremel Moto-Tool does much the same work the Foredom does, but it's usually used on a smaller scale. Because of its size, it is unable to accommodate the larger cutters shown in previous chapters. Another difference is, unlike the Foredom, the motor and chuck that hold the bits or other cutters are both part of the handpiece, eliminating the flexible shaft. (For more on the Dremel, read Gary Yoder's use of it.) Barth does, however, use a variable speed Dremel, saying: "I used to grind at the highest speed possible. Now I grind as slowly as possible. I thought that high speed was necessary for clean grinding, but I find I can grind cleanly at low speed. The stone bit rides lightly over the surface of the feather, leaving a texture behind. At high speed, it's hard to keep the bit from digging too deeply and changing the surface rather than just texturing it."

When it comes to painting a bird, Barth will use acrylics. He claims that painting goes quickly for him,

"but it goes with difficulty. Good painting can improve a mediocre carving. Bad painting can ruin a terrific carving. That's why, if the paint isn't enhancing the carving, I'll scrub it off and start again." He adds, "I want the painting to show up what I've done, not cover it up."

But Barth says that most of the birds he has done are soft-colored or brownish, such as the ruffed grouse, the owls, and even the woodcock. On doing an oriole, he says, "I'm normally a little bit scared of a bird with so much color." He uses another example of a wood duck. "It's gawdy. So even if you apply all the right colors where they should be, it can look fake because the real thing is so intense. So I've been scared of super brightly colored birds because it's hard at times to make them look convincing."

Shown here is the Dremel Moto-Tool he uses instead of the Foredom. Attached to a speed control rheostat, the tool has its motor in the hand-piece. Above the tool is a Northern oriole study skin.

Red Jungle Fowl, *Lynn Forehand*
Best in World, World Championship Class Decorative Lifesize, 1979
Photo by Steve Budman for the Ward Foundation

Cattle Egrets, *Lynn Forehand*
Photo courtesy of the Ward Foundation

American Coots, *Lynn Forehand*
Photo by Ronald Maratea

Mourning Doves, *Lynn Forehand*
Second in World, World Championship Class Decorative Lifesize, 1981
Photo by James L. D. Tatum

Spruce Grouse, *Ernest Muehlmatt*
First, Decorative Lifesize, Upland Game Birds, 1984
Photo by Ernest Muehlmatt

Woodcock, *Ernest Muehlmatt*
First, Decorative Lifesize, Shorebirds, 1983
Photo by Ernest Muehlmatt

Semipalmated Plovers, *Ernest Muehlmatt*
Photo by Ernest Muehlmatt

Miniature Woodcocks, *Ernest Muehlmatt*
Best in World, World Championship Class Decorative Miniature, 1979
Photo courtesy of the Ward Foundation

Ruffed Grouse and Song Bird, *Eldridge Arnold*
First in Show, Professional Decorative Lifesize, 1982
Photo by McCormick and Nelson

Wilson's Snipe, *Eldridge Arnold*
Photo by McCormick and Nelson

Screech Owl, *Eldridge Arnold*
Photo by McCormick and Nelson

Mourning Dove, *Eldridge Arnold*
Second in Show, Professional Decorative Lifesize, 1981
Photo by McCormick and Nelson

Sleeping Dunlins, *Eldridge Arnold*
Photo by McCormick and Nelson

Long Eared Owl with Mouse, *John Scheeler*
Best in World, World Championship Class Decorative Lifesize, 1976
Photo courtesy of the Ward Foundation

Louisiana Herons, *John Scheeler*
First in Show, Professional Decorative Lifesize, 1983
Photo by Kenneth Basile

Gyrfalcon, *John Scheeler*
First in Show, Professional Decorative Lifesize, 1980
Photo by Steve Budman

Ruffed Grouse, *John Scheeler*
Best in World, World Championship Class Decorative Lifesize, 1980
Photo by Kenneth Basile

Clapper Rails and Snail, *Anthony Rudisill*
Best in World, World Championship Class Decorative Lifesize, 1978
Photo by Steve Budman

Black Crowned Night Heron, Anthony Rudisill
Best in World, World Championship Class Decorative Lifesize, 1983
Photo by Kenneth Basile

Screech Owl and Polyphemus Moth (detail),
Larry Barth
First Place, Sculpture, National Wildlife Federation, 1983
Photo by John Lokmer

Screech Owl and Polyphemus Moth (detail),
Larry Barth
First Place, Sculpture, National Wildlife Federation, 1983
Photo by John Lokmer

Algonquin—Common Loons, Larry Barth
First in Show, Professional Decorative Miniature, 1982
Photo courtesy of the Ward Foundation

Eastern Kingbird and Goldenrod, *Larry Barth*
Second in Professional Decorative Lifesize Songbirds, 1983
Photo courtesy of the Ward Foundation

Mallard Pair, *Gary Yoder*
Best in World, World Championship Class Decorative
Miniature, 1982
Photo by M. C. Wootton

Pheasants, *Gary Yoder*
Best in World, World Championship Class Decorative Miniature, 1980
Photo courtesy of the Ward Foundation

Great Horned Owl, *Gary Yoder*
First in Show, Professional Decorative Miniature, 1977
Photo by E. Moses Yoder

Common Yellowthroat, *Gary Yoder*
First Place, Decorative Lifesize Songbirds, 1980
Photo by Steve Budman

Gadwall Drake, *James Sprankle*
First in Specie, Professional Decorative Decoy Marsh Ducks, 1983
Photo by David Evans

Redhead Drake and Hen, *James Sprankle, 1983*
Photo by David Evans

Hooded Merganser, *James Sprankle, 1980*
Photo by David Evans

Green-winged Teal Drake and Hen, *James Sprankle*
Third in World, World Championship Class Competition Grade Decorative Decoy Pair, 1982
Photo by David Evans

Hen Pintail, *Larry Hayden*
Best of Show Midwest Decoy Contest, 1975
Photo by Les Ward

Drake Wood Duck, *Larry Hayden*
Best Marsh Duck World Championship, 1974
Photo by Les Ward

Drake Old Squaw, *Larry Hayden*
Best of Show Canadian National, 1973
Photo by Les Ward

The underparts of the fox sparrow were done mostly with the stone, while the upper areas were textured with a burning tool.

For the base of the oriole, Barth chose the delicate top branches of a cherry tree. "When I think of an oriole," he states, "I think of it high up in a tree." And, he says, it is the voice more than the color that draws the observer's attention to it. Consequently, and in keeping with his thoughts about the bill, eyes, and feet, he has the oriole singing.

The branch the bird sits on is made of brass tubing, which he describes as a system of rods fitting into tubes. He finds the material very useful for stems because the telescoping effect can allow him to taper the tubing.

The leaves are formed out of thin sheets of copper and painted green. Barth explains that the green leaves complement the bird in terms of color, frame it nicely, and are in keeping with the bird's "natural history." He mentions that he had once seen a piece of marble, "an organic, natural material that was a deep, dark green." Running through it were bright, rusty-orange streaks. Seeing that piece of marble was in his mind when he developed the oriole composition.

Barth does, then, think a great deal in terms of color schemes. And he says, "the deep, rich green of the leaves of the oriole piece make the orange that much brighter."

Complex or Complicated?

Barth feels that regardless of how large or small a piece is, whether it is "powerful and dynamic, quiet and subtle, something about the piece must be simple." According to Barth, the viewer considers the overall appearance of a piece before he studies the details.

But the details and workmanship will eventually be scrutinized.

"In my work," he explains, "I try very hard to 'keep it simple.' It is a phrase I repeat over and over to myself, especially during the planning stages." By this Barth does not mean that large or involved pieces should not be attempted. He says that keeping things simple is basically keeping them under control, especially as more elements go into a composition. He goes on to say that the more involved a piece becomes, the more aware he is of a distinction he makes between two terms—complex and complicated. "A piece can be as complex as need be without affecting the unity of the overall design. But to me, the term complicated means that the various elements involved are not working together."

He uses his kingbird and goldenrod as an example. "Making the goldenrod was the most intricate and tedious thing I've ever done. I had to glue nearly 1000 tiny, delicate flowers, each one individually made from hot-melt glue, Super Glue, and dental floss. I think of the finished goldenrod as very, very complex, but not complicated. As complex as the plant is, the piece as a whole remains clean and simple. The word complicated alludes to confusion and disunity, whereas complex can go hand in hand with a strong, clean design."

Making Feet

There are other subtleties apparent in Barth's pieces, subtleties he spends a great deal of time creating. Again they have to do with the bill, eyes, and feet. These three have a disproportionate effect on the lifelike

Barth notes that when it comes to painting, he prefers to paint over stoned areas since they provide a better surface for acrylics.

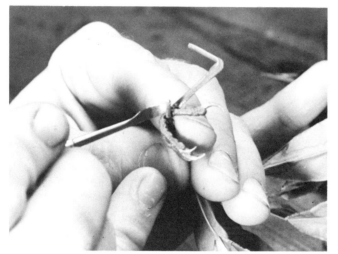

These are Barth's modeling tools used when it comes time to shape and detail the bird's epoxied feet. These he made himself.

appearance of a carved bird, he says. He points out, however, that the feet in particular "can say an awful lot about what a bird is doing," citing the ruffed grouse as one example. Plus, they can clutch and take different postures. With the oriole, Barth notes that the bird is not really clutching. "It's balancing itself, which indicates that it is not going to stay there a long time. This builds animation and movement into the piece even though the bird is stationary."

He recalls that at one time he hated making feet, especially when he and most other carvers were soldering toes to legs. Two-part epoxies have now replaced the soldered joints, and the feet have become one of Barth's favorite parts to make.

He uses a Duro product, the kind, he says, "you get at a hardware store where they tell you to use it for patching holes in your water tank." He feels this product is stiffer and has more body than other brands he has tried. When the epoxy's two parts are mixed together, they work like clay for about three-quarters of an hour. When applied to a piece of copper wire, which has been cut to the proper length with the claw formed at one end, it becomes a toe. Because of the epoxy's rather long hardening time, details can be pressed into it. If still more time is needed, Barth varies the proportions of the two parts. Once all the toes are completed, more epoxy is used to join them to the feet.

At one time, Barth used pins for detailing. But when he found them too hard to manage and hold, he made his own tools with long wooden handles that look

With the same tool, he can move the foot slightly to a new position.

This is the blade of a broken X-acto knife he uses to press detail into the foot.

something like clay sculptor's tools. Sometimes there is a problem with the epoxy sticking to the tools. To remedy that, he will stick the steel into a ball of Plasticene clay, which will leave an epoxy-resisting, oily film on the tool.

Barth used to make up and assemble the feet and all the toes at the same time. Now he does each piece separately "to break the assembly down into manageable units." Still, "it is important to mold the shape of the feet and toes before you start pressing details into them." He also notes that toes like the oriole's are not meant to do anything structural. "These toes don't support the bird. All they do is hang onto the branch. So a lot of strength isn't required."

What does hold the bird to its branch is a branch-and-leg assembly joined to the underside of the bird. This in turn is joined, given the telescoping effect of the tubing, to another branch.

Natural History and Artistic License

Like Scheeler and Rudisill, Barth is very conscious of a bird's habitat and peculiarities, or what he calls its natural history.

What Barth wants, then, is to put into a piece every attribute of the species he feels is important. He says, "I want to create the best oriole I can based on my understanding of what orioles are all about."

Yet, he believes there is room for artistic license provided it is within the confines of a bird's natural his-

Here is the assembly of bird, leg, and branch.

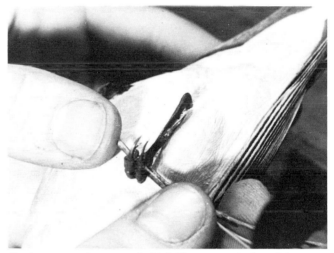

Barth composes the toes on the bird. The copper wire branch is permanently attached to the underside of the oriole.

With the knife, Barth removes excess putty from the copper wire leg.

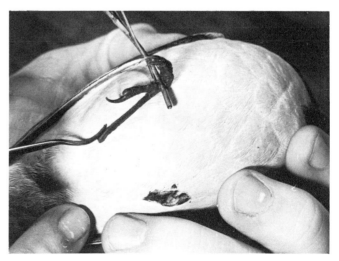

Since the epoxy is malleable for a time, he can continue shaping it on the leg and ankle.

With the oriole leg attached to the rest of the piece, Barth adds a small amount of putty to the ankle joint.

Barth points out that the bird is balancing itself, not clutching. The branch and stems of the black cherry tree comprise a system of rods fitting into tubes, while the leaves are made from thin copper sheets.

tory. This means that some birds do not go with some plants. "You don't have a downy woodpecker sipping nectar," he points out.

The problem of how much artistic license to take came when he was doing a woodcock sculpture. The typical woodcock habitat is fairly bland, he notes. These are low, squat ground birds that would be found among leaves and saplings. This he could deal with, but he wanted to "build some height into the composition, even though it's not characteristic of the habitat." Adding the branch he describes as artistic license, necessary in order to get the height he needed into the piece. He feels the branch balances the composition and points out how the shape of the branch "echoes" that of the bird.

The final step is positioning the toes. Since they do not support the bird, strength is not required.

For the fox sparrow, Barth says the legs and feet create a balance that is necessary for a lifelike appearance.

This composition of an American woodcock and cinnamon fern fiddleheads is a story of natural history. To make more than what is usually a bland habitat for woodcocks, he built height into the composition by adding the ferns and branch.

Barth made these fiddleheads for the woodcock piece, but later rejected them. They were done from basswood.

To recreate the gossamerlike substance of these ferns, Barth wrapped the wood with strands of hot melt glue.

Fiddleheads, Fluffy Feathers, and Whirlpools

Barth enjoys putting into his works what he describes as "structural elements in nature," whether they be leaves, goldenrod, fiddleheads, or streams. For the woodcock piece, he had decided on using cinnamon fern fiddleheads from the bird's habitat to complement the pale, gray colors of the woodcock's scapulars. Fern fronds are rolled up like watch springs when they emerge from the ground and before they uncoil. Because they look like violin heads, they are called fiddleheads. And the fiddleheads of this fern are coated with a gossamer substance.

To recreate these fiddleheads, right down to the coating, Barth started by carving their basic shape in basswood. Then, with a hot-melt glue gun, he made strands of glue, and, with a hairdryer, kept them from recongealing. This process left enough tack to the glue to enable him to wrap the wood ferns with the strands. The fiddleheads, he says, were their own composi-

When it came to recreating the fluffy feathers of baby great horned owls, Barth utilized short lengths of balsa wood. When they were boiled and chewed, the wood's fibers separated, giving the effect he wanted.

tional challenge. Also, he kept them lower than the woodcock. This way they would not compete with the bird for attention.

He is equally challenged in doing the water for his sculptures, particularly the kingfisher piece. For this, he tried to build a comparable situation in a stream to observe the circulation, but he admits he could not make visual sense out of the stream changing course. He even made a clay model, which, he also felt, failed to describe the water's action. Ultimately, "I winged it," he says. "It reads as water, so it works."

Another compositional and structural challenge was making feathers for his great horned owl sculpture. Barth wanted to recreate the fluffy look of feathers on young birds. This is something no other carver he knew of had been able to do or even had attempted.

Chewing the balsa, he discovered, when it was cut into manageable lengths, separated the fibers, an effect not unlike the fluffy feathers on immature owls. But it was difficult and tedious. And he needed a shortcut as he neared a deadline. Perhaps something he had

One of Barth's talents is using materials in unusual ways. This variety of plant parts was made from thin copper sheets, a material he used for the leaves of the oriole's cherry tree.

He finds the copper ideally workable for leaves and plant forms. A piece of the unformed copper is on the right.

The kingfisher's gaze focuses on the eddy or small whirlpool and also holds the viewer's eye. Attempting to copy a real eddy and not feeling he was successful, Barth still carved this base. He says, though, that the "water" is reacting in predictable ways.

Here he was able to make maple and beech leaves from the copper.

read about Thor Hyderdahl's balsawood rafts sinking only after being in water a long time affected his thinking. Whatever it was, he decided to boil the balsa. It was only after five hours of boiling that the wood sank —which indicated that the fibers of the wood were soft enough, so the time spent chewing was greatly reduced.

Templates of Clay

Like Scheeler, Barth makes his models from clay, but Barth makes a very detailed model. So precise can he model the anatomical shape of a bird he actually uses it as a template.

"I want a gesture, a basic form from the clay model. The details I'm content to work out in wood." Back to clay, Barth may run a piece of sheetmetal through the body and out as wings, "for the real thin parts of the bird," he says.

But after the pattern is made and transferred to a block of wood to be bandsawed, the model is not discarded. "If I didn't have the clay model," he says, "I'd have to sit there and stare at my wood block and try to visualize whether it's this way or that. But by working out the rough, bold form of the bird in clay, I have that to fall back on while the details such as the feathers can be worked out in the wood." And if he does encounter problems in the wood, he can go back to the clay to do his problem solving.

What happens for Barth is that the clay model re-

The clay can be used to plan out an entire composition.

Shown is a detail of a sandpiper grouping in clay.

Clay, when modeled, can become a template for Barth, to be traced onto paper and then transferred to the wood. This is a lifesize model he made of a screech owl.

Other sandpipers pick up bits of food in the surging water.

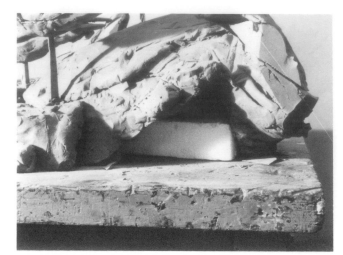

Styrofoam was used in places like this to cut down on the amount of clay needed.

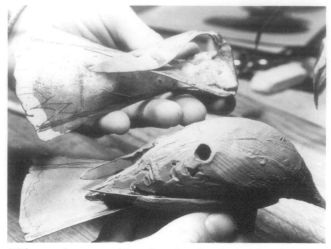

With areas that get too thin such as the tail and primaries, clay can no longer hold its shape. To compensate, Barth utilizes sheet metal that can be covered with clay.

Here is a clay model for a pair of goldeneyes, another model of a portrait in wood.

Here is a sheet metal armature for an Eastern kingbird. Compare the bird in the rear with the clay built up around the wings and tail.

Before Barth set his tools on the wood, he worked out in clay this model of his oriole. He strives to achieve a gesture, perhaps a basic form in the clay, with the exact details worked out in wood.

Using this oak tracing tool, Barth can project the side view from the model to paper. Here he traces the oriole.

mains not just as a visual reference, but also a template itself, one that he can go back to for measurements and proportions.

Roughing Out a Loon

A recent piece of Barth's is a pair of loons in water. Made of basswood, the birds float on bases made of cherrywood. Barth worked out clay models of the birds, bandsawed blocks of wood to shape, made the bases and joined the bases and the birds together with screws. Then he began the shaping. What sets Barth's sculpting apart from the other artists is that he uses neither the Foredom nor the Dremel for roughing out the wood.

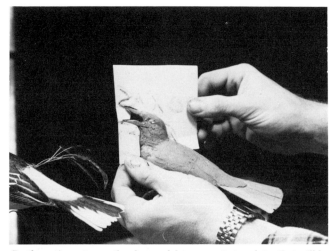

Barth continues to use the clay model to generate templates that will be used to check the accuracy and progress of the bird in wood.

The rubberband of this outliner, one that he designed, withdraws the pencil so the point does not get broken when it's not being used.

Here the cardboard template is compared with the finished piece. Note that the size of the bird's profile has not changed.

The result of the tracing is shown on a piece of tracing paper. Now the pattern can be transferred to wood.

A comparison of the clay model and the finished oriole shows how important the model is to Barth as a reference for measurements and proportions.

Barth uses a variety of carving tools—chisels and gouges, many of which are Swiss-made. With these he feels he has more control over wood removal than he does with the powered grinding tools.

He sharpens the tools by hand on a hard Arkansas stone.

He uses instead carver's chisels and gouges, most of them European made. In answer to why he uses them instead of the motorized tools, he responds, "I'd rather be carving off chips than grinding off dust, even though grinding tools may be faster." He adds that by being slower, he is allowed more control, "and things aren't gone before I know they're gone." Roughing out, then, is critical to Barth. "I used to think it was a carefree process. But I made a lot of mistakes that gave me trouble later on. I now think of roughing out as establishing the foundation which can make the project go smoothly."

There is another advantage to this slow carving time because it becomes time spent working out the composition of individual feathers and groups. "Maybe other carvers don't need it, but I require that time to make a super bird." He points out that the same tools and thinking are involved whether he is doing a loon on a base or an oriole.

Barth maintains a strong relationship between clay and wood, and he will actually draw reference lines and points on the clay model that can be transferred

One of the pieces he did with his carving tools is his pair of loons in water. This basswood bird rides in a water base made of cherrywood.

This is the bandsawed block for a single loon piece.

The bird is not immediately glued to the base; instead, it is temporarily joined to it with screws.

Here with the calipers he checks the length of the wood head.

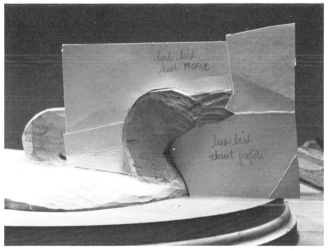

Barth will use these head templates surrounding the clay model constantly as he reduces the wood of the loon.

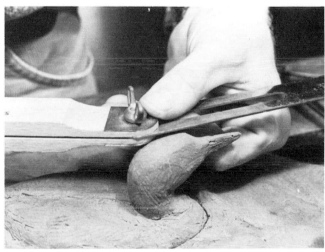

A sliding T bevel is used to determine the head angle relative to the body.

When the templates cannot be used, he switches to calipers and dividers to transfer dimensions from the clay to the wood.

With the same bevel he transfers centerlines to the wood.

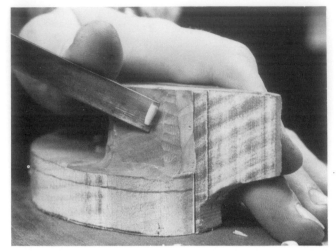

Carving begins with wood from around the head and neck area being removed first.

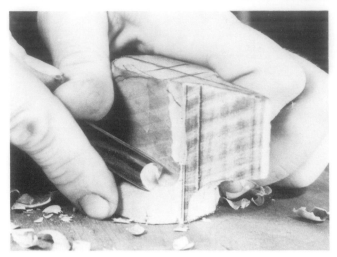

Continued carving gives definition to the neck area.

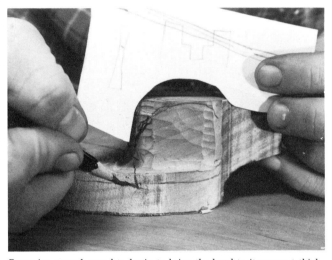

Removing enough wood to begin to bring the head to its correct thickness, Barth draws on the wood a profile of the head.

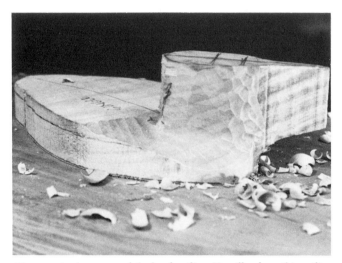

More carving has removed the head outline. He will redraw this outline as many times as it is carved away, since reference lines are critical to his technique.

A rounder gouge gives concavity to the shoulders.

Here he reduces the upper side of the loon with a flatter gouge. He prefers to leave as few concave marks as he can on flat or rounded areas.

Barth uses a large, flat chisel to reduce the concave marks left by gouges and remove more wood to help achieve a convex shape.

With a small gouge, the throat area of the loon can be shaped.

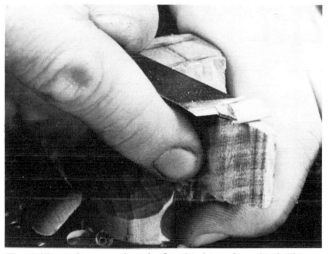

The tool he prefers more than the flat chisel is a skew chisel. This too removes gouge marks and creates flat areas. Here he uses one on the beak of the loon.

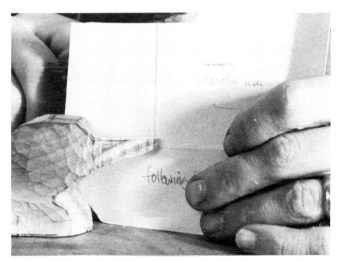

After the area of the beak has been considerably reduced, Barth comes back with a cardboard template. Now he sees that still more wood has to be removed.

Again, when a reference line such as this centerline is carved away, it is redrawn.

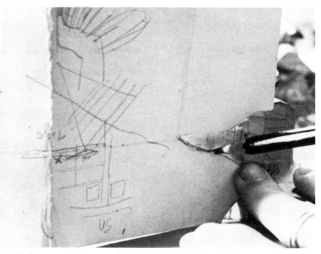

Barth draws onto the wood the beak line, indicating how much wood to carve away.

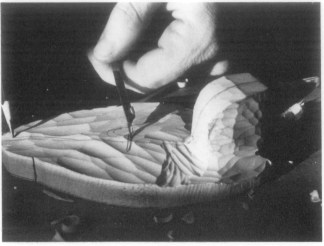

Carving continues on the body of the bird. Barth describes this procedure as rough shaping with a gouge for quick removal of wood.

He transfers with dividers the lines and points from the clay to the wood. All these build up a strong relationship between clay and wood until the feather patterns and other details are worked out.

Here he uses the heavy gouge to round off a sharp corner.

The grid lines are transferred to the wood.

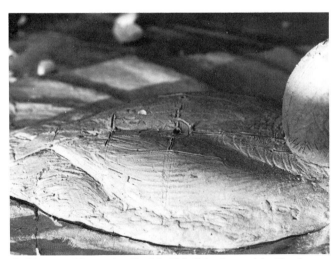

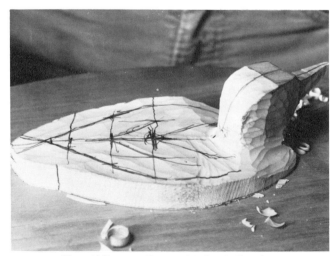

At this stage of the carving, Barth "grids" off the clay model with reference points and lines.

The grid lines are then used to locate the wings.

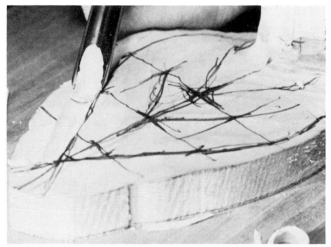

A gouge is used to define the wings by removing wood around them.

Barth feels he has better control over wood removal when he can get the piece off the bench and into his hands.

Reducing the area around the wings also removes the pencil lines. Again, for Barth to keep the plan of the bird in mind, he must redraw the lines.

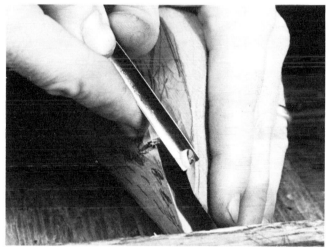

Barth demonstrates on another bird, not attached to a base, how he can hold the bird while carving it with a gouge.

After giving some shape to the loon's primaries, Barth begins shaping the bird down to the waterline.

To control the carving tool with both hands, he uses a benchstop which he can press the bird against.

to the wood blank. Plus, he will rely on the profile templates which he makes in cardboard from the clay model and uses them to check his progress in wood.

Barth puts even more time and thought into roughing out the block. He says that he sees birds in terms of geometric shapes such as intersecting planes, spheres, and cylinders. "I can only judge the relationships between different forms and masses if they are geometric. If I round the wood off right away, then I lose, say, the relationship the head has with the body. So I keep the wood chunky and boldly shaped a long time." And again he points out that the grinding tools "seem to get the piece free-form right away. I need more structure than that."

So Barth will cover a model like the loon with grid lines that are transferred and retransferred to the wood block as it loses its cubist shape in carving. Particularly important is the centerline which represents the silhouette of the bird and is the single most important reference line. After the centerline, there are many other reference lines and points, which he will redraw a dozen times if they are carved away that frequently. "It may seem redundant, but after doing it that many times, it starts to set in my mind and helps build up a fluency."

Nor is Barth content to keep a piece like the loon or any other locked up constantly in a vise. "I like to keep things in my hands so that I can always be turning them and looking at them from different angles. And it allows me to work on the whole bird simultaneously so that no one area gets too far ahead or behind." And small birds will also be worked out in his hands, though he may use what is called a bench hook as a backstop when removing wood.

After the loon is sufficiently roughed out, Barth can then start carving into the base to give definition to the water. For the water he picks cherrywood, a dense and very strong hardwood. He did, however, use walnut as the base for the kingfisher composition. He feels that walnut is too open-grained, which may be visually distracting when the glassy look of water is desired.

Is there a problem with joining a basswood loon to a cherrywood base? Barth says that glue joints are always a potential problem and admits he was especially concerned with this joint because two different species of wood were involved. But Barth glued the two pieces together with Titebond Glue and saturated the joint with Super Glue to stabilize and seal the joint. This also helped disguise the glue joint so it would not be obvious when the piece was finished.

Visit to a Banding Station

Barth would agree with other artists in this book that most beginning carvers go immediately to the block of wood and start cutting something out without having laid sufficient groundwork. So Barth, like the others, uses study skins and books and will spend as much time as possible in the field observing birds. He also visits a banding station, near his home in western Pennsylvania, where birds are netted and banded.

The banding station has given him the opportunity to make in-hand observations of live birds which, he feels, have helped him immeasurably. Much of his time at the station has been spent sketching directly from hand-held birds, concentrating on details that are not available from any other source. As he says, "there's just no substitute for the real bird." On several occasions he has sculpted a clay model directly from the real bird.

"The banding station has influenced my work a great deal," he says. "Without a doubt, the birds I've done since my association with the banding station have been my strongest and most accurate to date."

Anatomy

Barth doesn't limit his study to visits to banding stations. He has spent a lot of time formally in school and informally on his own studying the anatomy of birds. He feels strongly that one must have a good understanding of what is going on inside a bird in order to know what causes and affects its outward appearance. He notes that there are many things peculiar to avian anatomy that a bird carver should know. He says, for example, that humans can only drop their lower jaws. For birds, however, both the upper and lower mandibles hinge, "something I didn't realize until fairly late in the game," he says. "A bit of information like that makes a big difference when you're doing an open-billed bird."

He will draw accurate and detailed sketches of feet, bills, eyes, and feathers, done from the actual specimens he measures with dividers. And he will even plot out the roots of feathers inside a wing to help him place the location of a feather in a sculpture. So even when only the tip of a feather shows, he will have mentally traced it back to its point of origin. This, he feels, is especially important for wings and tails.

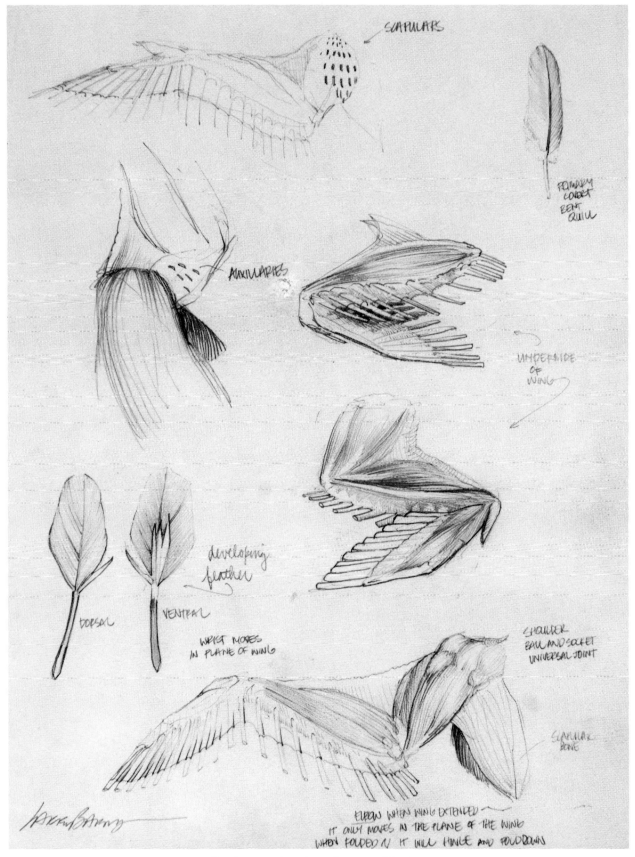

Sketches of various views of wings and feathers.

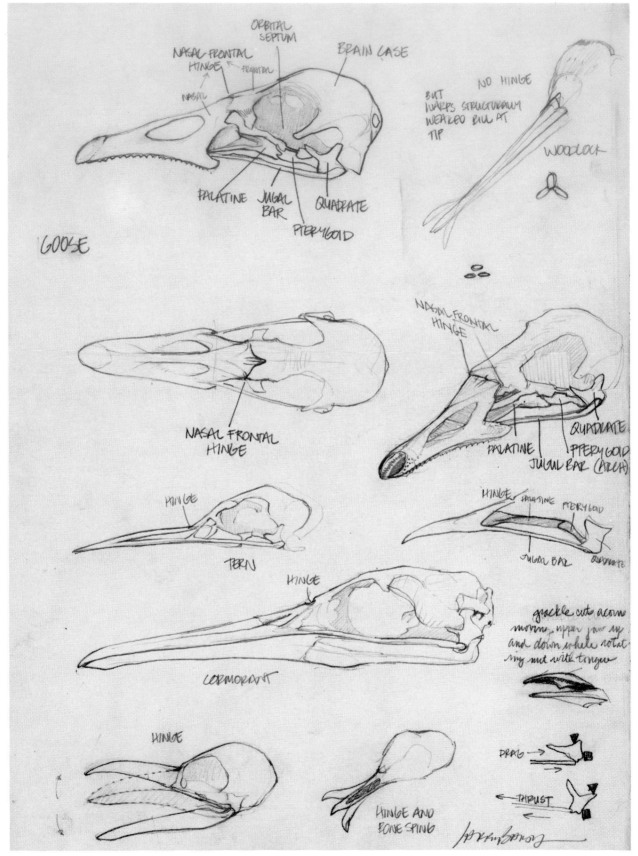

A page from Barth's sketchbook.

Study sketches of an Eastern meadowlark.

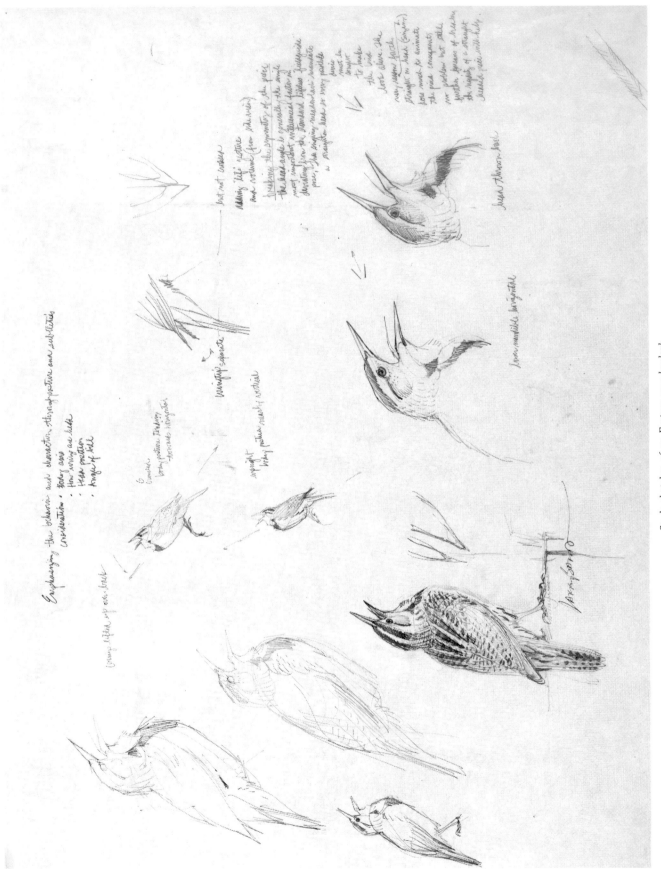

Study sketches of an Eastern meadowlark.

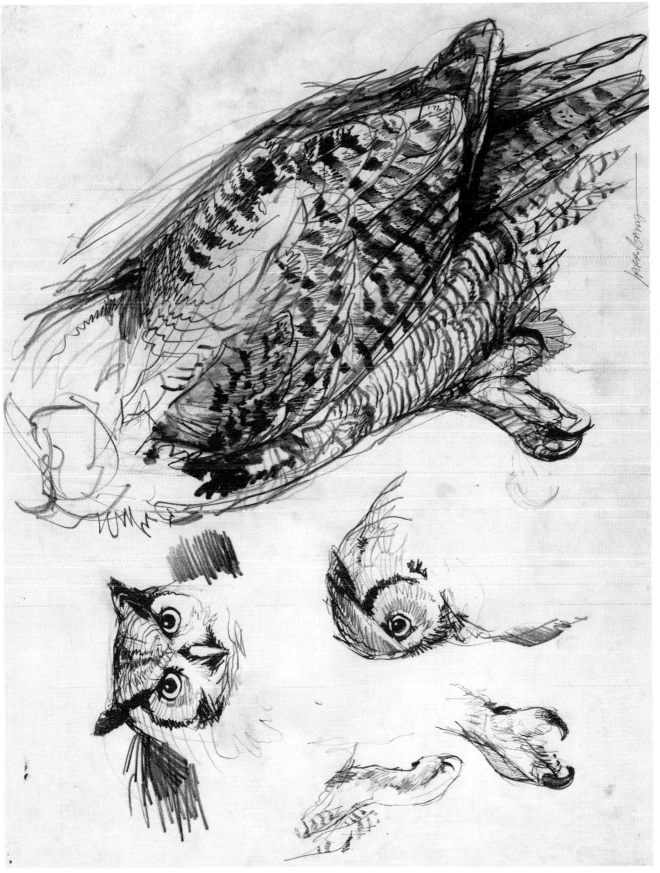

Working sketch of an owl pair.

The remaining space at top is filled with either foam rubber or styrofoam for cushioning.

To be able to ship or transport a piece to a show or customer, Barth has devised a floating box within a box. Inside is his loon pair. The base is held with wood wingnuts that will not damage the cherrywood.

Packing It Up

Often, a bird sculpture has to be shipped or transported to another location, a detail not always worked out by carvers, and one that has produced disastrous consequences. For a work like the two-loons piece, Barth constructed a wooden box floating within a slightly larger box. Securing the base with wooden wingnuts to the bottom of the inner box, Barth put his packing material of styrofoam pellets not around the carving but between the two boxes. This, he feels, will do a better job of asborbing shock. After a thick layer of foam rubber is placed over the lower inner box, the wooden cover is secured to the outer box.

To absorb shock, styrofoam pellets are placed in the space surrounding the two boxes.

With a sturdy wood cover screwed down on top, the box is ready for moving.

7

Gary Yoder
Birds Smaller than Lifesize

Even though Gary Yoder is the youngest of the nine artists, he is no neophyte to the field of bird carving. He has spent over half his lifetime sculpting birds, and miniatures are his specialty. In 1980, his pair of pheasants won Best in World for Decorative Miniatures in the World Championship Wildfowl Carving Competition. In 1982, he took the same prize with a pair of mallards flying over a marsh.

Sketching

Many bird carvers disdain doing sketches, claiming they are not representative of the three-dimensional subject matter. Yoder, however, is prolific with his drawing and credits Larry Barth with influencing his approach to getting under the bird's skin as a way of understanding it.

There are several goals behind Yoder's sketching. Since he puts some of his birds into flight, one goal is to determine how they will look in the air. He calls this implied motion, saying: "It's not stopping the bird in a moment of time. Rather, it's trying to get a feeling of motion." His sketches, for a pair of miniature pheasants for instance, are not confined to one view but include many, because as he walks around a sculpture, he gets different views of it. He says, that though "my carvings have had too much of a front side and a back side, my drawings don't necessarily have that because

they are two-dimensional." The first thing he tries to establish, then, is how the birds are moving.

Another goal of sketching pertains to the inner workings of the bird. He will make what he calls "moving sketches of a skeleton." He feels these are important when it comes to working out the basic proportions of the bird. For a wing, he may have not only bone structure, but also feather layout. For example, "it helps to draw the skeletal structure onto a wing, if you know that the bird's primaries are attached to the front part of the bone section and the secondaries are attached to the back."

It is not uncommon to find cubist or rectangular shapes drawn into these detailed sketches. These represent the blocks of wood from which different parts of the anatomy—the body, the wings, the tail feathers —will be carved.

Implied motion and anatomy are not the only aspects of the carving to be worked out in the sketches. Yoder also draws the habitat which, he says, cannot be separated from the birds. In a recent pheasant carving, he used cornstalks to keep the birds suspended in the air.

With the new pheasant pair, however, Yoder was not satisfied doing only drawings. For this composition he used styrofoam models, the first time he had done so. His are similar to others pictured in the book. Cardboard wings and tails are pinned to styrofoam bodies while heads are severed, only to be repositioned.

Gary Yoder is an accomplished carver of miniature birds. Here he works on a diminutive widgeon.

The finished widgeon drake, less than seven inches in length, was done in basswood.

Another Yoder miniature is this mallard drake, done in jelutong.

Yoder has constructed a model in styrofoam and cardboard of pheasants taking off. This is a help with basic composition, since motion is difficult to determine on paper which is limited to two dimensions.

The wings, partially made from styrofoam, are attached with pins.

On this bottom bird, the cardboard cutout indicates the location of the bird's ten primaries.

An advantage of styrofoam is that a head can be cut off and repositioned with pins to achieve a different attitude or pose, which is a great help when it comes to carving the bird.

Rough sketches for a pheasant layout.

Sketches of pheasants for wing position.

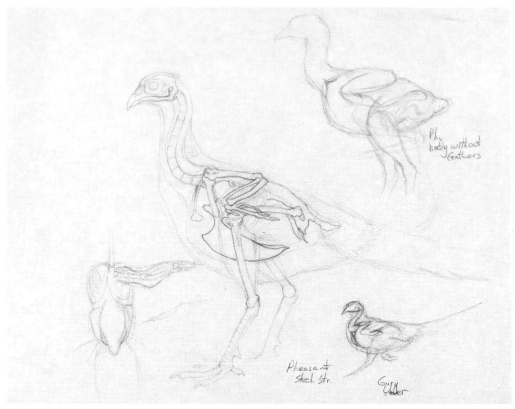

The pheasant's skeletal structure.

The pheasant's tail.

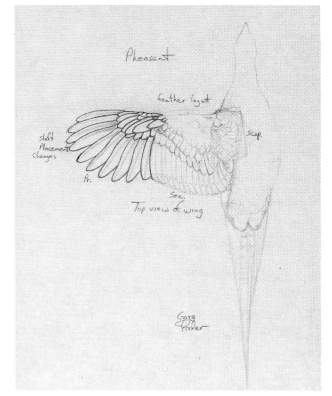

Top view of the pheasant's wing.

This bottom pheasant, made of basswood and partially finished, has its wings in the upstroke.

This upper pheasant has its wings in the downstroke. The primaries must be bent upwards, even more so at their tips, to achieve this effect. Bending can be done with the heat of a burning tool.

The joints visible here will be filled in with a plastic wood. Note the shelf at the bottom for the tail feathers and also the way the position of the head was changed by cutting it from the body.

"With these materials you can't tell too much, but to some degree it helps establish the size of the birds as well as the support systems," he says. It was also, he admits, an attempt to get somewhat away from drawings, especially since "models help me get away from a front and back side."

Implied Motion

There is another advantage, though far more subtle, to doing models, and it has to do with motion. Yoder feels his sculptures, like the pheasant pair, should imply motion, but he does not want his sculptures to look like stop-action photographs. He points out that when a pheasant takes off, it whips its tail feathers back and forth. "One of the reasons I chose the pheasants is because of the tail feathers," he says. "There's so much movement you can put into them." Another characteristic of all birds is the motion inherent in the wings, a feature which plays a strong role in his pheasant piece. He points out that when a wing is in the downstroke, all the feathers are laying flat and tight. And

This composition of swallows incorporates a series of Vs through the wings, tails, and even the grass that gives the birds support.

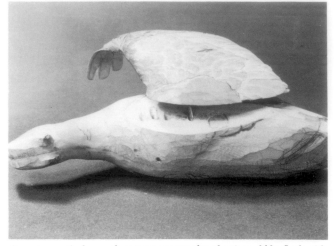

One wing on the lower pheasant was carved so that it could be flush with the body. The wire will be removed after the bird is hollowed to reduce its weight, and the wing will be glued in place.

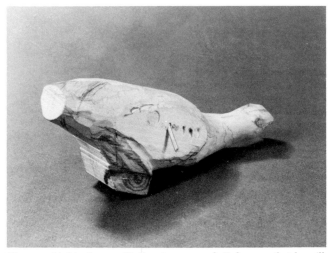

The same bird is shown with the wing removed. Yoder says that he will have to make the legs separately because of a defect in the wood. This can be seen where the feet are drawn in.

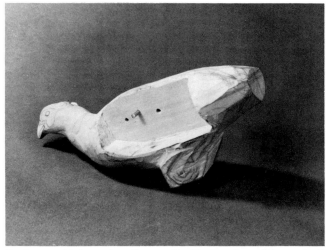

On the same bird seen from the opposite side, the wing will be mortised or "let in." This and the flush joint were both experiments in joinery on the same bird. The advantage to the let-in joint is that more wood is removed from the bird's interior.

when the wing is in the upstroke, the primaries in particular are just starting to separate to let air pass through them. Consequently, Yoder has one pheasant with wings in the upstroke, the other with wings in the downstroke. "It is," he states, "a flowing piece."

Even more subtle than wing and tail motion is the relationship of the birds to each other and how that generates implied motion. The pheasants are moving out of the cornstalks in a spiral, one which brings the eye up and around and back again.

Spirals are not the only means for implying motion in a sculpture that does not move. In a pair of barn swallows he did, motion is implied through a series of Vs. These figures, he says, are suggestive of arrows. The wings and the shape of the tails are "a series of V-systems," he explains, with even the blade of grass that supports the birds mirroring the angle of the wings. So instead of representing a spiral, this pair of birds suggests a linear, though no less static, kind of motion.

Shaping and Assembly

The problems of suggested movement are not the only ones the carver has to cope with. Roughing out the birds and putting them together are also a challenge, and no less so when the carver is working with the miniature size. As indicated earlier, Yoder did wings from separate pieces of wood. And though this is certainly not unique to carvers, what is novel is his joinery technique.

For a single bird he will let in a wing, that is, cut out a rectangular section to allow an equivalent rectangular wing end to be fitted in. On the other side of the bird, the joinery will be flush—that is, the side of the bird will be flattened to accept the flattened end of the wing. Both techniques, he says, were experiments, though he found the let-in wing had the advantage of providing an opening for hollowing out the birds to reduce their weights.

Wires extending out of the bird's wing or body help hold the pieces while they are being worked on. When finished, the pheasants will be hollowed and glued up and the wire pins removed. For even though their sizes are diminutive (the bodies are only six or seven inches in length), the weight is still a problem. The contact or support point is not on a wing or leg, but on the tail feathers. Yoder explains that the weight of a solid bird would make the tail feathers bend.

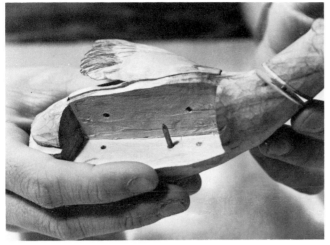

The same let-in joint was done on the upper bird. Another advantage to this type of joinery is that Yoder can carve the wing in place as part of the body block rather than carving it separately.

Here is an example of a textured pheasant's wing. The primaries and secondaries were done with a burning tool. The unburned areas, called the coverts, were done with a rotary stone first and will later be burned to refine the details.

The length of this basswood pheasant is only six inches.

This is the burning done on the underside. Note how relatively close the feathers lay on their downstroke.

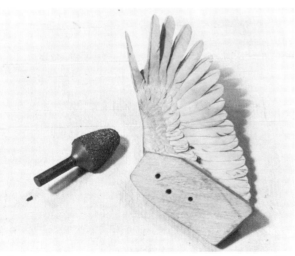

This grinding attachment or cutter can do much of the shaping of the wings, while a burning tool can do some undercutting on the small feathers above the primaries and secondaries.

The feathers removed from this wing were carved too thin, and a hole broke through them—a problem when working with a solid block of wood. Yoder, with careful gluing and painting, had to make the inserts look like the rest of the feathers.

The tail feathers on the upper pheasant were carved in groups. This allowed him to create the thin, hairlike edges that might not be achieved using individual feathers. One feather of textured steel will be attached to part of the habitat.

Why doesn't Yoder always do individual feathers for insertion instead of carving them and the wing from a solid block of wood? He offers several reasons. First, contrary to what he actually can do, he claims he is not good at making feather inserts. Second, he says that by making them, "sometimes it's like doing a jigsaw puzzle without seeing the overall picture, so you don't know what you're putting together until it's done. With a solid block of wood, you've got everything right there." And third, he gives credit to people like Barth, who has given definition to feathers from a single block, for having influenced his technique.

There are still other reasons for going to solid pieces. "I don't want glue lines," he says, relating them to what he calls transition lines or having one area stop as it joins another. "When you're carving a bird, you want to make everything work together. Transition areas stop the eye, focusing it on certain areas. So I try to blend everything together, even if I have to use separate pieces of wood."

For a pheasant wing, Yoder will start with a three-

inch-thick block of wood, one thick enough to give enough curvature and cup to the wing. Then, with a grinding tool, he will rough out the block until he gets the basic shape. From there, he will actually draw the bone structure on the wood and draw the feathers according to where the bones are. "I work on the top side first, then on the backside with the grinder. Holding it up to the light, I continue on the backside until I have it down to where light can pass through the wood." And he will carve in the shaft lines to help locate feather positions. Again, in defense of not doing inserts, Yoder says, "With a solid block of wood, you've got everything right there, with just a lot of undercutting."

In spite of this, problems will arise. Three of the feathers of a pheasant wing were carved too short. "So rather than throw the whole wing out, I burned a slot in and slipped three separate feathers in between." These inserts are remarkably detailed and accurate.

Yoder did the pheasants' tail feathers as groups of inserted feathers. Here he defends the insertion technique saying, "If you look at the edge of a pheasant's tail feathers, you'll see they're very hairlike, very thin. The only way you can capture that look is by supporting the surface of one feather with the feathers underneath. That was the reason for carving these feathers in groups, to get the splayed edges."

Also, because of the complexity of having the pheasants spiraling, Yoder felt the head of the upper pheasant did not have the right turn to it. "With so many angles, it was difficult to get the right look," he says. He removed the head, then, and turned it slightly, much as Forehand did with his miniature in chapter 1.

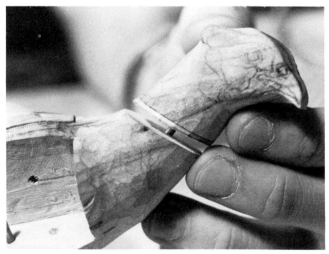

The head of this pheasant was severed and turned to give a better feeling of the bird "spiraling" up and out of the cornfield base.

After the wings and tails are shaped, Yoder then goes to the burning pen to put in the barb lines. Like Scheeler, Yoder is well aware of the effect of heat on wood feathers. He cautions that "burning distorts the shape of thin feathers because it removes moisture from the side you're burning on," warping their shapes. After the burning is completed, he uses Super Glue to harden up the feathers' delicate edges.

Flexible Basswood

It should be noted that for nearly all his carvings, Yoder prefers basswood. One of its attributes, he says, is its flexibility. He explains that it has some give to it, essential when working with such small pieces as miniature pheasant wings. A wood like jelutong he describes as too soft and too brittle. A wood like basswood, which is denser than jelutong and more close-grained, is ideal for him, so much so that he can even use it for parts of the habitat like the cornstalks the pheasants will be attached to. But most important, Yoder feels basswood is best suited for his texturing techniques.

Texturing and Exaggeration

Like Muehlmatt, Yoder says that a lot of his texturing technique is making feathers an exaggeration of what they really are. "When you look at a bird, it's pretty smooth. You're not going to see each feather shaped into it." But this is quite the opposite of what Yoder wants to achieve—which is the look and feel of individual feathers.

After penciling in feather layout, he will begin texturing with a Dremel Moto-Tool. Not happy with the lengthy flexible shaft of the Foredom (it has too much swing for him), he says the Dremel gives him more control because the motor is right above the tool bit and in his hand at the same time. With the Dremel turned to a high speed, Yoder will outline each feather using a small dental bit or burr. Then he will take out the high spots of the feathers. The next step is to use an even smaller bit and break up the outline of the feathers. This is done by putting in what looks like the barbs of the feathers, but making them splayed out. "It's a matter of going with the flow of the feathers, of putting some lines in long, some lines in short. This breaks up the visible outlines of the previous steps."

He will even put in feather splits. Using a scalpel he makes stop or straight down cuts, then goes in with

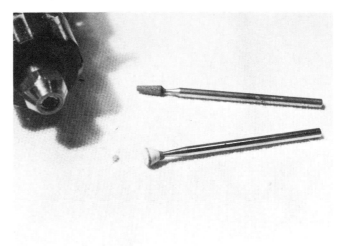
These grinding stones are used by Yoder for texturing, though he uses only their corners with the Dremel Moto-Tool at the left.

After drawing in the feathers on this widgeon, Yoder outlines and recesses them with this metal burr.

A light sanding after using the burr removes the tool marks. Yoder uses a 400-grit sandpaper.

Yoder softens and diffuses feather edges with a small dentist's burr. This also puts a heavy texture in the same direction as the barblines. These steps are exaggerations which, combined with the painting, will give his birds surface highlights and shadows.

Note how the lengths of the grooves put in with the dentist's burr are staggered. Yoder calls the effects created by stoning "peaks and valleys."

the knife at an angle to pop out tiny pieces. And he will use the same knife and technique to make undercuts. He explains: "Anywhere the feather looks thick, it has to be undercut. That creates the illusion of overlapping feathers."

A tiny grinding stone can also be used, not for undercutting, but simply to lower sections. This too will give the feathers a layered look. But Yoder notes that a stone is not used in the same way the dental bit is. "When stones are used to lower sections, it's all done as part of the texturing process. By stoning deeper at the base of each feather, you can get that lowered look without actually carving the feather in."

Stoning, that is, using a grinding stone, has decided advantages. It permits Yoder to create a variety of different effects. "To me the stoning gives a looser, fluffier look than the burning does." With the burning pen, he says, you can achieve a harder-looking surface. "Usually if a feather has a sharp, distinct edge to it, it is burned in. If it has a rounded, puffy edge, it is stoned in. With the burning, you achieve a sharper, more distinct texture line that will reflect light differently from a stoned line." (For more on stoning, see the chapter on Larry Hayden.)

Yoder uses the burning pen in texturing for exaggeration. By laying the tip down along the shaft lines, he can raise them, "making them more believable." It is this kind of burning, he says, that allows light to enhance his texturing techniques. "By burning deeper,

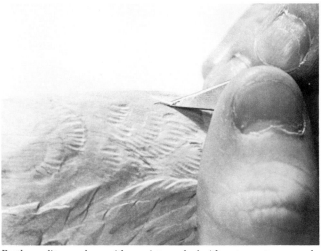

Feather splits are done with a pointy scalpel. After stop cuts are made alongside the splits yet to be done, the knife is laid down on the same level as the feather below, inserted under the wood, and lifted to pop the wood out.

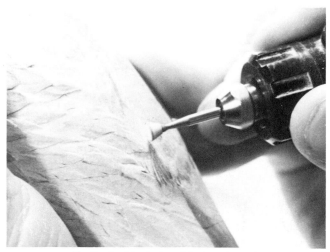

For the final texturing, this stone is used.

you can get a heavier shadow," he explains. On the other hand, by not carving very deep, "I get more light bouncing back."

Yet, there is still room for more exaggeration. He can carve what he calls "shallow S-curves." For this he will use a small veiner to make a "rippling effect," with the ripples running in the same direction as the barb.

Sometimes he will work with what he calls subgroups or areas of feathers, though, in fact, the bird has no such grouping of feathers. By working in sections, he can give definition to feathers with the scalpel, stone, and burning tool. He uses this technique to break up the relatively smooth surface of the bird.

Feather layout, he goes on to say, is actually more important than the shape of the feathers. "I try to keep them with a nice natural flow, but not arranged." He may, then, redraw them ten times or more. The results are what he calls an abstraction of feather shapes.

All this texturing for exaggeration, he says, "just takes forever to do." Yet, by doing miniatures, he notes, there is not a great deal of surface area to deal with. "Can you imagine doing large birds using these methods?" he asks.

However, texturing for him has to be done with some precautions, especially when working with such small pieces. "I should be working with gloves because sweat can come off my hands and onto the textured surface. When this happens, the grain pops up and you lose some of the detail you worked so hard to put in."

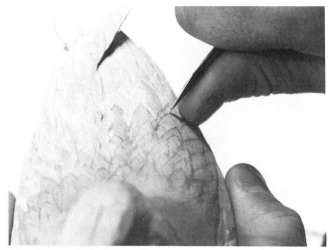

After drawing the feathers on the wood, stop cuts are made to give them a layered look.

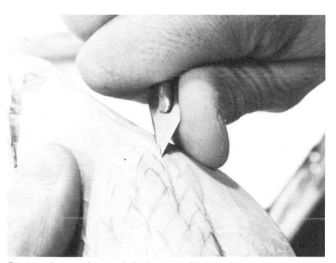

By removing wood around the feathers, Yoder achieves a layered look that gives the feathers depth.

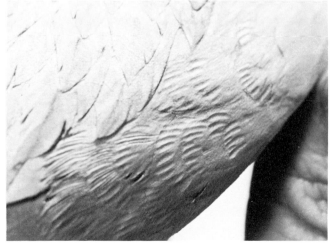

The result of the stone marks can be seen in the center of the photograph. Notice how they go in the thick lines left by a previous step.

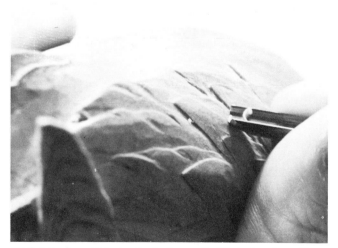

Feather ripples, which give the feathers a flexible look and provide an uneven surface for light to bounce off, are put in with a small gouge. When paint is applied, the feather is defined with highlights and shadows.

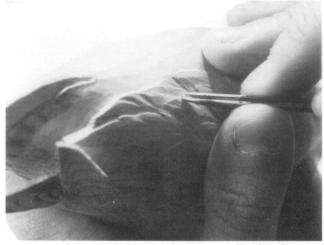

Even more refinement is achieved with a veiner smaller than the gouge. The ripples are exaggerated because texturing with the burning tool tends to flatten them out.

Here is the same area of the widgeon painted. Though much of the stoning would seem to be lost, the effect of light on the textured areas is not.

Here shown from left to right: the feather layout, the layered look of the feathers, and the ripples cut into the wood.

Another fine example of Yoder's texturing is this unfinished cardinal. Here it is ready for the detailing of the feathers.

Here is the effect of burning details on a tertial feather. To the left are the primaries, to the right the scapulars.

The Dremel and small burrs give the airy look to the tail without the use of a gouge or veiner. Also, there was a great deal of undercutting done on these feathers.

Light Sources and Painting

The process of giving shape to a feather does not stop with texturing. Painting is the next step in the long process. If Yoder is working with a subgroup of feathers instead of individual ones, he will paint the separate feathers in. "I'll take my brush and hit right on top of the stone marks. That is why the texturing is so important for the painting I do."

When he did a black-capped chickadee, Yoder cut in deep lines with a scalpel and burned over that from the front of the eyes to the feathers of the cheeks. This gave a shadowy and bristly look, in contrast to smoother sections elsewhere on the bird, where painting had more of an effect on feather definition.

"You can't start with just texturing," he says, "because everything relies on everything else for effect. If you didn't get the basic shape of the bird carved right, you're not going to texture right, and you're not going to paint right." So the first two hours of carving a bird are probably the most important. Yet, he says, perhaps ironically, that when it comes to getting the colors correct, there may not be a correct formula for painting.

He clarifies this statement by pointing out that the light source has a great deal of effect on a carving. In the previous chapter, Barth chose the oriole's coloration after he'd seen it "high up in a tree in the sun." Its colors would be different, then, if he'd seen it under flourescent lighting. As Yoder says, "You really have to pick your light source and then decide what color effect you want."

On these feathers, there is little undercutting. Yoder believes a strong light makes them look more undercut than they actually are.

This is the effect of burning on another cardinal. Note, in the middle of the photo, how the flow of barb lines changed on a feather that is normally hidden. This breaks up solid patterns and adds interest to an area but must be planned prior to carving.

On these undertail coverts, the splits were done with the scalpel.

The crest feathers of this cardinal must still be thinned out before texturing. To make these, Yoder plunges the point of the scalpel into the wood at different angles. Rather than slicing, he is digging out slivers of wood.

In texturing this chickadee to give it a shadowy and bristly look prior to painting, Yoder carved in the bristles with the scalpel in a circular flow. This diffused light and helped avoid a hard, shiny look. He then burned in lines over the head to contrast that area with smoother sections done with the stone.

The defuzzer is used in the Dremel, after texturing and after applying the gesso, to remove the fuzz that is inherent to ground basswood.

In preparation for vermiculation, the wavy, tracklike lines on some birds, Yoder works up two different colors that will be mixed.

What helps Yoder determine the colors he chooses are not paintings, but black-and-white photographs. Working from these, he can get the light and dark values of the bird correct. "To me it's a degree of subtlety and variation. That's why I can't say there's a right way or a wrong way to painting."

And how does he go about creating subtleties and variations? Like Muehlmatt and others, Yoder prefers to paint transparently and apply different shades of the same color to get the effect he desires. Starting with a base color to make a flat background, "you start painting strokes over that of different lengths." If he wants a shinier effect, he will mix a gel medium solution into his acrylic paints. Using this mix for a mallard duck, he could achieve the almost neon bluish-green color on the head. If he wants to tone a color down, he will apply watered-down paints over it. And sometimes he will apply pure colors side by side, as in an impressionistic painting. "I let the eye do some of the mixing," he says.

When it comes to painting basswood, however, Yoder has found, as have others, that it is difficult to get the wood smooth for a painting surface. "One of the characteristics I don't like is the fiber in it," he says. "When you take a sharp knife and cut it, there is no problem. But when you take sandpaper and cut it with that, it raises a soft fuzz, even with 600-grit sandpaper," an extremely fine paper. He has a couple of remedies before painting. One is to use an attachment to the Dremel he calls a defuzzer, which has a slight abrasive to it. With that, he can stroke the wood lightly to remove as much fuzz as he can. Then he will apply a lacquer and a gesso paint over that. And again he will use the defuzzer. "That way I won't lose any of the carved features." (Compare Sprankle's and Hayden's techniques in the following chapters.)

Vermiculation

A number of birds have as part of their coloring wavy lines called vermiculation. For painting these lines, Yoder uses a very small, pointed brush. He says that the most important aspect of this technique is the consistency of the paint. "If it's too wet, it will run, if too dry, you have to push too hard on the brush and you can lose control."

Also important is the preliminary texturing, which he will make heavier than normal. On a miniature vermiculated bird, he will burn in rather than stone the texture. Burning, he says, puts lines straight down into

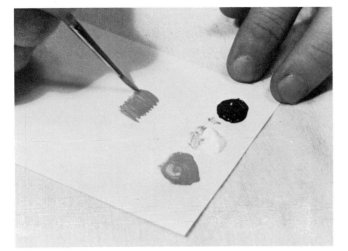

The result of the mixing is a base coat.

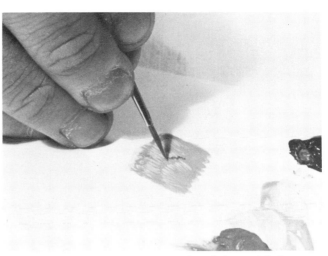

Vermiculation begins as a series of small dots and dashes.

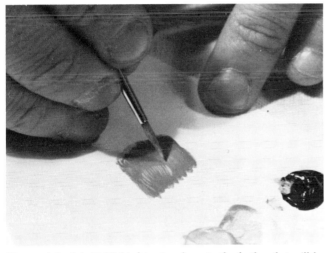

Here each barb is highlighted to give shape to the feather that will be vermiculated.

The sizes of the dots and dashes are extremely important to create the overall balance of light and dark.

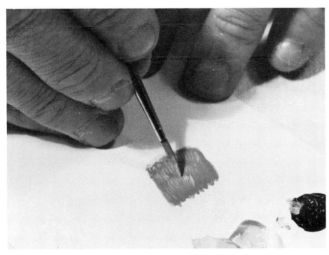

By continuing to paint rows of lines, Yoder is establishing a feather pattern.

An example of vermiculation done by Yoder is this experimental feather of a ruffed grouse. It is made of maple.

To keep the lower bird of the barn swallow pair suspended, a blade of grass was made from brass with a stiff wire running through its center.

The feet and toes of this bird were carved from basswood with dentist's burrs and a knife. They were then glued to the legs which were then glued into the basswood body.

All the primaries and secondaries were inserted on the swallow, including the tail feathers. Yoder carved the body and head from a single block of wood. He made three attempts before he got the head turned the way he wanted.

The texture on this bird was entirely burned in, with no sealer applied over the wood before painting. The burning seemed to have kept the grain from rising when the paints were applied, Yoder says.

The last two feathers of the wing, partially shown at the top of the photograph, are brass. At the contact point on the lower bird's wing, he made two other brass feathers and textured them with dentist's burrs so they matched the wooden feathers around them. Silver solder was used at the contact point.

No gesso was used on the swallow, and the first coat of paint was very dark and flat. Highlights were picked up with lighter colors mixed with a gel medium to make them shinier and more transparent.

the wood and leaves small, flat areas between the burn lines. These create an ideal surface for painting what he calls "the dots and dashes of vermiculation." "The whole trick is to get the right pattern and size to the dots and dashes," he says. "Too far apart between the vermiculation lines and the whole bird looks too light. Too close together and it's too dark."

Swallows, Kestrels, Chickadees, Widgeons, and Mallards

Yoder limits how he uses study skins. He notes that they can be distorted and rearranged when pushed from the inside. "They're just a reference to look at, more for feather work than anything else, and for a painting reference." When working with a study wing, for example, the first thing he does is count the feathers, noting that each has a distinct shape, and sees what order they are in. Typical of what he has done with study skins is his pair of barn swallows. These were done from a single skin, he says, but because of its condition, "all I could get from it were the tail and wing feathers."

This was his first set of flying birds, made in 1979. For the pair, he did make individual feather inserts. And to support them, he ran a support system of brass through the birds.

A year earlier he carved his largest bird, a kestrel. In this piece are some twenty-five pieces of wood, with such areas as the wings and tail feathers carved

Kestrels have always been one of Yoder's favorite birds. He even nursed a pair of them back to health. It is, then, a bird he is very familiar with.

The brass feathers designed with tab extensions run through the wing and into the body of the top swallow. The tab fits into epoxy putty put into the hole while it was still soft and then backed out. This made a rock-hard slot to slide the wing in and out of.

This bird was shaped and rounded with a knife and burr. The entire bird was then burned with the burning tool. This he did in 1978 before he started developing his stoning technique.

He did make feather separations on the breast, however, to give the illusion of depth. The beak of the basswood kestrel was roughed out with a knife and then detailed with dentist's burrs.

as separate pieces. An interesting feature of the bird is its lack of stone texturing. The feathers and other definitions were all done with a burning pen with the paint applied last. He did not use a study skin, but instead, he had two live kestrels in his workshop with him.

Yoder will also do songbirds such as chickadees. Describing them as "lively little birds with strange shapes," he likes the character of the bird and its coloration. On this bird, the back, breast and side feathers were stone-textured, while the black areas were burned with a burning pen.

When doing feet on birds like the chickadee and a Caroline wren he made, Yoder's technique is the same as Barth's. For the armature he used steel wire for the

Here is a more recent kestrel Yoder is working on. For this one he carved both the head and body from a single block of wood. Lifesize, the bird has feathers roughed out with a metal burr.

All twelve tail feathers were inserted as separate pieces in the kestrel.

The feathers were drawn in with a pencil. The very dark lines indicate the separation of feather groups. These also indicate where he will cut deeper for feather layering.

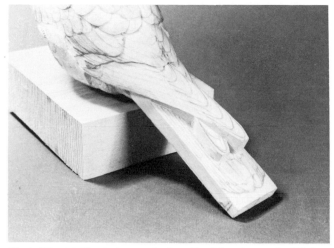

Most of the detailing is done on the top side of the wings and tail before undercutting between feathers is done.

Here Yoder is cutting the final outline of the primaries.

Here are Yoder's typical carving tools, including gouges and an all purpose knife with a removable blade in the center of the photo.

Shallow stop cuts are made on the primaries so the knife cuts do not show through the feathers after texturing and painting.

This is a typical knife-carving procedure for outlining the tail feathers of a kestrel.

The black-capped chickadee, branch, oak leaf, and acorn were all carved from basswood.

The wing feathers were carved with a skew chisel that allowed shallower cuts and more control of depth than a knife would. The sides and back were done with a dentist's burr.

Though the head for this chickadee was done as a separate piece to protect the beak from grain changes, the body, tail and crossed primaries of the wing tips were done from a single piece of wood.

Since Yoder did not want a lot of individual feathers showing on the back, he did little carving here.

The metal toes for this bird were soldered to the leg wire.

Putting light edges on these feathers made it possible for him to leave them uncarved. A light edge against a dark base can fool the eye, he says.

Yoder remembers trapping a Carolina wren like the one above in his garage one winter as it was looking for food among the beams. Small incidents like this can trigger the idea for a carving many years later, he says.

The beak of the bird was carved, sanded, and soaked in Krazy Glue to harden it and give it a boney look. When dry, the break can be sanded smooth.

This dentist's tool can put in the groove down the side of the wren's leg. It can also shape and detail features.

Feathers with sharply defined edges are carved with a scalpel. Notice the different variations in feather depths and the diminishing thickness at the base of each feather. Each feather was carved convexly to give it "vitality and life."

This widgeon is twice the size of the photograph. It was highly textured because the dark lines of vermiculation that go across the barb lines tend to counterbalance the depth of the texture lines. The dark tertial feathers and primaries were lightly textured for a harder look.

The leg wire of the wren is soft, annealed steel, while the toes are electrical copper wire with the insulation stripped off. Each toe was done separately, covered with epoxy putty, and left to harden. After the leg wire was puttied, the toes were stuck into the leg while the epoxy was still soft.

The head Yoder considers the most important feature of a bird carving, and more specifically the eyes. He tries, then, to make the life of the bird come out through the eyes and face.

Yoder notes in this photograph that it is important to get the correct drapery of feathers and the right flow to them.

The body of this mallard drake was heavily textured to hide the open grain of the jelutong.

This is the way the widgeon drake appeared before it was textured and painted.

Very short, deep lines were burned on the head with no gesso or sealer used. The first coat was flat and dark in color. Then lighter colors mixed with a gel medium were applied to make the head shinier.

This is the pattern for the widgeon. Note that Yoder plans to carve from a solid block of wood.

Yoder compares doing this carving and feather placement to painting a landscape, which means working from the simple to the complex features. He started with major feather groups, broke them down into subgroups, then into individual feathers.

The primaries of the mallard were undercut with a knife and dentist's burrs.

Here is the same view of the mallard before painting. The two curled tail feathers were inserted.

A mallard pair.

legs and applied an epoxy ribbon (that comes in two pliable, putty-like strips) over them. And the toes, made of copper and done individually, were put on with the epoxy putty instead of solder. To help him shape these parts of the anatomy, he used dentist's tools.

Yoder would agree with Barth when he says that "legs and feet are a lot like human hands. They're very expressive." This, he says, is especially true of the toes, which can be bent like the knuckles of a hand. How much time does Yoder spend making toes and feet? He devotes nearly two days to the wren's legs.

Much less work would seem to be spent shaping waterfowl. "With the small ducks," he says, "it's almost pure technique. I just sit down and do them." He explains that it is a matter of simply working the wood, that habitat and motion do not have to be accounted for. The widgeon drake and mallard drake are examples of his small ducks, both measuring only seven inches in length. It was the widgeon, though, that was carved from a single block of wood instead of using a separate piece of wood for the head as he did with the mallard. He says, "I still struggle with this, but I get a nice smooth flow from the cheeks into the neck and body with a single piece. It's a much more natural look." The mallard is his most recent piece, and he says the feathering was quite deep. Also, because of the bird's vermiculation, he spent some five days painting it. The mallard, he adds, is one of his most highly textured birds.

Detailed sketch of a green heron.

Detailed sketch of a redtail.

Snowy Owl
Gary Yoder
Nov. 1980

Detailed sketch of a snowy owl.

8

James Sprankle
Waterfowl Alive and in Wood

The Challenge of Waterfowl

James Sprankle traces his interest in waterfowl back to his preteen years when he hunted ducks. "Since I was that young," he says, "I had wanted to carve my own gunning decoys, and those were the first birds I carved, with heads turned for more realism," adding that store-bought decoys come with stiff, straight-ahead poses.

Carving decoys is not the only aspect of his past that has led this artist on to win nearly sixty blue ribbons at the Ward Foundation's World Championships alone, with eighteen Best in Show awards at major shows. As a teenager he learned taxidermy, and the only kind of bird he ever mounted was waterfowl. "I carve ducks today because they're something I've grown up with," he says. "And now, to be competitive and to make a living, I stay with waterfowl, not other decorative birds." He is known as a waterfowl artist, doing birds like gadwalls, green-winged, blue-winged and cinnamon teal, buffleheads, wood ducks and shovelers.

Sprankle states, in spite of what he has seen other artists sculpt, that creating waterfowl in wood is more difficult than doing other families of birds. He says that "people seem to know more about ducks than they do about songbirds, so you have to be more accurate." He points out that there are many more references available on ducks than on all the other kinds of birds combined. "With something like a cardinal, you don't see books devoted to their anatomy. But I can show you

With generations of woodworking tradition behind him, along with early-age adventures in duck hunting and a background in self-taught taxidermy, James Sprankle brings a lifetime of interest to waterfowl carving. He now devotes all his working time to carving waterfowl. Here he works on a shoveler duck.

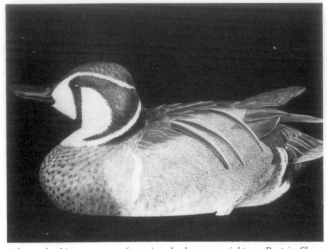

After only thirteen years of carving, he has won eighteen Best in Show awards in major competitions. Typical of Sprankle's work is this baikal teal, done from one of the live birds he collects. Photo by David Evans.

Another bird done from his aviary collection is the green-winged teal drake carved in 1981. Photo by Michael Hopiak.

Enclosed with wire mesh, Sprankle's aviary measures 14 x 18 feet and contains a fiberglass pond which is small enough to enable him to get the birds in front when he photographs them.

book after book devoted to ducks. So it's tougher to fool people with waterfowl."

References to him, as to the others, are vitally important to his carving. Yet, despite the fact that he still does taxidermy work on specimens brought to him, and may refer to skins when painting, he will never refer to a mounted bird or a model when carving. Live birds are Sprankle's preference, ones that he himself raises.

Aviary Photography

Sprankle uses an aviary, cage or wire enclosure in which live birds are kept, as a source and resource for his work. He credits Larry Hayden and Jim Foote, both of Michigan, for its use, saying that Hayden had told him that after one year with an aviary, Sprankle's carvings would improve thirty percent. "I said I can't get thirty percent better," Sprankle recalls. "But the first year I brought my birds to a show on Long Island (New York) and took eight First Place in Species ribbons and Best in Show." Again referring to Hayden, Sprankle says, "When Hayden and Foote carved something, you knew the bird was anatomically correct because of their aviaries." And studying live birds, he adds, "is a science that makes what I'm doing beyond being a craft."

But it is not the feeding and observing of penned-in birds alone that make Sprankle's work so lifelike. It is the camera that makes it possible to get the poses he feels are so critical to his work. The aviary Sprankle presently has measures 14 x 18 feet. "By having one that size," he explains, "when I walk into it, I have those ducks so tame I can photograph them from twelve to eighteen inches away. With a small aviary, those birds are automatically going to walk in front of me into the water, and they become tame that way."

Sprankle feels it is difficult to tame birds in a larger aviary. "The birds get in behind you and won't get in the water," he says. Still, he is critical of his present setup. "I have too many birds for what I want to do. You really need only two birds to work with at a time. Otherwise, other birds swim in front of what you're shooting." He suggests that two aviaries, one as a holding pen, with a trapdoor between, may be the answer. "Then I can move two birds into the shooting aviary without other birds getting in the way."

If this is not possible, he advises there should be only four to six birds in a small enclosure. He says that though you may not have the number of birds you want, you can always rotate them with other birds after extensive photographs have been made. "All my birds have been raised in captivity," he adds, "conditioned to a nonhostile environment. This is what helps in photographing them." Outfitted with a cedar box sunk three feet in the earth, the aviary is a place where Sprankle can photograph at eye level, though with another aviary he had, he could get above the birds with his camera for top views of the ducks.

And what benefit do photographs, slides in Sprankle's case, provide? Working with a projector, he can reduce or enlarge the projected images and make patterns from them. A slide then, can be translated into side and top profiles of a duck that can be put on a block of wood before bandsawing. And he can take measurements of a bill or get a paper pattern for feather layout.

Using a telephoto lens, Sprankle recommends ASA 200 color slide film. What he does not suggest, however, is using the slides as color references. There are too many processing variations, he says, and rarely can an accurate color be obtained.

Sprankle points out that aviary photography is not just going out and shooting rolls of film. "I've seen guys shoot five rolls of film in a half hour. You really have to wait for a side view or an unusual thing that the bird does." Behavior that he might photograph, then, would include how a bird takes a drink, preens itself, how it holds its head, how it rests with head under wing. "Maybe I'm just looking for side feathers drooping down," he notes. "If I get two good photographs with a roll of film, I'm pleased," he says. Of this kind of reference material, he explains, "When you see a photograph of a live bird, you can say 'There's something I want to incorporate into my next carving.' Maybe it's just the way the head is setting on the body, or the way it's tilted." Yet he adds that the aviary, though available to relatively few, may not be for the beginning carver. "Maybe you've had to have carved a bird before you photograph it," he says.

He sees the aviary as an educational experience for those who have one. And for those who do not, he suggests a zoo as a place to go for photographs. Of photos of stuffed birds, he says they are of no interest to him. For as a taxidermist, he discovered that it is easy to stretch a skin, making it as much as twenty-five percent larger in size than it really is. "When judging a show," he says, "I can tell when a person was working off a poorly mounted bird because of the mistakes copied."

If study skins are used, Sprankle advises they be

Hidden in a sunken cedar box, Sprankle can photograph his birds with a zoom lens at ground level. Sprankle uses the photos for reference material, and, in addition, he uses them for carving patterns.

Typical of the birds in the aviary is this black duck, which has just taken a drink of water.

Here is the same bird in a resting position. Attitudes and poses like this are carefully considered when Sprankle decides on a carving.

The side view of this cinnamon teal drake, in a very relaxed position, is what Sprankle looks for when choosing a pattern from a slide projection.

kept in plastic bags with newspaper wrapped around the bodies, especially if they are new. The paper will absorb moisture, and by keeping them in a freezer, the colors will hold up better. He does admit that if study skins are relatively new and taken care of this way, a carver can use them as references for painting.

Sprankle's reference materials, files of patterns, dimensions, and slides, are present when he carves a duck. He will even have photos made from the slides which he will pin up on a wall in front of him. "I can then pick up the bird at any point in the carving," he says, "and compare it to the photographs. I can even sketch an area of feathers on the bird from them." And if he reaches a critical stage, he can go out to his aviary and refer to the live bird. The photos, he says, are really general kinds of illustrations of what he is doing rather than hard and fast references.

Even with so much material, Sprankle will still update his slides and photos, constantly building up his library. And it is not uncommon for him, during the actual carving, to be taking notes, changing patterns, writing down colors. When he does the bird again, he believes, he can make the changes that will improve the carving.

Highland Basswood

Of all the woods Sprankle has worked with, he feels basswood is the easiest for him to carve. "With it you

Another bird in his aviary is this pintail drake. Sprankle, always looking for new reference material, is especially interested in the way the feathers droop.

The dead-on view of the pintail's head will make a good photographic reference.

can cut cross-grain and it won't check on you," he explains. But he indicates there are two types of the wood—a highland and a lowland variety. The highland, he notes, is harder and yellower, while the lowland basswood, usually found in damp or swampy areas, is whiter and softer, with a tendency to raise a fuzzy grain after grinding and sanding. He prefers, then, the highland wood because of its lack of fuzz, which is a help when painting, and its hardness, which lends itself to better texturing.

Still, Sprankle has a technique for getting the carved wood as smooth as possible. After sanding thoroughly, he will spray the wood with denatured alcohol from an atomizer bottle. This brings up any latent fibers and dries immediately. After this happens, he can give the carving a final sanding.

Of pine, which was once the only wood used for carved birds, he agrees with Barth that its sap or resin tends to bleed through even numerous coats of paint. And it is harder to texture because the burning point tends to build up with the sticky substance. He has used tupelo gum, but feels there are many pieces around that are just too hard to work. He has also experimented with jelutong, but he is uncomfortable with its pockets or internal holes and its porousness, which he feels would be a detriment to his painting.

For him basswood seems to work under any conditions. "I learned with basswood and will continue to use it as long as I have a source for it," he states.

Here is the same bird with a good head profile.

When carving and painting, Sprankle will have these photographs, made from slides, readily visible as references.

Here is a canvasback duck in a sleeping position.

The photographs, with a study mount of the bird and an unpainted shoveler hen, are of a cinnamon teal hen.

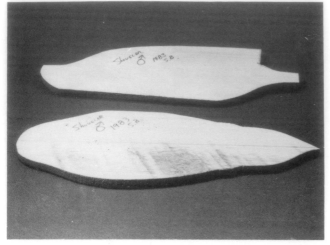

Because they hold up better and are more permanent than paper or cardboard, Sprankle works with wooden patterns.

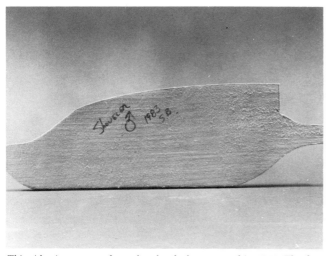

This side-view pattern for a shoveler drake was used in 1983. The date is significant because Sprankle constantly seeks to revise and update patterns.

Separate Heads, Feathers, and Feet

Though Sprankle works from solid blocks of basswood for the body of a bird, he will add feather inserts, the primaries in particular, and the head and feet as separately carved pieces. Still, he does not do as many insertions as other carvers in the book. At one time he inserted tertials as well as primaries, but he now feels these feathers are more realistic when carved out of the bird.

Patterns are a help for all parts of the anatomy, with the bandsaw cutting them to shape. For the body, he will tilt the bandsaw table and use a skip-tooth blade that acts like a rasp, while moving the bird back and forth at different angles to shape it. Further shaping is done using a pneumatic sanding drum and Foredom tool.

When it comes to the head, Sprankle has a technique for flaring it into the body that requires no extensive carving. After both the head and body have been shaped, but not textured, he flattens out an area where the head will be with a Forstner bit in a drill press. This bit removes wood evenly and leaves a flat surface. Then using a five-minute epoxy (he prefers Devcon because of its holding power), he joins the head to the body in the attitude he wants. After the glue has dried, he uses a wood filler to cover the joint.

Many carvers have found that a plastic wood filler will not burn for texturing, so they will not use it. Sprankle says, however, that it can be used if the burning tool is turned down to a low intensity of heat. The brand he uses is 3-in-1. "I've tried most wood fillers,"

Here the side view of the shoveler drake has been bandsawed to shape. The part on top was reattached with nails to provide a flat surface for the pattern since his technique also requires a top view to be bandsawed.

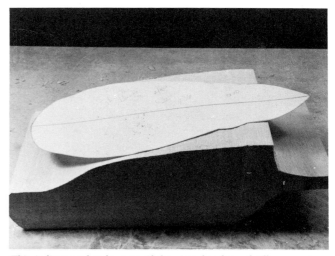

This indicates what happens if the piece bandsawed off were not reattached.

he says, "but this brand is the easiest to use and set up." He also points out that it is not as grainy as some other products of this kind.

To eliminate many carving problems when using the filler, Sprankle applies a coat of the brand's solvent. With it he can feather or smooth the plastic wood with a sable brush. So effective is this, he rarely has to sand out imperfections, though he may remove any excess with a knife and do some shaping with a small carving tool. "The wood fill saves a lot of aggravation of trying to get everything to match up perfectly," he says.

He uses filler around the eyes and feet as well, noting that if a mistake is made, it can be corrected by adding wood fill. And when he does need sandpaper, he uses a cloth-backed 100-grit variety given him by John Scheeler. Made in Switzerland, it has a longer life than other papers and it smooths the wood fill without cutting it up.

For the feet, Sprankle uses the real feet of a duck which he can attach with pins to a block of wood. He keeps the feet frozen until he is ready to make the pattern, then he softens them with water. By mounting them, he can trace both the top and side views and cut the block to shape with a bandsaw. Calipers will take the measurements of webs and the lengths of toes and nails. The toes can be refined with an X-acto knife with a no. 11 blade. He says it has a very sharp point, and it is one he can throw away when dull. "I'd rather be carving than sharpening," he says. A ruby carver and other grinding attachments give the foot definition, while the burning pen can actually shape and harden details like the bird's toes and nails.

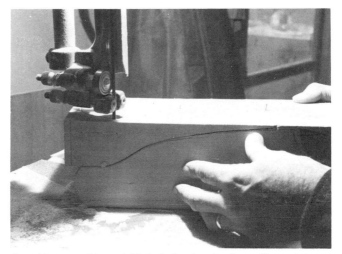

Sprankle uses a skip-tooth blade for bandsawing the profiles and shapes of the head and body of a bird.

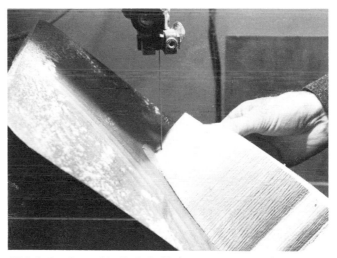

With the bandsaw table tilted, the blade can remove some sharp corners of the wood. This step would take a great deal more time with a grinding tool.

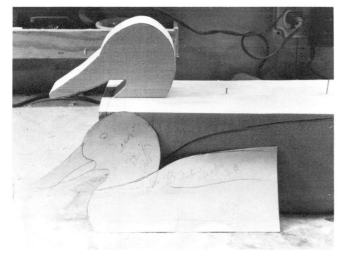

This shoveler drake head pattern indicates how the head will come off the breast. The wood cutout is above.

Only a light touch is needed to push the wood through the blade.

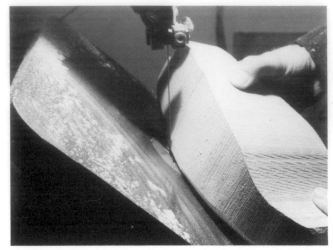

The skip-tooth blade can actually do some shaping because its teeth act like a rasp.

The drum will not burn the wood and can give a great deal of contour to the block.

Here is the result of bandsaw shaping, with a great deal of wood removed.

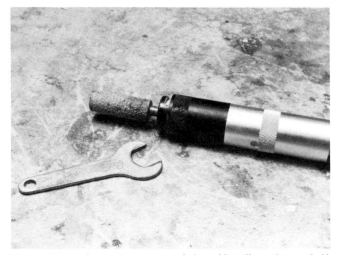

For roughing and removing more wood, Sprankle will use this one-half-inch diameter carbide bit.

A pneumatic sanding drum is used for sanding the body before the feather layout is determined. Sprankle uses a 120-grit sleeve.

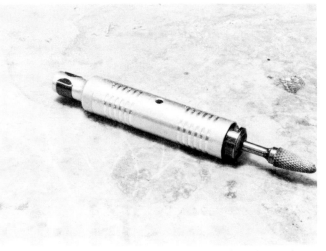

A carbide cone bit is a favorite tool for smoothing the wood.

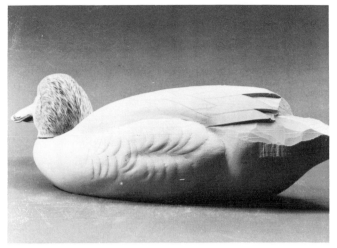

These feather patterns were done with a cone-shaped ruby carver.

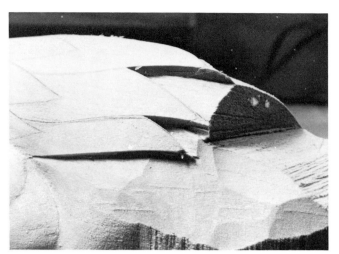

These tertial feathers were cut in with a knife.

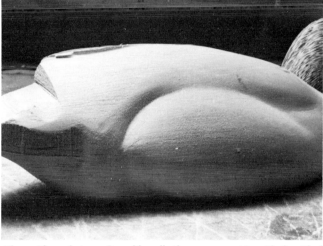

These side pockets, as Sprankle calls them, were put in with the aid of a rasp and then the Foredom

As can be seen here, part of the body will have to be flattened out for the head to sit correctly.

Here the wood for the tail must still be taken down more before the feathers are laid out.

Study bills, cast from freshly killed ducks, can be purchased for nearly any species. Sprankle finds them an invaluable aid for carving bills since they give exact shape and features.

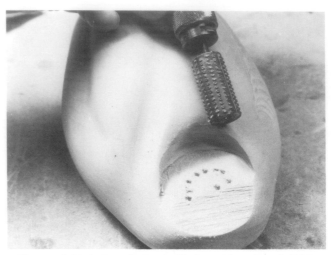

Here he uses the study bill as a reference before removing more wood.

The area behind where the head will sit must be enlarged slightly.

A Forstner bit in a drill press will remove large amounts of wood while leaving a flat surface. Sprankle uses this tool when he shapes the area for the head to rest on.

Used for the enlarging is this three-quarter-inch diameter rasp and Pfingst & Co. handpiece. The rasp can also be used for roughly shaping the body and head.

The shoveler's head has most of the detail carved and burned into it. Sprankle finds it easier to do detail work on the head before it is attached to the body.

The first step in attaching the head is mixing the two-part, five-minute epoxy.

The Devcon epoxy Sprankle uses is applied here with a plastic coffee stirrer.

Sprankle points out that texturing to this extent actually retards the drying time for acrylics and lengthens the period of time the paints can be blended.

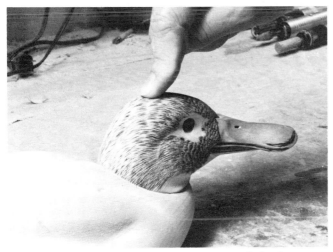

A light but constant pressure insures a tight bond.

To make the eye socket, he first used a one-half-inch diameter ball-shaped cutter and then a cone-shaped one.

Here are the patterns propped against the carving of this shoveler duck.

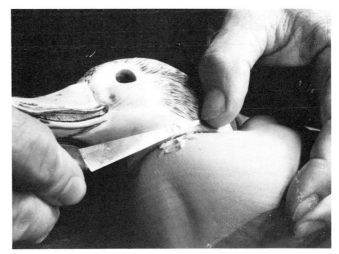

Excess wood is removed with a knife before the wood filler is applied.

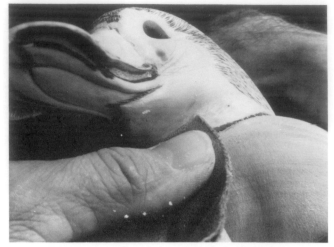

A 100-grit sanding cloth removes the knife marks.

He will also smooth out as much of the plastic wood as he can with the chisel.

To flare the head of the duck into the body, Sprankle uses a plastic wood filler and its solvent which will keep the filler soft and pliable.

A sable brush dipped in the solvent smooths out the plastic wood. A little saliva on the brush also helps.

He roughly applies the filler to the neck area with a carver's chisel.

Here the neck area is filled. Little sanding is necessary.

The next stage of development is putting the glass taxidermy eyes into the shoveler duck. Seen here are two birds, one before the eyes are set in and one with the eyes in place.

Epoxy must fill the hole well before the eye is set in.

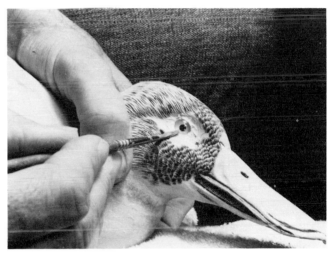

It is accidental that the eye sockets went from one side of the head to the other. Each was drilled in separately, as he advises, after the head had been given most of its shape. Drilling them in and through a band-sawed block may not be accurate, especially if the piece is not perfectly square.

Again, wood filler is used to close up the gap between the eye and its socket. Here Sprankle smooths the filler with a sable brush and solvent.

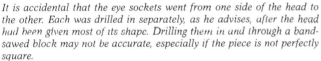

For setting in the eyes, a two-part plumber's sealer or epoxy is used. Sprankle mixes the two parts on a plastic chopping block.

Excess filler can be removed with a small gouge.

Before applying more plastic wood around the eye, he checks them front on to see that they are set in properly. Sprankle is trying to achieve the look that the duck is watching him.

One final check confirms that both eyes are the same distance from the end of the bill.

More filler is applied and smoothed out with the solvent that keeps the filler damp and workable.

The eye areas are now ready to be textured with a burning tool turned to a low setting.

Again, a small gouge can remove excess filler while smoothing it.

One texturing technique of Sprankle's is using a #9 lead pencil. With it, he can impress wrinkles on a bill before painting.

Sprankle will do feather insertions. The basswood feather at top is for the tail. The lower one is a tertial.

Sprankle advises setting in the primary feathers after the bird has been completely painted. This way, it is easier to paint the tail area without the primaries getting in the way.

This photo shows the location of the tertial feather on a finished shoveler.

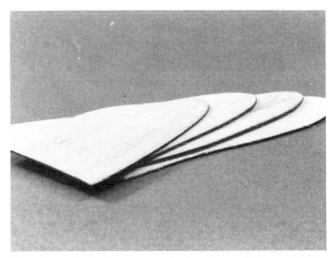

The primary feather inserts comprise four pieces of basswood. They were traced from actual feathers.

This photo shows where a group of primary feathers is inserted on a cinnamon teal drake.

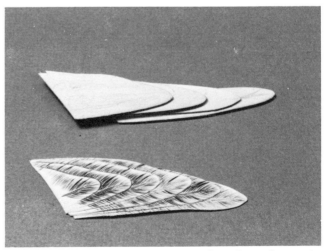

The four feathers are sanded thin and glued together and textured.

Pictured is a set of tail, primary, and tertial feather patterns.

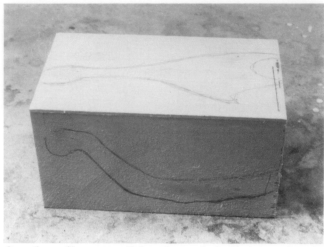

Once the profiles are penciled on the wood, the block is ready to be bandsawed.

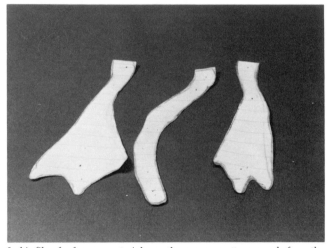

In his file of reference materials are these paper patterns made from the feet of a gadwall drake.

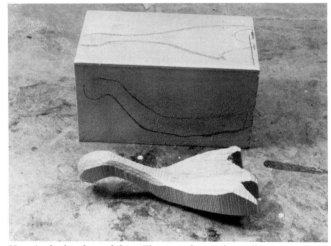

Here is the bandsawed foot. The procedure is basically the same one used for the body. The part bandsawed away is reattached so the top profile can be established.

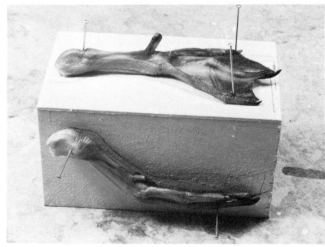

Sprankle does not use paper templates, however, for making the webbed feet that he puts on some of his ducks. Instead he uses real ones, which he keeps frozen until he needs them. These he pins to a block of basswood to obtain the top and side profiles.

This sanding drum in the Foredom handpiece gives shape to the features of the foot. It even defines leg muscles.

The same sanding drum gives the foot its cupped appearance.

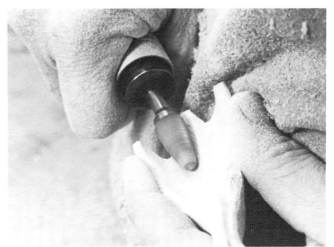

Being a smaller bit than the sanding drum, the carbide cutter can be used in more confined areas.

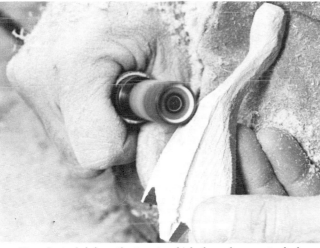

Here the tool defines the toes to which the webs are attached.

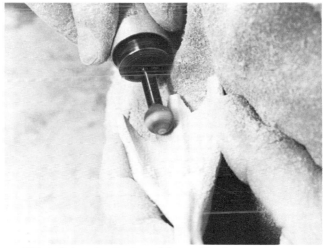

This ball-shaped cutter is used for working in concave areas.

This carbide cutter is used for fast wood removal.

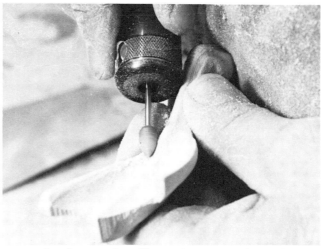

The ruby carver Sprankle uses does not tear the wood.

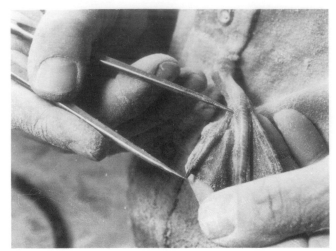

Calipers are used to check the length of the toes and claws on an actual foot.

This knife is used for defining the toes and cutting the claws to shape.

Measurements are then made on the wood.

Using a pencil to outline the toes so they can better be seen, Sprankle also uses it to remove bits of wood that are lodged in these areas.

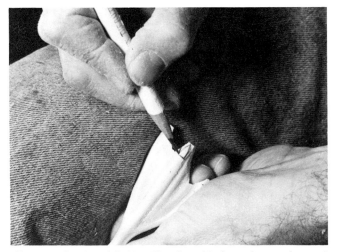

Claws are also given definition. Here Sprankle draws them on the wood.

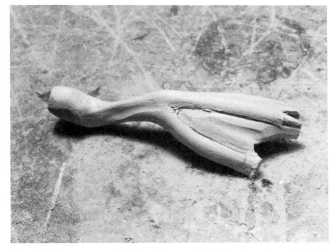

Here is the amount of shaping done so far. Note how the nail of the center toe is cut to shape.

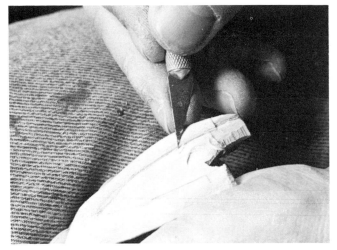

An X-acto knife gives final shape to the toes.

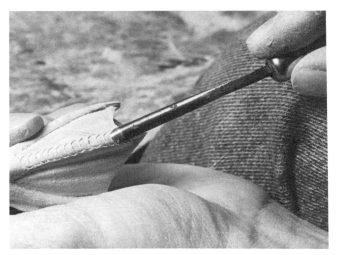

A gouge is used to put the scaly effect of the toes into the wood.

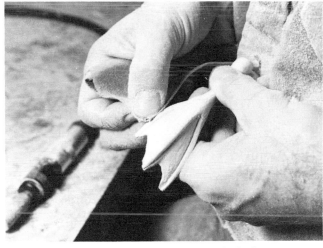

A cloth-backed sandpaper cleans up the knife cuts.

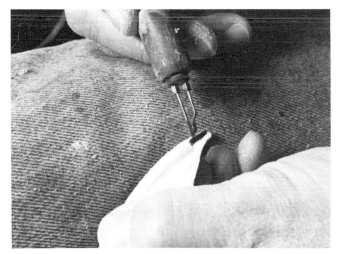

The burning tool not only helps define the claws, but it also hardens the wood.

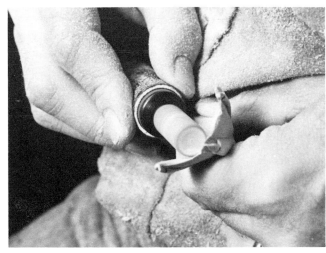

To get the webs as thin as possible after the toes and nails are defined, Sprankle goes back to the sanding drum.

The burning tool is also used to put in the tiny notches at the edges of the webs.

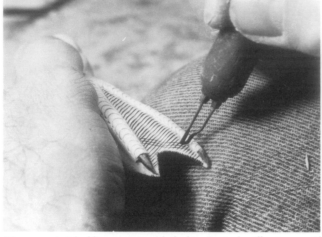

These crosshatched lines, put in with the burning tool, will act as a grid for paint. Into each diamond Sprankle will put a drop of gesso primer. When hardened, the paint will give the foot a scaly look.

This is the other foot of the same gadwall. The tiny toe in the back of the leg was added.

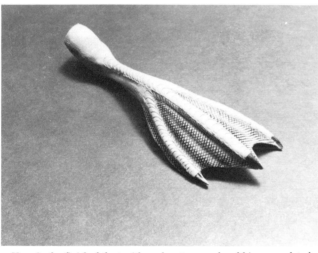

Here is the finished foot with scales, toes, and webbing completed.

Here is the foot of a redhead drake.

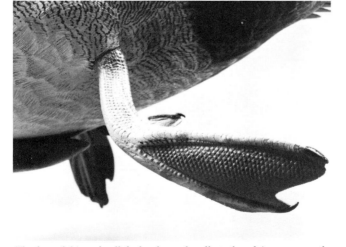

Sprankle points out that ducks have different types of feet. A puddle duck such as a mallard, one that feeds on bottom vegetation, has a smaller foot than a diving duck, a merganser being one, that can go after fish at great depths. So knowing what kind of feet you're working with is important, he says. And if there is a question of size, he prefers to have a foot slightly smaller. "It's more lifelike," he says, "especially when it's in a tank of water."

Texturing Waterfowl

The foot of this gadwall drake shows the effect of applying gesso on the burned-in diamonds.

Critical to Sprankle's waterfowl carvings is texturing, and he will spend from twelve to twenty hours putting texture on a single bird. What may cause him to

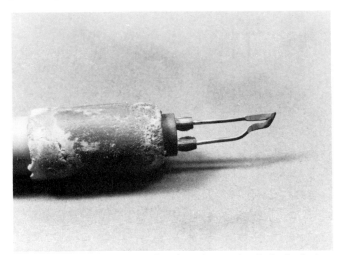

Sprankle uses this burning tool and tip for nearly all the feathering. Extremely sharp and thin at the tip, it is especially useful on the head and cheek feathers.

This shoveler hen, completely burned, is ready for a coat of Deft sanding sealer and gesso before acrylics are applied.

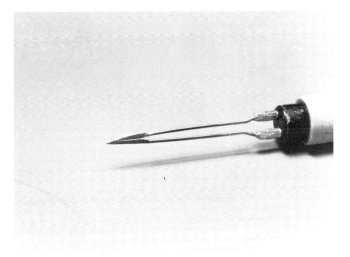

Not all burning tips need be used for feather details. This one can be used for removing small particles of wood under feathers that have been undercut instead of inserted. An example would be the tertials.

This is an area on the back of the shoveler hen. Note how Sprankle is careful to stagger the quills so they do not run into each other. Also note the overlapping feather splits.

spend more time than other carvers is his observation that different ducks have different kinds of feathers. He notes that birds like shoveler and pintail hens have twisted flow lines on their breast feathers, while most diving ducks have straight breast feathers. On those with symmetrically straight breast feathers, Sprankle will burn heavily at the base of a feather and lighter at its edge. He will not undercut that edge, because, he says, that would give it a fish-scale appearance.

When laying out feathers, which he does with a no. 2 pencil, he will put in splits, which he can accomplish with the X-acto knife. Quills he will put in with the burning pen. These, he advises, should never be put exactly in a line. Instead, he runs the quill of the underneath feather upward so it will not run into an adjoining one.

When doing primary feathers, it is not necessary to burn the entire insert if part of it will not be seen.

Note on this closeup of the same bird how Sprankle avoided a fish-scale effect when laying out feathers. He did this by not only staggering them, but also by making their exposed parts different sizes.

The top bird is a blue-winged teal drake; the lower a cinnamon teal drake. Hollowed bodies enable them to float for competition purposes, a carryover of traditional hunting decoys. Photo by Michael Hopiak.

Not all details are done with a burning tool; texturing on the head was done with a grinding stone. The nostrils and eyelids were built up with an epoxy sealer. Note how effectively the wood filler was textured where the head joins the body.

Another technique of Sprankle's is texturing the head before it is glued to the body. It is much easier, he finds, to work detail on a separate head, especially the many little feathers on the face and the lines on and under the bill. He says he can spend a couple of days working on the head alone.

Hollowed Birds

Other carvers like Rudisill and Yoder will hollow a bird to reduce its weight, especially if it is to be suspended in flight. Sprankle, however, hollows to remove wood from the interior of a bird to facilitate its floating. He does this for competition birds because they are judged floating in a tank of water. Sprankle explains this is a carryover from the use of hunting decoys. It is a tradition, he says, in many contests, and "seeing them floating has an appeal." These decoys must be perfectly balanced, which means they cannot list to one side, nor can the heads or tails be too deep in the water. He has found the more wood he can take out of them, the lighter they are, and the better they ride in the water.

The Forstner bit, which is used to remove wood and make a flat surface for the head, now has another function—the hollowing of the floating bird. By attaching the bit to the drill press, Sprankle can remove wood to two different levels because of the way the duck's body slopes from the tail toward the head. In drilling out the bottom, he is careful to leave half an inch of wood along the bird's bottom perimeter. After cleaning out the inside with a die grinder and a one-inch

The head of this canvasback drake shows a strong combination of stoning and burning for texture.

A similar pair of floating basswood ducks are these black ducks. Photo by Michael Hopiak.

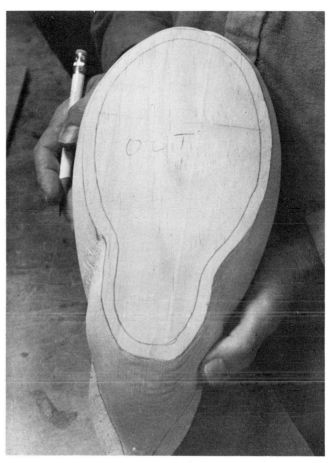

In preparation for hollowing a floating decorative duck, the area that is to be removed is penciled on the bottom of the bird. This amounts to a one-half-inch border. Wood will be removed inside that.

ball rasp, he divides with pencil that half-inch band of wood in half. He then bevels the inner quarter inch to a forty-five-degree angle with a rasp drum attached to a Foredom. It is this bevel that will allow him to fit a half-inch-thick wooden plate into the bottom, thus sealing the bird.

After making a paper pattern of the beveled perimeter, Sprankle traces it on the wood which in turn gets beveled, not with the Foredom but with the bandsaw. But permanently sealing that plate or plug cannot be done just yet. He explains, "How the bird rides in the water is important in the competitions. Even a quarter of an inch can make a difference in the pose or in making the bird look as though it is 'moving' through the water." And without some additional material, this attitude or pose cannot be achieved by simply plugging the bottom of the hollowed bird.

What Sprankle calls corrections in pose are made with small pieces of lead. When attached to the inside of the plate, they can make a bird swim lower in the water near the head or correct an imbalance owing to how it was hollowed.

Sprankle has devised his own technique for determining the position of the lead. Securing the plate to the bird temporarily with a rubber band, he will float the decoy in a plastic basin or busbox (used in restaurants for collecting dishes) filled with water. But to keep the bird from taking in water, Sprankle floats it on plastic. Using the plastic from a dry cleaning bag, he says it is the finest plastic he can find which facilitates a free-floating posture. Some carvers he knows use Saran Wrap to cover not the water but the bird.

The Forstner bit, used to remove wood on the body for the head, is also used for boring out the bird. Since the depth of the shaped block is not the same everywhere, Sprankle determines, while the bit is next to the bird, how deep to bore.

Continuous, overlapping holes are bored with the bit. A block of wood under the head section gives support to the body.

Sprankle believes as much wood as possible should be removed from the bird. Here he stands it on its tail end to hollow out that area.

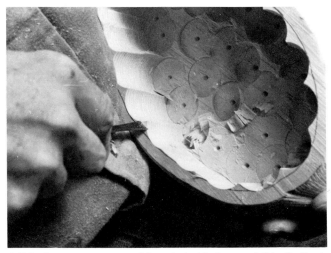

A fishtail gouge removes wood from the inside that was left by the Forstner bit.

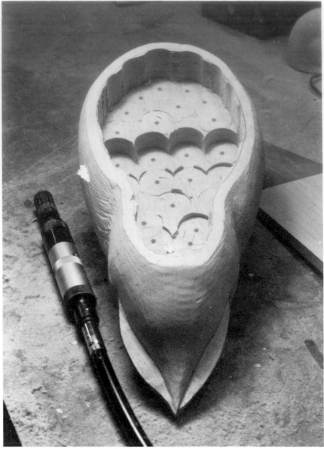

As much wood as possible was removed with the Forstner. The two levels on the inside reflect the outer shape of the bird.

A rotary rasp and Foredom, shown in the previous photo, coarsely level the walls of the hollowed duck.

The one-half-inch border which is left is divided in half. The inside half will be beveled.

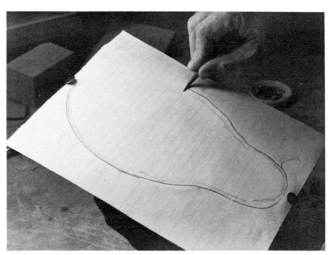

The pattern for the bottom plate is made by tacking a piece of paper over the bottom of the decoy and drawing over the beveled outline.

Sprankle uses the same rotary rasp to bevel the inner border. This will keep a wooden bottom or plate from falling into the body.

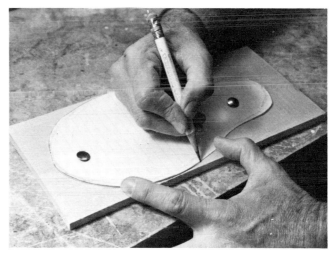

The cutout pattern is then transferred to a one-half-inch thick piece of basswood that will become the plate.

After the bevel is established, the final removal of interior wood is done with a one-inch diameter ball rasp on a die grinder. It is especially useful when grinding away wood in the tail area.

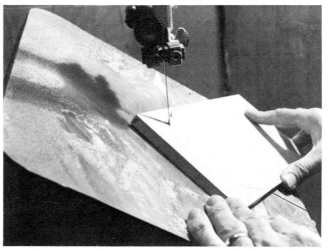

The plate is beveled by cutting it on the tilted table of the bandsaw.

Finished, the plate is ready to be fixed permanently to the body.

By doing it his way, Sprankle says, he does not have to peel the wrap off each time he wants to get at the lead weights. All he needs to do is remove the rubber band to adjust the lead. When that has been done, he fastens the plate to the body with a five-minute fiberglass compound, and after it has dried, he runs the bird over a jointer to make the plate flush with the body. He does caution, however, that great care must be had in making the bird watertight. For once water gets into the decoy, the base will invariably pop off. In competitions, during which a bird may be in a tank for several hours, he has seen this happen.

Gunning Decoys

Occasionally, Sprankle will make gunning or hunting decoys, which are also hollowed out. The very first decoys he made were of this type. They are functional, not decorative. Made with a bulky look with a heavy bill and tail, they have no feather inserts. They are made this way to protect the delicate feathers and features that could be damaged when decoys are sacked and carted off for hunting.

Lead weights, like the ones pictured, are fixed to the inside face of the plate. These will give the bird balance and poise in the water and replace the need for having a keel on the bottom of the duck.

The bird is floating on dry-cleaning plastic that covers a basin of water. The rubber band, which holds the plate to the body, makes for easy removal so the lead can be repositioned if need be. The plastic keeps the bird from getting damaged by the water.

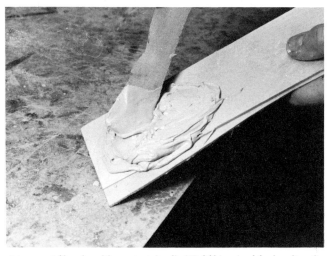

A two-part fiberglass-like material called Tuf-fil is mixed for bonding the plate to the body.

The fiberglass must completely fill the gaps. If water were to enter the floating bird, the plate would come off.

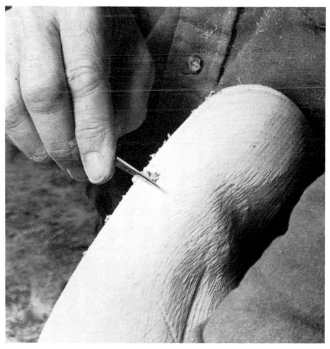

Excess Tuf-fil is scraped away with a knife.

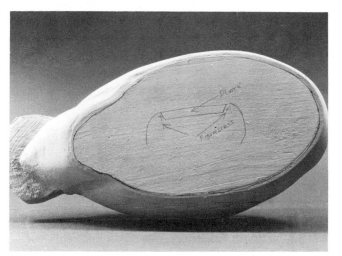

Here the plate is permanently affixed to the hollow body. Since the fit may not be flush, it may be necessary to run the plate over a jointer to even out the bottom.

Occasionally, Sprankle will carve gunning decoys like this one of a black duck. Note that the feather tips and bill are made somewhat bulky to prevent breakage. The small anchor in front of the bird keeps it from floating away when it is put in water.

Details are painted on this gunning or service decoy, but no burning is done. All feather tips were put on with a Prisma-color pencil.

Essential to most carvers is gesso, a thick undercoating for acrylic paints. This will give the bird an even color tone, and its light color reflects the acrylics. The unpainted bird is a shoveler hen.

Why the white background? Sprankle answers that white is a natural color and that the acrylics he mixes are transparent, so the white comes through. Mixing the paints on a white background is closest to what actually happens when he applies the colors on the white gesso undercoat. So in working this way, Sprankle is getting not only a truer color, but also a close approximation of how the color mixes will look on the bird.

Yet, glass and white backgrounds are not the only aids Sprankle uses to get the right colors. Proper lighting is another. He notes that under flourescent light he has difficulty mixing paints, but with natural sunlight he feels he can be more accurate with colors. For this reason he avoids painting at night when he must rely solely on artificial light.

His application of acrylics is not unlike Muehlmatt's in that he puts on successive washes, building up the color with six to eight thin washes, and sometimes as many as ten or twelve. As Muehlmatt does, he uses a

Nor are these birds weighted, having, instead, keels to which small anchors can be attached when they are set out to attract waterfowl. The keels, Sprankle says, are usually offset to enable the birds to be self-righting, since wind and water can turn decoys over.

Another feature of working decoys is their lack of texture. Instead of being burned in, feather tips can be put on with a Prisma-color pencil, which leaves an indelible line.

As simple as they are, gunning decoys are still collected because many people cannot afford to buy the decorative pieces. There are carvers doing them for competitions, with the major criterion being that they are simple enough for easy replication. The World Championship Wildfowl Carving Competition has a category for them called "The Lem and Steve Ward Shootin' Stool," stool meaning a group of birds. Sprankle suggests this may be a good category for a beginning waterfowl carver to try.

Painting on Glass

All nine artists featured in this book have their own techniques for mixing or blending paints. Some mix the paints on the bird itself, others start on a palette. Sprankle prefers to begin on glass.

He explains that by mixing his colors on a clear piece of glass with a sheet of white paper underneath, he is able to see what he calls a true color. "I'll even bring inside a live bird," he adds, "and while I mix colors, compare them to the bird's."

A piece of clear window glass with white paper towels underneath provides a surface on which to mix paints. The combination of these two materials will duplicate the gesso on which the acrylics will be applied.

Sprankle begins mixing paints on the glass, taking gobs of color directly from the tubes.

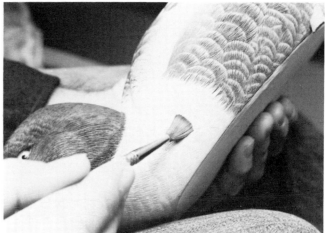

Here Sprankle demonstrates wetting an area lightly with water so adjoining areas of different paints can blend together more easily.

hairdryer between applications. What is different is his "watering" process. Sprankle says that where there is water, paint will not stick. He waters down an area he does not want paint to adhere to. This may be an area already painted or one unpainted. He can then work on a section that hasn't been coated with water. The alternative to this way of working, and one most of the other carvers use, is the blending of colors in the areas where they meet.

He points out that blending acrylics can be difficult, so he blends or pulls them together by "blending to water" as opposed to blending color to color. He uses the shoveler duck as an example. The top third of the bird's side has a yellow cast to it. This mix of yellow

ochre and white, watered down, is put on first. Then he wets this area, but does not make it so wet as to have it run. Dampening, he feels, is a good way to describe it. Then he can apply a mix of burnt sienna, ultramarine blue, burnt umber, and a small amount of yellow ochre to the adjoining area, the rump, which is rust-colored.

Another tip which is helpful in painting a waterfowl is epoxying a wooden keel to the bottom of the bird. Sprankle can hold onto this keel when he is painting and he can remove it when he is finished. He points out that grease from your fingers can cause the paint to go on unevenly or "slide off" in some areas. He suggests spraying Windex that has ammonia in it lightly

Since paints straight from the tubes are too difficult to blend and work with, they are mixed with water. Sprankle uses a ratio of 80 percent water, 20 percent acrylic to make a thin wash.

Like many painters of wood birds, Sprankle uses a hairdryer between the application of washes.

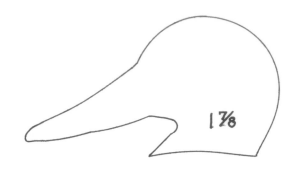

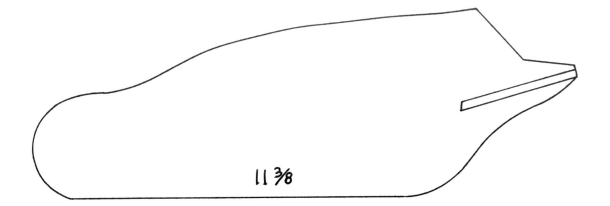

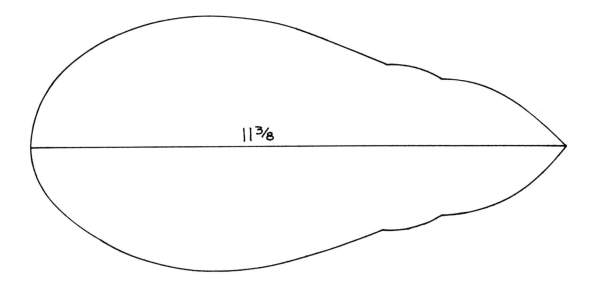

Working patterns of a shoveler drake, pictured as one-half the actual working size.

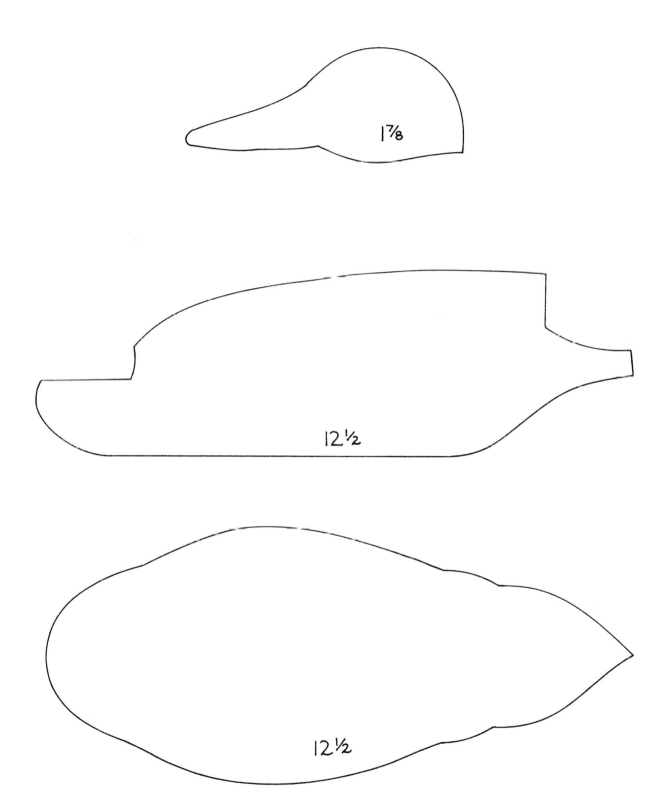

1⅞

12½

12½

Working patterns of a shoveler drake, pictured as one-half the actual working size.

Shown here is a lifesize shoveler drake done by Sprankle. It won First Place in Species at the 1983 World Championship Wildfowl Carving Competition.

On these side areas of the shoveler, Sprankle used a combination of yellow ochre and white with a small amount of burnt umber.

The small amount of vermiculation, seen in the left center of the photo, and behind the dark of the head, also center, was done with a rapidiograph pen with a #0 point. The vermiculation was then fixed with a light coat of Krylon #1311 Matte Spray.

on the wood and wiping it off with paper towels. This will eliminate most of the grease before the paints are applied.

Painting a Shoveler Drake

As has been discussed throughout this chapter, Sprankle finds references such as photos, patterns and notes essential for all phases of bird sculpting, from anatomy to feather layout. The same is true of painting. Besides referring to the live bird, he maintains an updated notebook of painting instructions. Each part of the bird, from sides to rump to feet and head, is detailed with what colors to use and how to blend

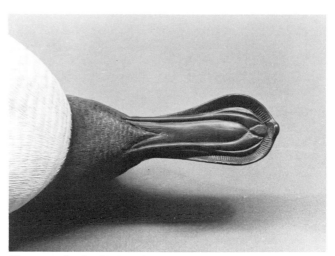

The area under the chin has a brownish shade, with white applied to the feather tips. Then washes of burnt umber were put over that.

The back of the duck was done with a mix of raw umber and black, with the tertial area darker. For the tail Sprankle used a mix of white and raw umber, with straight white on the feather tips.

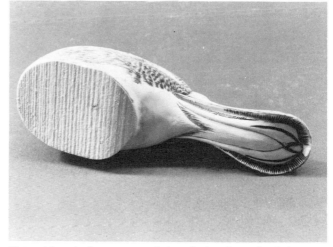

Pictured here is the same area before the burning and painting were done.

The bill of the duck was painted with a mix of ultramarine blue and burnt sienna. The breast was painted a gray shade first, with straight white put on the feather tips.

Sprankle may refer to a study skin when painting. To the right is the skin of the shoveler drake, to the left the painted bird.

Sprankle constantly strives for new poses and looks for his carved ducks. Here is a gadwall drake he did.

On the back of the same bird, note how carefully the feathers are laid out.

them. In the margins, next to the coloring text, are splotches of paint for additional reference.

The notes that follow explain the painting of a shoveler drake. When asked about the characteristics of the duck and why he chose to carve and paint one, he says that though he has one in his aviary that is four years old, it is a bird not often seen or available to hunters. It is rare to find a shoveler on the Atlantic flyway, a coastal migration lane used by ducks.

A shoveler in an aviary, he says, will spend ninety-five percent of its waking time sifting water with its bill down in the water. He has, in fact, carved shovelers with their bills down as if sifting. They are not the kind of birds you would see in a field eating corn, nor would you see them eating fish. Their colors are "pretty and bright," almost to the point of being gawdy.

An Eye for Detail

Sprankle believes many qualities go into making a good bird carver. One of them is having an eye for detail. Though he will not comment on his own talents, he does say that artists like John Scheeler and Larry Hayden "look at something, pick up and retain details, and they recreate them." He believes this is something almost God-given and perhaps helps define what an artist is.

He sees an artist as needing the ingredients of dedication, sacrifice, and intensity. The last, he says, is defined by how badly a carver wants to do his work. "If you're going to do something, why not be the best,

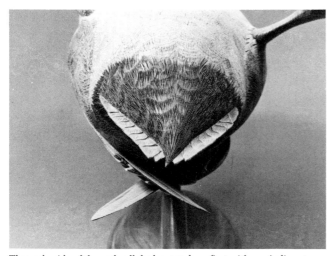

The underside of the gadwall drake was done first with a grinding stone, and then reworked with a burning tool.

Another photo of the gadwall drake shows the wrinkles around the base of the bill that were put in with a hard lead pencil.

SHOVELER DRAKE 1983

Undercoat thin gesso – two coats of Deft brand

Sides 2nd step, apply white and small black mix on lower and rear corner

3rd step, to one-third top area apply yellow ochre and white mix (more white than yellow); add small amount of burnt umber (may need a wash of it)

Rump 4th step, apply a mix of Liquitex burnt sienna, ultramarine blue, burnt umber, and a small amount of yellow ochre; water this into blue area

Breast paint area with white and Grumbacher gray; follow with straight white feather tips; use washes of white for desired shade

Head put a thin wash of gesso and a thin wash of yellow ochre over entire head; start with thin coats of two parts of thalo green, one part of Hooker's green, one part of black over entire head; for highlights, put yellow ochre on first, then thalo blue wash over entire head; crown is black and under chin is black (burnt sienna and ultramarine blue); put all white feather tips on crown of head now (white mixed with raw umber); put brown umber on crown and under chin; thalo blue and black on bluish area; wash of thalo blue and one wash of black over entire head

Bill paint lower mandible with a mix of white, cadmium red, and small amount of black (ultramarine blue and burnt sienna)

Back paint area raw umber and black; then paint tertial area darker; tertial feathers have a greenish cast on lower half – use thalo green and black; put washes of raw umber on white feather tips; splits done with ink pen; quills are darker; quills straight white on tertials

Blue on Sides apply gesso first, then ultramarine blue and white; then add burnt umber; apply straight ultramarine blue on upper part (watered into lighter blue area)

Speculum gesso first, then paint whole area with cadmium yellow; mix or blend in thalo green and Hooker's green and black and bronzing powder; then apply wash of straight black; white on edges

Tail paint entire tail area white and burnt umber and a small amount of black; for darker areas, add black; spots are blended in with this darker mix; straight white goes on feather tips; then apply wash of burnt umber

Wings apply burnt umber, white and small amount of black; feather tips are darker, so add more black to the mix; greenish cast is gotten with thalo green and black; quills are darker (more black to original mix); then apply burnt umber washes; white on feather tips (white and burnt umber)

Vermiculation ink pen used on sides; matte #1311 sprayed on sides; then a wash of burnt umber

Feet Hansa orange, white, cadmium yellow mix; then apply a wash of burnt umber

Most of the head of this redhead drake was done with a stone and then a burning tool.

When dealing with thin feather areas, such as these primaries and tail feathers, Sprankle will apply a couple of drops of a penetrating glue such as Super Glue to reinforce them.

A side profile of the same bird shows how the head-to-body joint disappeared because of the way Sprankle textured the wood.

This cinnamon teal drake in a sleeping position took First Place in Species at the 1983 World Championship Wildfowl Carving Competition.

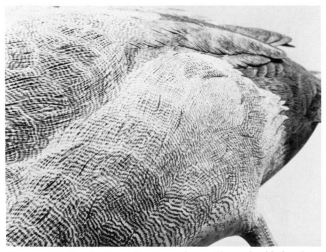

The vermiculation for the redhead was done with a red sable brush instead of a rapidiograph pen.

A pose like this one of the bill under the feathers was taken from an aviary bird. Note the position of the taxidermy eyes.

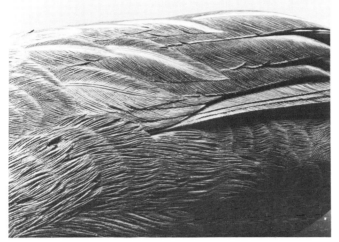

The feathers of the cinnamon teal drake appear rough. This is the way they would look when wet.

This is another duck based on an aviary bird, a baikal teal. This is an Asian breeder and an occasional visitor to Alaska. There are many different types of teal, and Sprankle hopes to carve all of them. Photo by David Evans.

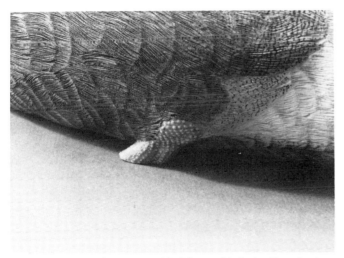

Sprankle does not always put webbed feet on his ducks. Here the foot is partially showing on what he calls a flat bottom decoy carving. The bumps on the legs were made with drops of gesso that were painted over.

Sprankle will carve a duck because it offers something unusual or different. He did this hooded merganser because of the crest feathers on the head and the duck's soft colors. Photo by Michael Hopiak.

The primaries of this cinnamon teal drake were inserted.

whatever that may be. Get to the top," he advises, "and maintain what you're doing."

He admits ribbons are important, but they are not an accurate way of telling what a carver does in his art form. "Yet ribbons mean a lot to people who want to buy my birds," he says.

To explain what his art means to him, Sprankle relates the story of a man he knew, Ken Harris of Woodville, New York, who carved for years. And though he fathered two career people, Harris knew he would be remembered after he died longer than his children would be. Sprankle adds, "I like to think that after I die, people will be able to see my carvings for years and years, see my name, and remember me."

9

Larry Hayden
Waterfowl in Living Colors

The Evolution of Realism

For the thousand years or so that birds have been recreated in this country, changes have been few. The Indians made their waterfowl decoys out of bulrushes and feathers, and later Americans turned to wood as a means of attracting birds from the sky. Birds did get a little fancier with feathers painted on the wood, and perhaps an insertion or two, but the basic gunning or service decoy remained somewhat stiff and static well into the 1960s with little hope of changing.

But evolutions start with small but significant steps. One of them was what we now take for granted, the texturing of the wood surface to define feathers. Until 1970, texturing was unheard of at competitions, even those sponsored by the Ward Foundation. Birds were carved smooth, and that was all that was acceptable. In that year Larry Hayden put a wood burning tool to a decoy he had made and entered it at the World Championships held in Maryland. "It was a drive to make a decoy more realistic looking," says Hayden. "But it was only slightly done. I didn't want to shock anyone too much." The race for more and more realism would seem to have begun.

Painter, Carver, Teacher, Best in Shows Winner

Hayden is no newcomer to the world of art. A commercial artist for twenty-five years, most of them spent in Detroit, he has spent his entire life in Michigan, a state once famous for market hunting, owing to the Great Lakes and the Mississippi flyway. In fact, the first factory-made decoy was manufactured in Detroit. Without formal art training, he worked in an art studio in that city as an apprentice and worked his way into commercial art. Hayden has illustrated nearly every commercial product from Waikiki dancers to tractor trailers, but his introduction to waterfowl and their reproduction came well after he began his career as an illustrator.

Hayden explains that a friend working with him in the art studio was a duck hunter. This friend invited Hayden to go duck shooting. What appealed to Hayden, more than the actual shooting, was using the decoys. Deciding to make his own decoys, he soon discovered he was shaping and painting them better than they really needed to be. After friends started encouraging him to compete in decoy shows, he entered a decoy in the Ward Foundation competition. It won Best in Show. So successful has he been with his carvings, he has won thirteen national Best in Shows consecutively. "I probably come from a competitive family, so I'm proud of what I've won," he says, especially the Best in Shows.

Talking about his accomplishments, Hayden echoes John Scheeler. "It's nerveracking after winning so many shows just to start the decoy. You go to a show and you're not happy you won, you're relieved you didn't

A nationally recognized painter and carver, Larry Hayden specializes in waterfowl paintings and has designed duck stamps for four different states.

His most recent painting is titled "A Flurry of Wings," picturing pintail ducks on the rise. These birds, he says, will not come into heavily covered areas.

The pintail drake is shown here. The rendering he does of such a bird is not very different from what he does on wood.

Pictured is a pintail hen.

Another fine example of Hayden's decoy art is this pintail hen.

One of the earliest of the factory-produced decoys is this one by the Mason Decoy Company of Detroit, Michigan, now owned by Larry Hayden.

Partially textured is this decorative basswood decoy of a mallard drake carved by Hayden.

In striking contrast to the factory decoy of the middle and late 1800s is this canvasback hen done by Hayden.

Another unfinished decoy of his is this wood duck drake.

lose." He advises people with a competitive nature that "if you don't win, you've got to look harder at the next bird you do. Maybe you'll notice the head was lopsided, that the eyes weren't put in right, or you missed the likeness of the bird."

Teaching carving has become an important avocation for him. He says, "I like sharing this knowledge with other people so it becomes appreciated by the public." Success has touched him here as well for students from his classes have won six Best in Shows in decoy contests, in novice, amateur, and even the highly competitive open class.

Though he docs appreciate the highly intricate and decorative works done by the other artists in this book, Hayden feels his real love is for the decoy. With it, he says, "you've got a real legitimate form of folk art." He goes on to say that with the other types of sculpture, there is little room for mediocre carvers. "You've either got to be very good or forget it." Yet, like James Sprankle, he sees the decoy as having "a legitimate place on someone's shelf," even one done by a novice.

His advice to someone wanting to carve decoys is fairly simple. "The first time you do a decoy, the worst thing that you can do is try to make one like mine. You've got too much to deal with." He advises, then, attempting something like a gunning decoy, because "you've got to familiarize yourself with the tools. Then go into an intermediate decoy where you start putting a few feathers on the bird."

A Study in Subtleties

Hayden, who prefers to call his carvings decoys instead of sculptures, strives for simplicity and subtlety. Yet there is no lack of realism in his waterfowl. In doing decoys he says that "you have to look for the little, subtle things on a bird that you can use to bring realism into your carving. There's no big spectacular thing on these birds, so you look for things like wrinkles or indentations on the bills, or the shape of the eyelids." These are what he calls the small details that have to be captured in the carving.

When asked if he exaggerates these details, Hayden answers that you cannot with competitive waterfowl carvings. "The puffiness of the feathers might be exaggerated," he says, "perhaps more pronounced. But in the competitions, you're judged on realism and exactness."

The most important single aid in bringing out the subtleties he aims for is the study bill. Hayden points out that the bill of a live bird is very fleshy. Yet, when

Since decoys are usually smooth, Hayden looks for the subtleties in his ducks to recreate in wood. On this wood duck bill, the nostril was an important part of the bird.

On the bill of this canvasback hen can be seen not only the attention to nostril detail but also the wrinkles he puts in at the base of the bill.

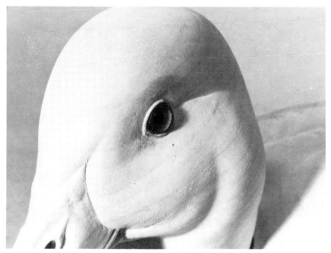

On this mallard drake, the eyelid, a subtle detail, was shaped from Thermoset, a wood filler.

On the left is a study bill, cast soon after the duck was killed. It is compared to the bill of a pintail mount. Note how the mount's bill has shrunk.

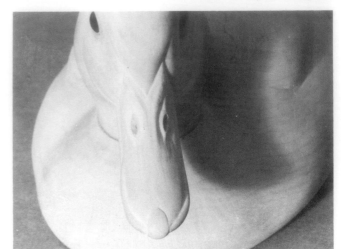

Compare this carved bill of a mallard with the study bill in the previous photograph.

the bird is killed and prepared by a taxidermist, it shrinks, "almost like a fallen leaf," losing shape and detail. "So to carve one, you have to have the fresh bill." And what has made this possible for carvers are study bills. (A supplier of these is listed in the appendix.) A study bill will show up even the most minor details, as well as the prominent wrinkles at the base of a duck's bill.

Hayden recalls, with humor, how at an early competition, he had entered a decoy on which the bill measurement had been taken from a live bird. A judge told him it was much too wide and should be disqualified.

Hayden would agree with nearly all the other artists featured in *HOW TO CARVE WILDFOWL* that most of the bird's realism comes from the head. In his case,

Study bills, like this one of a mallard drake, can be purchased for nearly any species of duck.

this is especially true of the eyes as well as the bill. After being extremely accurate with the positioning of the eyes, saying that a hair width off on the vertical axis is a great deal, he will go to the trouble of putting eyelids on the decoy. To do this he uses a brand of filler called Thermoset. Most other fillers, he claims, tend to be too thin and cannot be modeled easily. Thermoset has a slow drying time and is more like a modeling clay. He can work it with a knife, in a manner similar to the way one works with clay sculpture. Then, after it has dried, he can apply finishing touches with the knife and a piece of sandpaper.

Texturing Without Burning

In creating subtleties in his decoys, Hayden does not stop with the head. He works with the entire piece to achieve what he calls a soft, yet animated carving. He says that feathers do not lay flat like shingles. Instead, they are cupped to shed water that might otherwise get underneath the feathers and onto the skin. Hayden animates the feathers of the decoys he carves by giving them a puffy look with the Foredom tool and grinding stones. He says with certain stones he can initiate a convex shape to them. Then he can sand down the feathers' edges to give them high spots (not unlike Gary Yoder's techniques in chapter 7).

He does not use a knife for feathers. He says that a knife-edged feather tends to stay where it is, that is, "sometimes you want to wash out the edges, or literally make them disappear, when you apply your paint. With the stoned edge, I can come in and sand and wash out

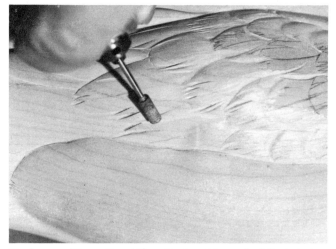

Hayden uses this small carbide cutter to put in much of the texturing. Rarely will he use a burning tool. With a bit like this one, he can give the feathers an animated, fluffy look.

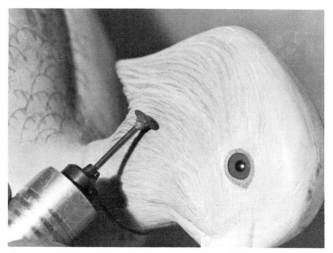

Here he demonstrates another stoning attachment he can use with the Foredom. This is a typical tool for doing fine texturing.

Shown on the same head are the results of the stone texturing.

the edge so you can hardly see it. All you may see is the puff of a feather."

This technique is not unique. In fact, Muehlmatt does the same thing to a more exaggerated degree. It is interesting to note that Hayden rarely uses a burning tool for doing shaft and barb lines. "The advantage of using the stone is a wider range of texturing," he says. "I use a stone predominantly and use the wood burner to a real minimum. Maybe on a little feather on a primary section." Hayden cites other reasons for avoiding the burning tool. He points out that with a stone, he can get a smoother surface for painting. With the texture created by the burning tool, especially for

By not having sharp divisions between feathers, and by sanding out the ridges left by the cutter, Hayden can achieve a fluffy look. These splits, done with a knife, are difficult to deemphasize when a subtle look is warranted. He advises using a stone for the splits.

Hayden textured the breast of this pintail hen with the stone. Notice how the feathers "lace together" to create a continuous flow.

The breast feathers of the canvasback hen were also done with the stone attachment.

Hayden believes in making things as mechanically as possible—that is, working out the carving and painting well in advance. He will have templates not only for the body but for the feather layout as well. This is a typical pattern.

vermiculated areas, he says that the paint tends to bleed down between the burning strokes, resulting in a blotted look.

He adds that with the burning pen, he is limited to the degree of depth he can get. He notes that a wood duck has coarse and deep texturing on the sides of its head, and with the stone, he can achieve that look. He also indicates that the burned lines tend to be stiff and do not animate the texture.

With the Foredom and stone, then, Hayden starts putting in his texture lines lightly and then goes deeper as the strokes progress. At the same time he is blending the lines of adjoining feathers together, what he calls "lacing them into the next feather." He describes this as a kind of overlapping, something he can achieve with the stone but not with the burner.

"Woodburning is boring," Hayden states. "The stone gives you more freedom." And, he adds, it gives the bird a more lifelike appearance. The only problem he sees in using this technique is having the confidence to do it, and he suggests that a beginner practice on scrap wood. He has, in fact, convinced experienced carvers in his classes to use grinding stones for texturing. "Once they try it, they put away their wood burners and never use them again," he says.

Feather Templates

Few of the other artists go to the extent that Hayden does in laying out feather patterns. Most carvers sketch these freehand directly onto the wood and start carving or burning. But Hayden is different. He says, "I'm

an artist, but I do as little freehand work as I possibly can. For if you're off a little bit, it will wreck the likeness of a duck. So I plan out all my steps to avoid those little mistakes of being a little too small or a little too big."

Feather layout for Hayden begins with a photograph of a live bird and a mounted one. The former, he says, will not give him well-defined feather shapes. Starting from the back of the bird, he will plot them out. Taking a real tertial feather, for example, he will measure off its length and width with dividers. Then he will draw its shape on tissue paper. But this is not the final

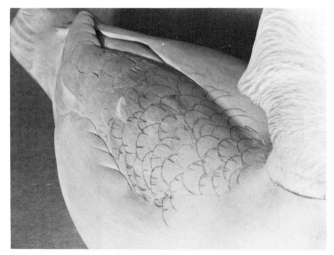

This view of the back of the wood duck shows a feather pattern transferred from tissue paper that had been carbon-blacked on the reverse side. This leaves an imprint on the wood.

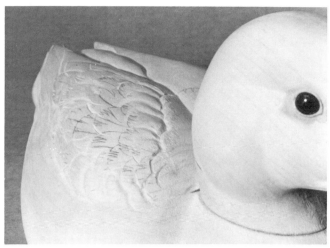

After the pattern had been transferred, this outlining with a stone is the first step to animating feathers before the fine texturing is done.

drawing. He might go through three different ones, putting one sheet of paper on top of the previous one, before he gets the one he wants (not unlike Lynn Forehand's technique described in chapter 1). He will do this for the entire back and sides.

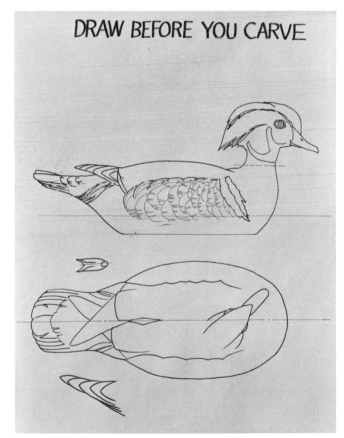

A centerline on the back of the bird is important for positioning the template or feather pattern. The same is true on the sides. For this, the duck's waterline is used.

The next step is transferring these blueprint-like drawings onto the rounded decoy. Starting on the top, he will do only one half of it at a time, tracing the feather layout onto the wood (penciling in the outlines on the back of the tracing paper leaves carbon that will adhere to the wood). He will then go over the outlines left on the wood so they do not rub off. Crucial to this technique is having a centerline down the back. Lines along the sides are called water lines. These will help center the tracings that are held to the wood with masking tape.

He will also use transparent acetate templates of the bill profiles and apply them to that part of the anatomy as he shapes it. He may do the same for the primaries or large tertial feathers. He uses these devices and makes the procedure as mechanical as possible to avoid any freehand drawing or carving errors.

It should also be noted that Hayden feels strongly about having a study mount. In fact, he says it is impossible to do a fine, decorative decoy without a mount. "But you don't use one for the shape of the head or muscles. For that you need a live bird and good photos if possible."

Crossed Primaries

Hayden will insert primaries on his decorative decoys. Many carvers do this for decoratives, but for gunning decoys, most will carve these feathers flat with no undercutting. Hayden is different. Even for his gunning birds, he will carve the primaries from

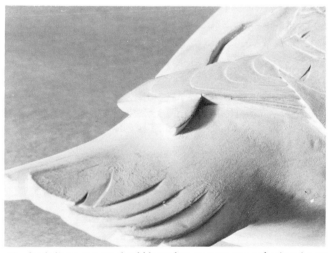

Hayden believes carvers should learn how to carve crossed primaries on a decoy rather than, or before, they try inserted feathers. These were done on the wood duck decoy.

Hayden will do insertions as he did for the primaries of this pintail hen.

the solid block of wood and have them raised. On first sight, the feathers might even appear to be inserted as separate pieces. Hayden takes care to shape them so they are neither fragile nor bulky. "In my case, I don't want to lose the likeness of the bird," he says. "A lot of carvers are going into decoy-making and inserting the crossed primaries, but I think it's important for a carver to learn how to carve them from the block." He goes on to say that he feels all carvers should be able to carve feathers from the block so that the tradition of making hunting decoys is maintained and perpetuated.

Preparing the Carving for Painting

Hayden points out that a residue is usually left on the decoy after it has been sanded. To remove dust

The primaries of the canvasback hen decorative decoy were also inserted.

specks, he uses a stiff toothbrush. But the wood still must be sealed to make it impervious to water, since the acrylics he uses are water-based paints. He first applies a good brand of sanding sealer for the waterproofing. He will put on two or three thin coats of sealer mixed with lacquer thinner, noting that a heavy coat would clog up some of the delicate carving details.

After the wood is sealed, he puts on a primer of Liquitex gesso, again using thin coats. Because gesso comes as a thick paint, Hayden mixes it with equal parts of water and applies it in the direction of the texturing. Gesso, he says, gives him a good surface to paint on. It is a flat paint with an almost chalky base to it and it absorbs somewhat of a sheen that comes with using acrylics. "It leaves a flatter finish that's closer to what a duck's feathers are." He cautions, however, that "if you don't have enough gesso on the bird, and you start painting, you can get an unnatural sheen with acrylics, an almost porcelain look."

Color Study Boards

Hayden has an axiom concerning painting. He says, "If you don't have a nicely animated carving, you are not going to do miracles with the painting. Yet, on the other hand, poor painting can blur the look or wipe out the features." He concludes, simply, that he cannot separate the carving from the painting.

What he does, then, is not unlike what he does in preparation for his feather layout—he determines well in advance of painting the decoy what its colors will be and comes close to actually rendering the entire bird on illustration board. This he calls a color study board.

He says that like carving, where "carvers are anxious to get in and start moving wood around" without preliminary steps, painting is usually done without adequate preparation. He puts it another way, "The more steps you do, the more you're familiarizing yourself with the bird."

On his study boards, besides rendering in paints different areas of the bird, he breaks a color into three different values. These are light, dark, and medium.

As some of the other carvers have pointed out in this book, many colors are achieved by mixing paints, and rarely is a single color used directly from a tube. The same is true of Hayden's three values of color. Using a plain brown that he might want on a feather, as an example, Hayden would begin with a mix of raw umber, white, and water. ("Colors straight from the

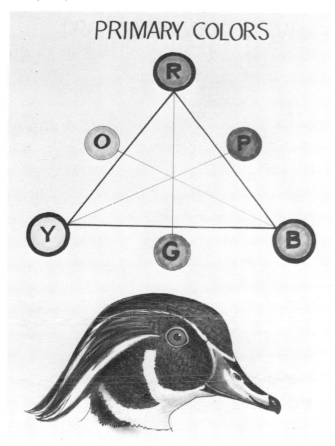

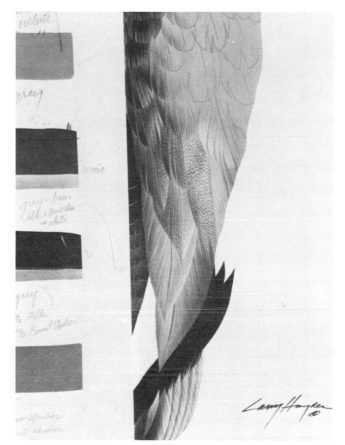

When painting, Hayden follows the color wheel when mixing his acrylics. The primary colors are red, blue, and yellow. Mixing red and yellow makes orange; red and blue makes purple; blue and yellow makes green.

In working out details for the back of the mallard, Hayden had decided on five different colors to be used.

To determine how the duck will be painted, Hayden uses a study board like this one for a mallard. Note how finely rendered the bird is, especially the head, and the color combinations on the border, his "painting notes."

Here is a color study board for a canvasback hen.

This closeup of the same board shows that seven different colors were decided on for the back. Note the vermiculation rendered.

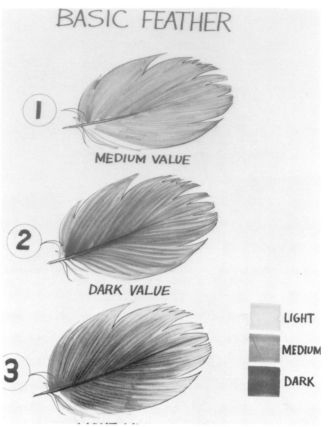

Basic to Hayden's mechanical approach to painting, where details are worked out well in advance of approaching the decoy with a brush, is the color value. He has three values for any color.

tubes are too thick to mix," he says.) Depending on how much white he adds to or substracts from the raw umber, he can achieve the medium, light, and dark values. The rendering, he says, is "a process of laying on transparent washes to build up depth." And all this is worked out on that all-important color study board before he goes to the bird.

Are there set formulas to follow after this? Hayden answers that there are not. "There are a million combinations of color that can be experimented with," he says.

As an example of how he might use these different values on a bird, he may begin with the medium value as the first application on the gesso primer. Next, he would take the dark value and do some rendering with it – he may create small edges to the feathers or shadows down in the grooves. Last, he would use the light value for highlights or light feather edges to give some depth to the effect, as the previous color rendering will show through.

When determining what paint to use for a brown feather, which might be a mix of raw umber, white, and water, Hayden will come up with a medium value as the first wash to be applied.

DARK VALUE

By varying the mix of burnt umber and white, he can achieve a darker tone of brown or a dark value. This would be the second phase of rendering a feather, but would be confined to the inside, not the edges, of the feather.

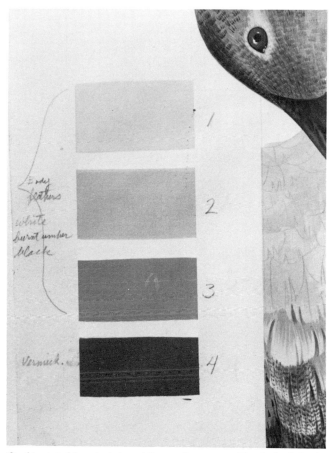

DARK VALUE

LIGHT VALUE

The third wash to be applied would be the light value. This would be confined to the tips of the feathers

On this pintail hen study board three values are used for the body feathers. Hayden used a combination of white, burnt umber, and black.

Deciding on values Hayden describes as organizational work, saying that the study boards "eliminate having to think how the bird will come out when painting." He also feels that "my painting is kind of mechanical. It's something you can learn, because I

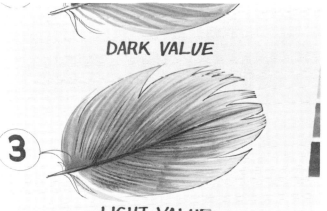

In this color study Hayden shows how medium, dark, and light values of paint are used.

Though this mallard head appears dark, with no gesso coming through, three different color values were still used.

Hayden will also work out on a study board vermiculation for a three-valued feather.

The back of this pintail hen demonstrates how the three values of color were put to use.

Here Hayden points to an area where the dark value was applied.

On this illustration which Hayden did for lecture purposes, he demonstrates the painting of white feathers on an old squaw drake.

Hayden points to where the light edges of a feather were rendered. These are done last so they "clean up" a previous feather edge, as Hayden works from the tail to the head.

teach this in my classes to the guys without any artistic talent and they paint pretty nice decoys."

On the board, then, he can experiment with bringing together different colors, mixing them, and determining their values and where they go on the carved bird.

Highlights and Shadows

To help in understanding the application of color values, Hayden utilizes highlights and shadows. Simply, he takes his textured decoy and holds it up to a light source. As the light shines on a side of the wood bird, he can see what areas are accented by the illumination and what areas have shadows. These highlights and shadows, then, must be *painted in*. He explains, "You can't always depend on natural light to highlight some areas and shadow others because your carving may be in a muted-light room. So decoys have to be painted with highlights and shadows on them." He compares this to painting a picture, saying, "You've got to do this because your carving is going to be in many different lightings."

This is an example of underpainting highlights and shadows with vermiculation applied afterward.

In this illustration, Hayden shows how highlights and shadows look when the three values of colors are applied. Note the highlighted areas on the top of the head and bill.

He notes that a bird out-of-doors always has the same light shining on it—the sun. To simulate that effect, he advises, "Visualize your sun coming down from one side on the decoy as you hold it up to the light." Then he says to turn the decoy around and determine the highlights and shadows on the other side. His mallard study board is a good example, he says, of how he determines these lighting effects.

Dealing with Colors

Like Ernest Muehlmatt, Hayden is conscious of color complements, especially for what he calls "graying down a color," whereby a color can get "shadowed" instead of highlighted. He uses the example of the red of a wood duck drake's bill. "You would not use black to gray it down in a shadow area, you would use its complementary color, green. Otherwise, you would get a muddy color."

Another example is with a yellow that would be found on a mallard drake's bill. Instead of putting black into it to gray it down, purple would have to be used. Black would turn the yellow greenish in color. But by putting in a purple, a rich yellow is achieved, a color that suggests it is in a shadow area.

Hayden also says it is important to know the difference between warm and cool colors. For a warm gray, for example, he would make a brownish gray. For a cool gray, it would be a bluish one. He adds that it is important to understand that practically all waterfowl feathers are composed of warm colors. "So you avoid having your colors bluish looking."

He advises that a burnt umber will "warm up" a color. For a white, however, he suggests using raw umber. Even for black feathers, he says, he will mix in burnt umber to warm the color.

When asked the difference between raw and burnt umber, he says, first, that they are both earth colors. The difference between the two is that the burnt umber has a reddish brown cast to it and the raw umber has a yellowish brown cast. The color Hayden uses most for waterfowl is raw umber.

Jars of Color

Since acrylics dry quickly if mixed and left on a palette, Hayden will mix the colors that he has created on the color study boards and put them in jars which he has previously labeled. He points out that rarely will he paint an entire bird in one day. With the colors premixed and ready in these jars, he can use the same colors for a month or so. For a duck like a mallard, then, he may have a dozen different jars of colors. With these on hand, he says, "I'm not involved with the mechanics of matching or measuring colors. Think how awkward it would be to mix them up every day. This way, I'm just involved with the rendering. And

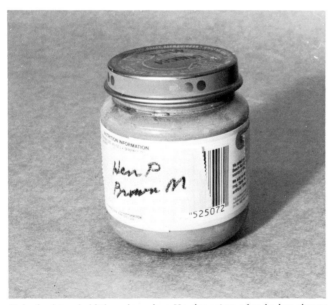

Baby food jars hold the color values Hayden mixes after he has chosen them on the study boards. Storing paint like this will keep it fresh for a month or so, making daily mixing of colors unnecessary.

with the charts, if I do a similar duck or the same one again, I have them for references." But he qualifies this statement by saying that he will not do all the colors quite the same way again. Instead, he will look for improvement, referring to notes he has written on the study board indicating whether something turned out well or poorly.

Iridescence

Perhaps the most critical aspect of painting for a carver to deal with successfully is iridescence, the lustrous, rainbow effect of colors in certain birds. To create an iridescent effect, Hayden begins with what he describes as "an opaque style" of painting.

He likens the opaquing technique to painting the interior walls of a house in order to cover old coats of paint. "It's putting on a coat of paint without letting the surface show through," he says. For Hayden, this means the gesso is covered with successive washes until it is no longer visible. Opaquing sets the stage for the rendering, which is also done with washes.

Using the wood duck as an example, Hayden divides the bird's iridescent green head into his three different values of light, dark, and medium green. The shadow areas he will paint in as opaque colors, which will not vibrate from the highlights and will be more subdued in color. He will paint the shadow areas in dark greens and blacks. When he gets to a highlighted green area, he will make use of powder metallics, also known as bronzing powders, that come as ground-up particles. As a medium for the powder, to hold the bits of metal, he uses a flat varnish. Still, he says, "they don't thin out, and they're hard to apply with a brush. Sometimes you have to use an airbrush and blow them on because they're not very brushable."

If the powders are so difficult to work with, why does Hayden go to so much trouble to use them? First, he says, there is not a good acrylic-based iridescent paint on the market, though hopefully one may soon be developed. A second reason is the iridescence makes a wood duck look far more lifelike than a duck painted without it.

Since metallics will tarnish, is it reasonable to expect that the color will fade after a number of years? Hayden says that he has never had that happen to one of his decoys because, with the metallics, he uses a very thin varnish. The only problem he claims to have had is that the colors wear off when the decoys are handled.

Even iridescence, the shininess of some birds' feathers, must be worked out on a study board like this rendering of a wood duck's head. Hayden uses an opaque style of painting, one that is not transparent like the previous examples of color value combinations.

Hayden points to the fine detailing he can achieve on the bill of his pintail hen.

When a thin layer of varnish is applied, "it's not really durable," he says.

Bill Subtleties

The bill is part of the anatomy where carvers can achieve a great deal of realism, Hayden says. On the bill color values change subtly from one area to another. Acrylic paints, unlike oils, are not easy to blend together. This is particularly true, in the places where Hayden wants to make slight changes, so he may use an airbrush to achieve some of this blending or he may use oils, because their wetness makes them easy to

Bill studies must be worked out in advance. He may use oil paints on a bill because they can blend together better than acrylics, and he can apply a coat of dull, flat varnish over them to give the bill an eggshell appearance.

Even under a totally different light, the bill of the same pintail hen has the same highlights and dark areas, the results of his painting techniques.

blend. Over the paint he will apply a coat of dull, flat varnish, an effective means for giving a bill its "egg-shell appearance."

Painting Sequence

Hayden begins to paint from the rear of the duck at the tail, works toward the rump, then off onto the back, the sides, works up to the breast, and does the head last. The reason for this sequence, he says, is the overlapping effect of the feathers. "This way you're never painting a feather ahead of another one. It's the same when painting a picture." He describes this process as "cleaning off previous feather edges" with strokes that redefine the edge of the feather next in sequence. If he does not paint in this way, he would have to take extreme care in where he ends each feather and begins another.

Of painting in general, he says, "You can't learn by listening to lectures. You learn by repetition, especially because it may even sound easy when someone tells you what to do until you actually try it."

Brushes

Hayden uses a Liquitex brand brush. For the rendering of the feathers, he uses a no. 2 and a no. 3. For mixing paints, he uses a no. 8. An important quality of brushes used with acrylics, he indicates, is how they point up. A brush that will point up is made so that the combined hairs are narrow at their base. This area has to be narrow, he says, "because acrylic paints bloat the brush up at the base. If initially the brush were too heavy there, you wouldn't be able to bring it to a point."

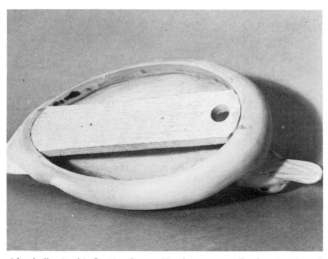

After hollowing his floating decoys, Hayden temporarily glues in a board.

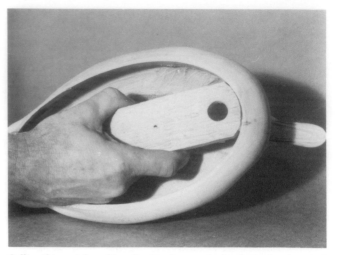

Calling this an inboard handle, Hayden says he has better hand control over the bird when texturing and painting than he would with a keel.

Getting a Handle on the Bird

Hayden's carved birds are hollowed like Sprankle's. And, like Sprankle, Hayden removes the wood before he does all the detailing because putting the bird on the drill press to hollow it out might damage some of the detail. What Hayden does differently, however, is put a narrow board temporarily across the bottom of the bird before he attaches the full bottom plate. He says this gives him a better handle on the decoy than a keel attached to the plate, and it's especially helpful when he's painting.

Kiln-Dried Wood

As six of the other artists do, Hayden prefers using basswood for his decoys. But he does look for what he describes as kiln-dried lumber. Kiln drying is a relatively rapid process for removing moisture from wood which is stored in a room in which the heat is thermostatically controlled. The other process is air-drying, allowing sunlight and its natural warmth to remove water from the wood. Air-drying may take as long as a year per inch thickness of wood. Hayden has found air-dried basswood to be too soft for initiating his subtle details. "You can't get the real high detail if the wood's too soft," he says. "On the other hand, you don't want something as hard as Masonite." He says he sent a piece of Michigan kiln-dried basswood to John Scheeler who found it to be the best he has worked with.

If artificially dried basswood is not available to the carver, Hayden suggests using a sanding sealer that "can stiffen up a soft piece of wood."

Study Bills

Hayden maintains his own aviary. In fact, he may well have been the first carver in North America to have done so. His aviary is an important source of reference material, especially for pictures of ducks. He prefers photographs to slides, noting that they are easier to sort through. He will take top and side photos of the birds that can be turned into patterns for the wooden duck. But an interesting problem arises, and that is, how does he determine how large to make the photographs for pattern purposes?

Hayden says he needs some measuring device as a reference, and for this he uses the study bill. Pointing out that it is accurate because it was cast from a "fresh duck" (one dead only a few hours), he can have the photo blown up to correspond to the bill's size. This should make the rest of the bird fairly exact in proportion. When it comes to the top-view photo, he measures the enlarged picture from the breast to the back and has the top profile blown up to correspond to that measurement. This method, he says, will give an exact width.

He notes that when taking flat-on shots of the bird's body, it is almost impossible to get an accurate one of the head at the same time. So he will take a photograph of the head separately and combine that with the body shot. For getting the top view, he simply puts a board across the top of the aviary so he can get above the bird, something that cannot effectively be done while standing on the ground.

Aviary Maintenance

Typical of the birds Hayden has in his aviary are canvasbacks, wood ducks, blue-winged teal, mallards, shovelers, and pintails. Pintails are his favorites. Being wily, pintails are not easy for a hunter to kill and they are hard to attract with decoys. Their streamlined look and their coloration give them an aesthetic appeal. Hayden has had a pair of pintails since he started his aviary some fifteen years ago. He says that after feeding birds nearly every other day for that many years, he could not help but learn something about them.

"You've got to study the birds to do a good job on decoys," he says and the easiest way to study them is to have an aviary. "If you have to depend on going to a bird sanctuary, you'll forget what you might have learned by the time you get home. Here it's right in front of you on a daily basis."

Hayden's aviary, measuring 20 x 30 feet, is enclosed on all sides and the top with chain-link fence. Close to his house and facilities to make winter maintenance easier, it features two fiberglass ponds.

Maintaining the aviary is vitally important. He advises that "correct maintenance is keeping the ducks healthy and in top condition. If you don't, you won't get good pictures. And if you can't get that, it's a mistake to have an aviary."

Hayden's aviary measures 20 x 30 feet and has two fiberglass ponds in it. Purchased from a livestock company, the ponds measure 4 feet long x 6 feet wide x 18 inches deep, and they are a full one-quarter-inch thick. He points out that four ducks will get the water dirty enough to require changing it every three days, something which must be done if the birds are to remain in good condition. But he points out that in northern

Seen through the steel tubing of the gate are two canvasbacks in one of the pools. The cable seen above the ducks leads to a submersible pump which keeps the pool ice-free.

A typical bird in Hayden's aviary collection is this pintail hen.

climates such as where he lives, in Michigan, a heater may be required to keep the water ice-free. Hayden uses a commercial livestock tank heater, the kind used to keep watering troughs ice-free. Hayden's heater, a submersible one, has operated at −20°F., maintaining the water temperature at one degree above freezing. The floating varieties of heaters, he has found, take up space in the pond that could be used by the ducks, and they do not seem to be as effective.

Besides having a good drainage system, the aviary should be as close as possible to water and electric facilities. You should also think about the distance between the aviary and your house, especially in winter, when going back and forth long distances is a definite drawback.

Hayden has enclosed the sides and top of his aviary with narrow gauge cyclone fence. The most important reason for doing this, he says, is keeping predators out. One of the worst, he notes, is the raccoon, at home even in suburban areas. If a raccoon gets into the pen, it may kill all the birds. In some rural areas, foxes and minks, especially hungry in winter, will seek out ducks. Hawks and owls can also be problems, and even rats may be a threat if they discover that food is being put out for the ducks.

Keeping birds in an aviary, Hayden says, "is not like having a pet canary where you can go and pull the paper out from the bottom of the cage. They have to be fed every day, and if you go away, you've got to have a babysitter." He adds that whether you have two ducks or eight, it is the same amount of work. "You've got to have a lot of dedication," he says.

Other Bird Resources

Hayden notes that in North America there are well-stocked public and private collections of waterfowl, ones that he himself may visit. "I don't limit myself to studying just the ducks I have. That's a mistake because ducks vary, like people. You can't look at one duck and say that is the perfect example of the bird. You want to study as many of a particular species before you decide what is the average representative." Apart from color differences varying from light to dark, there are also great variations in size. "So you don't want to carve the large or the small example of the species."

Aside from traveling to other duck collections, he will also photograph waterfowl in the wild, especially flying ducks which he will incorporate into his paintings. He uses a 400 mm lens on a motor-driven camera. He praises Kodak's 1000 ASA film, especially when lighting is poor, as it usually is in the early morning hours or late afternoon.

In addition to wildlife trips, he will even use books as a reference. Hayden recommends Frank Kortwright's *Ducks, Geese, and Swans of North America* for the excellent biological descriptions of birds that can even help him determine whether a specimen is a juvenile or an adult.

Bibliography

Wildfowl Books Recommended by the Artists

Bahrt, Sidney, and Jex, Hope S. *A Wilderness of Birds*. Doubleday & Company, 1974.

Birds. Hamlyn Publishing Group Ltd., 1965.

Birds of North America: A Personal Selection. E. P. Dutton & Co., 1972.

Ching, Raymond. *The Bird Paintings*. William Collins Sons & Co., 1978.

Kortwright, Frank F. *Ducks, Geese and Swans of North America* (revised edition). Stackpole Books, 1976.

Lambert, Terence, and Mitchell, Alan. *Birds of Shore and Estuary*. Charles Scribner's Sons, 1979.

Lansdowne, J. F. *Birds of the West Coast*. Houghton Mifflin Company, 1976.

————. *Birds of the Eastern Forest:* 2 vols. Houghton Mifflin Company, 1970.

————. *Birds of the Northern Forest*. Houghton Mifflin Company, 1960.

Nicolai, Jurgen. *Bird Life*. Putnam, 1974.

Parry, Gareth and Putnam, Rory. *Birds of Prey*. Trewin Copplestone Publishing Limited, 1979.

Queeny, Edgar M. *Prairie Wings: Pen and Camera Flight Studies* (reprint of 1946 edition). Schiffer Publishing Ltd., 1976.

Stout, Gardner, ed. *The Shorebirds of North America*. Viking Press, 1968.

Terres, John K. *The Audubon Encyclopedia of North American Birds*. Alfred A. Knopf, 1980.

Todd, Frank S. *Waterfowl: Ducks, Geese, and Swans of the World*. Harcourt Brace Jovanovich Inc., 1979.

Tunnicliffe, Charles. *A Sketchbook of Birds*. Holt, Rinehart & Winston, 1979.

Additional Reading

For more on the artists Grainger McKoy and Gilbert Maggione, read "Wood Takes Wing," by Tom Brakefield, *Sports Afield*, May 1978.

For a technical article on Grainger McKoy's work, read "Grainger McKoy's Carved Birds: A Wooden Covey on Springs of Steel," by Roger Schroeder, *Fine Woodworking*, January/February 1982, No. 32.

Sources for Supplies

Carving Tools, the Foredom and Dremel Moto-Tools, and Accessories

Catalogs are available from the following:

Albert Constantine and Son, Inc.
2050 Eastchester Rd., Bronx, NY 10461
Phone: 718-792-1600 / 718-792-2110 (fax)

American Sales Company
Box 741, Reseda, CA 91335
Phone: 213-881-2808

Buck Run Carving Supplies
781 Gully Rd., Aurora, NY 13026

Carvers' Corner
153 Passaic St., Garfield, NJ 07026
Phone: 201-472-7511

Cascade Carvers Supply
198 Galaxie Rd., Chehalis, WA 98532

Craft Cove, Inc.
2315 W. Glen Ave., Peoria, IL 61614
Phone: 309-692-8365

CraftWoods
2101 Greenspring Drive, Timonium, MD 21093
Phone: 410-561-9469 / 410-560-0760 (fax)
Also has study bills, cast feet, glass eyes, and a variety of woods including jelutong.

Electric Tool and Service Co.
19442 Conant Ave., Detroit, MI 48234
Phone: 313-366-3830 / 313-366-1855 (fax)

P.C. English Enterprises
Rt. 1, Box 136, Fredericksburg, VA 22401
Phone: 703-786-4717
Also carries Karbide Kutzall cutters and Tuf-Carv filler.

Exotic Woods Inc.
2483 Industrial Street, Burlington, ONT, CANADA L7P 1A6
Phone: 905-335-8066 / 905-335-7080

The Foredom Electric Company
16 Stony Hill Rd., Rt. 6, Bethel, CT 06801
Phone: 203-792-8622 / 203-790-9832 (fax)

Garrett Wade
161 Ave. of the Americas, New York, NY 10013
Phone: 800-221-2942 / 212-807-1757

J. H. Kline Carving Shop
P.O. Box 445, Forge Hill Rd., Manchester, PA 17345
Phone: 717-266-3501

Jennings Decoy
601 Franklin Ave. NE, St. Cloud, MN 56304

Lewis Tool and Supply Company
912 W. 8th St., Loveland, CO 80537
Phone: 303-663-4405

Little Mountain Supply Co.
Rte. 2, Box 1329, Front Royal, VA 22630
Phone: 703-636-3125

McGray Wildlife Sculpture
1-167 Island View Dr., R.R.2,
Wiarton, ONT, CANADA N0H 2T0

MDI Woodcarvers Supply
228 Main St., Bar Harbor, ME 04609

Nelson Carving Supply
2680 S. McKenzie, Foley, AL 36535
Phone: 1-800-44-DUCKS

Quality Carving Supplies
28 Riverfront Dr., Venice, FL 34293

Stuarts Woodcarvers Supply
107–180th Ave., Kirkwood, IL 61447

Warren Tool Company
2209-1 Rte. 9G, Rhinebeck, NY 12572
Phone: 914-876-7817

WASCO (Wildlife Artist Supply Co.)
1306 West Spring St., P.O. Box 967, Monroe, GA 30655
Phone: 1-800-334-8012 / 1-404-267-8970 (fax)

Waterfowl Study Bills, Inc.
P.O. Box 310, Evergreen, LA 71333
Phone: 318-346-4814 / 318-346-7633 (fax)

Welbeck Sawmill Ltd.
R.R. 2, Durham, ONT, CANADA N0G 1R0
Phone: 519-369-2144 / 519-369-3372

Wildlife Carvings Supply Headquarters
114 Amber Street, Beach Haven, NJ 08008
Phone: 609-492-1871
Also has cast legs and feet, glass eyes, acrylics, mounting
bases, carbide burrs, and Langnickel brushes.

Wood Carvers Store and School
3056 Excelsior Blvd., Minneapolis, MN 55416
Phone: 612-927-7491 / 612-927-0324 (fax)

Wood Carvers Supply Inc.
P.O. Box 7500, Englewood, FL 34295

The Woodcraft Shop
2724 State St., Bettendorf, IA 52722

Woodcraft Supply Corp.
210 Wood County Industrial Park, Parkersburg, WV 26101
Phone: 800-225-1153

Burning Tools

Annex Manufacturing
2 Hillview Drive, Barrington, IL 60010

Chesterfield Craft Shop
20 Georgetown Rd., Trenton, NJ 08620
Phone: 609-298-2015

Colwood Electronics
15 Meridian Rd., Eatontown, NJ 07724
Phone: 908-544-1119 / 908-544-1118 (fax)

Hot Tools, Inc.
24 Tioga Way, P.O. Box 615, Marblehead, MA 01945
Phone: 617-639-1000 / 617-631-8887 (fax)

Brushes and Paints

Beebe Hopper Arts
731 Beech Ave., Chula Vista, CA 91910
Phone: 619-420-8766

Christian J. Hummul Company
P.O. Box 1093, Hunt Valley, MD 21030
Phone: 1-800-762-0235

Cast Feet

Richard Delise
920 Springwood Dr., West Chester, PA 19382
Phone: 610-436-4377

Taylormade Bird Feet
165 Terrianne Drive, Taunton, MA 02780
Phone: 508-824-3337

Cast Bills

Bob Bolle
26421 Compson, Roseville, MI 48066
Phone: 313-773-3153

Highwood Bookshop
P.O. Box 1246, Traverse City, MI 49684
Phone: 616-271-3898

Oscar Johnston Wildlife Gallery
Rt. 2, Box 1224, Smith River, CA 95567
Phone: 707-487-4401

Carving Wood

The Duck Butt Boys
327 Rosedown Way, Mandeville, LA 70448
Phone: 504-626-8919

Glass Eyes

Carver's Eye Company
P.O. Box 16692, Portland, OR 97216
Phone: 503-666-5680 / 503-666-5680 (fax)

Hutch Decoy Carving Ltd.
7715 Warsaw Ave., Glen Burnie, MD 21061
Phone: 301-437-2501

G. Schoepfer Inc.
460 Cook Hill Rd., Cheshire, CT 06410
Phone: 1-800-875-6939 / 203-250-7794 (fax)

Tohickon Glass Eyes
P.O. Box 15, Erwinna, PA 18920
Phone: 800-441-5983 / 215-294-9483

Ruby Carvers

Elkay Products Company
7240 Northeast Drive, Dept. 255, Austin, TX 78723
Phone: 512-928-1224

A Sampling of Competitions and Exhibitions

World Championships
Ward Foundation
P.O. Box 2613, Salisbury, MD 21801
This show is held in late April in Ocean City, Maryland.

Easton Waterfowl Festival
P.O. Box 929, Tidewater Inn Association, Easton, MD 21601
This is an early November townwide wildfowl art exhibition.
A number of the artists in this book exhibit their work there.

Louisiana Wildfowl Carvers and Collectors Show
615 Baronne Street, Suite 303, New Orleans, LA 70113
This guild show is held in late summer.

U.S. National Decoy Show
The South Shore Waterfowlers Association
P.O. Box 36, Brightwaters, NY 11718
Held in late March, it is the oldest show of its kind in this
country.

The Wausau Show
Birds in Art, The Leigh Yawkey Woodson Art Museum
12th and Franklin Streets, Wausau, WI 54401
This show may come the closest to treating bird sculpture as
an art form. It is held mid-September through late October.

North American Wildfowl Carving Championship
4510 Kircaldy Road, Bloomfield Hills, MI 48013
Point Mouille State Game Area is the site for this key show
in late September.

International Decoy Contest
Affiliated Woodcarvers Ltd.
P.O. Box 406, Davenport, IA 52801
Held in early August, this competition has been in existence
since 1964.

Pacific Flyway Waterfowl Festival
P.O. Box 536, Quincy, CA 95971
Head to Sacramento in late June for this major Western show.